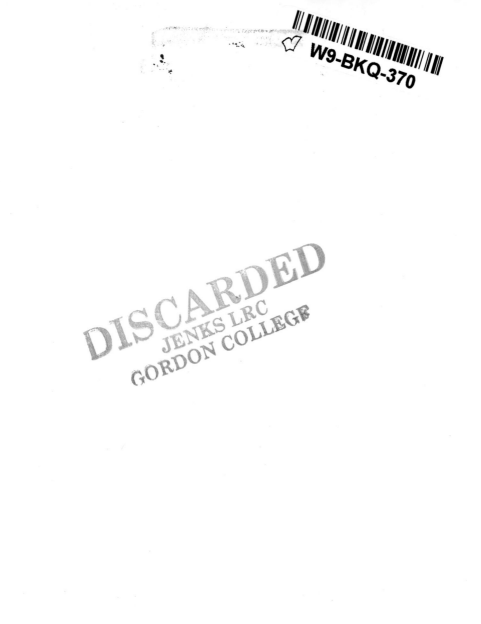

SEMANTIC STRUCTURES
Advances in
Natural Language
Processing

SEMANTIC STRUCTURES
Advances in
Natural Language
Processing

Edited by
David L. Waltz
Thinking Machines Corporation and
Brandeis University

LEA LAWRENCE ERLBAUM ASSOCIATES, PUBLISHERS
1989 Hillsdale, New Jersey   Hove and London

Lawrence Erlbaum Associates, Inc., Publishers
365 Broadway
Hillsdale, New Jersey 07642

Library of Congress Cataloging-in-Publication Data

Semantic structures.

  Bibliography: p.
  Includes index.
  1. Natural language processing (Computer science)
2. Programming languages (Electronic computers)—Semantics. I. Waltz, David L.
QA76.9.N38S46 1989   006.3'5   88-33420
ISBN 0-89859-817-6

Printed in the United States of America
10 9 8 7 6 5 4 3 2 1

Contents

Preface

I want to build a machine that will be proud of us.
                                                —Danny Hillis

Natural language (NL) understanding is central to the goals of artificial intelligence. Any truly intelligent machine must be capable of carrying on a conversation. It would be difficult to ascertain that a machine was "proud of us" unless it could tell us, both directly, and indirectly via paraphrases under questioning. It is not essential that conversations be in spoken language—they could be in sign language or via a keyboard and screen—but the machine must be able to converse.

Dialogue—in particular clarification dialogue—is essential if we are to avoid disasters caused by the misunderstanding of robots and other intelligent interactive systems of the future, designed to carry out actions on our behalf. One-way communication won't do. Machines that speak (or print) the contents of their own memory are already with us, but no one considers them to be intelligent. We would be very impressed by a mute computer that could carry out linguistic instructions with perfect reliability, but I do not think that it is possible to build such a machine, for the same reasons that human assistants can not work satisfactorily (except for trivial or repetitive tasks) unless they are able to engage in discussions about their assignments. Computer programs that can describe their surroundings will also need to be conversationalists: To be convincingly intelligent, such programs must be able to perceive and interpret the events around them with respect to the goals they permit or prevent; moreover, they must be capable of interpreting events from different perspectives as goals shift. A machine that always describes the world from a single perspective will not seem particularly intelligent or interesting.

This book is an interim report on the grand enterprise of devising a machine that can use natural language as fluently as a human. What has really been accomplished over the nearly 40 years since this goal was first formulated (in Turing's famous test)? What obstacles still need to be overcome in order to achieve this goal? This preface offers a broad perspective on these questions and uses this perspective as the setting for the five chapters that comprise the rest of this volume.

KNOWLEDGE

First, and perhaps most critically, intelligent conversational programs must have knowledge. Natural conversation depends on a vast body of shared knowledge of word meanings, concepts, conventions, and strategies for expressing these concepts in language. Conversations may also require quite specific knowledge on the conversational partner's goals, propensities, and history, as well as knowledge of the situational context, potentially including knowledge of the perceptual world. Sentences within a conversation are not, in general, self-contained. They express meaning only to the extent that a listener can be convinced that he or she has been able to identify the right topic of conversation and decipher what comment the speaker has made about this topic and why.

Exactly what knowledge must a system have? How can such knowledge be collected, represented, and learned? I will return to this topic. Much of this book, including the chapters by Dyer, Lehnert, and Loiselle, Alterman, and Neumann, is concerned with knowledge—especially knowledge about relatively large units of natural language, such as stories or conversations, as opposed to knowledge of phrases or sentences. Berwick's chapter shows how word meanings can be learned from text.

Architectures and Algorithms

This book is also concerned with mechanisms and architectures for natural language processing (NLP). In some areas of artificial intelligence—mathematical reasoning, problem solving, vision, and games, for example—it may be possible to build systems that perform at or above human levels, yet operate by different principles. However, using language truly fluently and appropriately requires a system to make the same inferences, to be surprised, amused, or confused at the same points, to be reminded of the same shared knowledge and to make the same judgements about listener's reactions to its utterances that a human language user would. Thus, I believe it is very unlikely that we can build a machine that understands and generates natural language without modeling human language processing mechanisms, and memory structure, in some detail.

What are these mechanisms and structures like? In the years since I first began to study artificial intelligence (AI), I have gone from a belief that natural language understanding is possible on any universal computer by direct modeling of human behavior and the stream of consciousness—modeling of The Knowledge Level (Newell, 1981)—to a belief that, while we probably won't need to model the full detail of the brain's neural action and connectivity, we will probably need to use massively parallel, Society of Mind-like models (Minsky, 1987) that embody some deep correspondences with the "modules" and architecture of cognition.[1]

The need for such models is inspired in part by what is known about the brain, but important influences also come from introspection and from observations of human behavior: The sheer speed of language understanding—in sharp contrast with the slowness of individual neurons—argues strongly for a massively parallel system where different aspects of processing (e.g. phonetic, syntactic, se-

---

[1]In the Society of Mind model, systems are comprised of very large numbers of independent agents, each of which connects to and communicates with a number of other agents in the system. Each agent is active whenever the concept, percept, or feature it represents is recognized, suggested, or hypothesized. Agents become active through the influence of other agents and/or sensory inputs. Each communication link between agents carries very simple messages, encoding the level of activation of the sending agent. Groups of interconnected agents are organized via hierarchy and other structuring patterns into "agencies," modules that are responsible for classes of functions and actions.

mantic, pragmatic, and memory operations) are handled by different agents (Waltz & Pollack, 1985). Both the triggering of particular "free associations" and memory items and the selection of appropriate meanings for sentences strongly suggest the joint action of a great many semiautonomous influences, many of which exert very subtle influences.

An important consequence of Society of Mind models is that different meanings are represented by different distributed patterns of activity across the *same set of agents;* that is, meaning is represented "in place." In contrast, traditional AI (and von Neumann machine) processing paradigms assume a central processing unit that selects and processes items from memory, one at a time; items must be moved out of their places of storage to be processed, and only one (or a very small number) of memory items can be considered at any given instant. Thus, if the Society of Mind view is correct, the vast amount of attention expended in AI on heuristics, knowledge representation schemes, and algorithms for finding the most important memory items is largely irrelevant to actual natural language processing—no correlates will be found to exist in the brain for such functions and structures. However, knowledge representation remains a central issue—perhaps *the* central issue in natural language processing. Only the portions of the field concerned with efficient implementations of search on von Neumann machines can be scrapped.

The Society of Mind theory, along with massively parallel connectionist or "neural net" architectures (Rumelhart & McClelland, 1986; Waltz & Feldman, 1988) have played important roles in stimulating the development of massively parallel computers, such as the Connection Machine (Hillis, 1985). These architectures follow in the tradition of perceptrons (Minsky & Papert, 1969; Rosenblatt, 1962) and are inspired, in part, by neurophysiology (although they so far bear little resemblance to actual nervous systems). Natural language researchers who want to use such models and hardware have been required to dramatically rethink their algorithms and data structures. Parallel hardware seems destined to become much more important in the future, not so much because it matches the mechanisms and structure of NL processing in the brain, but because these architectures are the only ones we know that can scale to arbitrarily large size and power, and because such architectures promise to be far more cost-effective than serial machines. Natural language algorithms that match or can be adapted to parallel hardware will dominate serial implementations, and only the nonparallelizable remnants will still be carried out on serial hardware. Fortunately, most semantically-oriented processing, including nearly all the research described in this book, can be relatively easily parallelized: For example, individual word senses can be assigned to processors or connectionist nodes, or such concepts can be represented as distributed patterns on parallel networks (Rumelhart & McClelland, 1986). Special-purpose speech processing chips, based on analog, rather than digital, processing, have already been constructed (Hopfield, 1988). However, syntactic processing has so far resisted significant parallelization, though there are promising methods for aspects of syntatic analysis (Church, 1988; Ejerhed, 1988; Selman & Hirst, 1985; Small, 1983; Waltz & Pollack, 1985).

NATURAL LANGUAGE KNOWLEDGE

There are two kinds of science: physics and stamp collecting.
                                                                      —E. Rutherford

For the last 35 years, natural language processing has more closely resembled stamp collecting than physics. An early hope and expectation (Simon, 1965) was that a relatively small number of basic powerful principles would suffice to achieve artificial intelligence. For example, much early effort centered on heuristic search in AI and transformational grammars in linguistics; both these are more akin to physics than stamp collecting. It now seems clear that intelligence in general and natural language in particular involves vast numbers of facts, procedures, rules, heuristics, and so forth, none of which is in itself very significant. Moreover, it is unlikely that this body of material can be reduced to a small set of primitives or operations.

To the extent that phenomena reminiscent of physics have been discovered in the study of natural language, they have concerned primarily the syntactic regularities of language. Noam Chomsky has argued that the structure of any language can be characterized by a quite small number of innate parameters. For example, parameters may specify such items as the ordinary order of sentences: SVO (Subject Verb Object) as in English versus SOV as in German; or the standard order of nominals and modifiers: ⟨adjective* nominal⟩ as in English versus ⟨nominal adjective*⟩ as in French.[2] Each individual

---

[2]⟨adjective*⟩ represents zero, one, or many adjectives concatenated together, as in the phrase: "the *big white run-down* house".

learns such aspects of his native language by setting the appropriate values for these parameters.

There has also been some physics-like success in the area called "lexical semantics" (Pustejovsky, in press; Jackendoff, 1983). Lexical semantics postulates that all language is based on a very small number of primitive semantic objects (e.g., states, actions, and state-changes) and relations between them (e.g., temporal succession, agentive actions, and causality). Any verb is associated with a particular structure of these objects and relations, along with a set of particular mandatory and optional features that constrain the ways in which the word can participate in sentences. Although there are some regularities in the lexicon, most words are idiosyncratic and must be learned one by one.

Words alone comprise a large body of data. The Random House Unabridged Dictionary (Stein & Urdang, 1981) defines roughly 300,000 words. Because, on the average, each word has 3.7 senses, on the order of a full-fledged NLP system must be able to handle about 1,000,000 distinct meanings. (A reasonable guess for the vocabulary of an educated adult is probably about half this number. These estimates omit many phrases and proper nouns that could be considered lexical entities.) All these estimates contain many phrases and proper nouns. Each word sense may in turn require the storage of a large amount of knowledge. For example, consider a verb such as "eat." In order to use "eat" appropriately, we need to know when its use is literal, metaphorical but familiar, novel and meta-phorical, inappropriate, and so forth. A program will need to understand that "the man ate hay" is unusual, whereas "the mouse ate the cheese" is a cliché. We know about hundreds of kinds of eaters, human and animal, and hundreds of foods, leading to tens of thousands of possible eater/food combinations. Although "eat" may be a particularly difficult example, even if we only store on the average of 10 facts about each word sense, this would still lead to as many as 5 million basic word facts.

Moreover, we each know a great many particular facts about history, geography, politics, entertainment, literature, sports, games, industry, and so forth, which are important to include if we are to be able to understand or generate appropriate linguistic references for natural conversation. We can estimate an upper bound on the amount of such knowledge: Assume that we were to learn one chunk of 100 bits every second for 16 hours every day for 20 years; we would learn 50 billion bits (Hillis, 1988). This amount of information does not seem to present an obstacle for hardware—a current Connection Machine can store 4 billion bits of information in its fast memory, and denser memory chips should allow 64 billion bits of fast storage by the early 1990s. However, collecting, representing, and using this information seems a very daunting task indeed.

How could we get this information into a machine? One possible answer is to gather a team of "stamp collectors," and there is a real-life example of this approach: Doug Lenat and a number of coworkers are building CYC, a system into which they are placing, by hand-coding, all the information in an encyclopedia (Lenat et al., 1986). Lenat estimates this will require 10 years and cost $50 million. Lenat is using a frame-based representation language (Brachman & Levesque, 1983; Minsky, 1975) to encode the information. He hopes that his group can use information in the system to accelerate the learning rate of the system as the project comes closer to completion. However, representing basic knowledge of language itself seems substantially harder than representing facts; we do not know what structures and operations are appropriate for expressing linguistic and lexical knowledge, and there is no organized respository of knowledge. In addition, finding and using pieces of encyclopedic knowledge to help encode new encyclopedia entries is a much easier task than using this knowledge to support the understanding of general conversations or text passages. A very different technological alternative to hand-coding is discussed in the last section of this preface.

Learning (or knowledge acquisition) thus presents a set of key problems that must be solved if we are to build natural conversational systems. Each chapter of this book bears in some way on this issue. Berwick's chapter deals with learning directly; Neumann shows methods whereby perceptual inputs can generate linguistic descriptions and appropriate corresponding memory structures; Dyer, Alterman, and Lehnert and Loiselle each deal primarily with representation of knowledge, and thus implicitly constrain the types of linguistic learning that will be needed to build a full-scale system. Each of this last group also offers novel insights into the evolving of meaning structures, in parallel, in a Society of Mind-like understanding system.

UNITS OF KNOWLEDGE

What are the natural units of knowledge that constitute and support natural language understanding? I will argue here that such units span a large range of sizes and types. At the highest level, entire topics can be "primed" by context. For example, the sentence "the group lacked an identity" will quite effortlessly evoke one interpretation if its context is mathematics; quite another if its context is psychology. (See [Waltz & Pollack, 1985] and [Bookman, 1988] for some proposed mechanisms to handle such phenomena.) At the finest levels language can interact with perceptual and mental imaging processes. This is necessary to explain how we judge the meanings of descriptions, such as the shades of difference between "over," "above," "just above," "somewhat above," "far above," "almost on top of," and so forth. Such distinctions can force crucially different inferences: "Just above the roof of the house" suggests quite different inferences from "the shelf just above the desk." The issues are explored in Neumann's chapter in this book. (See also [Herskovits, 1985; Langacker, 1986; Maddox, 1988; Talmy, 1988; Waltz, 1981a, 1981b, 1982; Waltz & Boggess, 1979]). Between these extremes lie the types of units that introspectively seem most critical: stories, sentences (or predications), phrases, and words. Most of the chapters in this book are concerned with these units: Berwick with words and phrases; Dyer, Lehnert, and Loiselle with stories; and Alterman with words, sentences, and sequences of sentences.

WORDS

During the 1970s and part of the 1980s, much of the AI natural language processing world used "primitives" and structures of primitives to represent word (and sentence) meanings. Proposed primitives include those of "conceptual dependency" (Schank, 1975; see also Dyer's chapter in this volume for a history and explanation of CD); "preference semantics" (Wilks, 1975); and the LNR system (Norman, Rumelhart, et. al, 1975). Primitives are special sets of irreducible word-like units, chosen so that, ideally, structures built out of them can represent all possible linguistic meanings. In practice, primitives have actually proved limited, though less so than one might imagine. (See the illuminating discussion in Winograd, 1978, as well as Wilks, 1975 and Jackendoff, 1976. Because many different words can collapse into the same primitive or structure of primitives, primitive-based representations express paraphrases naturally. However, they may not allow a system to express important distinctions in text. Thus, for example, in CD "eat," "nibble at," "wolf," "smoke" (as a cigarette), "inject" (as a drug), and many other words are all represented by a single primitive—INGEST. Although one would want to be able to make some inferences that are common to all these cases (i.e., some substance is at first outside and later inside the agent's body), INGEST is too crude to allow importantly different inferences. For example, "wolf" suggests that its agent was hungry or in a hurry, whereas "nibble at" suggests its agent's disinterest in or dislike of the food (Waltz, 1982).

As mentioned earlier, most natural language researchers have abandoned primitives and now make the assumption that each word is distinct, requiring its own, substantially more elaborate, structure (Jackendoff, 1983; Pustejovsky, 1988; Small, 1983). Berwick's chapter in this volume deals with the acquisition of relatively elaborate structures to represent word meanings. In the work reported in Alterman's chapter, each word is represented in terms of the network of other words (or concepts) closely related to it (e.g., subsequences of actions, situations that hold before or after actions, goals or reasons for actions, etc.). I expect this current trend will continue toward finer-grain representations, specialized for each word, and linked into networks (Brachman & Levesque, 1983; Sowa, 1984; Woods, 1975).

STORIES

Stories seem uniquely important because they are apparently the mind's preferred unit of memory: Stories are important carriers of cultural wisdom in a form that seems compelling and easily digested. It is instructive to compare their palatability with the oppressive pedantry of lectures of prescribed rules of action (Brewer & Lichtenstein, 1982; Dorfman, 1985; Dorfman & Waltz, 1981; Wilensky, 1983). Proverbs, a particularly valued form of language, encapsulate stories (Schank, 1986). I will not elaborate further here on the representation of stories, because they are so extensively and well treated in the chapters by Dyer, and Lehnert and Loiselle.

AUTOMATING THE BUILDING OF FULL-SCALE METHODOLOGIES FOR NATURAL LANGUAGE SYSTEMS

For most of its history, AI has been concerned with "toy problems." This is true of the chapters in this volume: All deal with specific natural language passages, chosen to be representative but still limited. Scaling up presents difficulties: At the two extremes of the spectrum, one can hand-code (as in CYC [Lenat, et al, 1986]), or one can use methods to automatically build NLP systems. To date there have been very few practical applications of natural language processing,[3] and this fact has dampened the enthusiasm of funding agencies and companies that support research in this area.[4] Fortunately, there are signs that this situation can be improved by strategically merging AI/NLP and Information Retrieval (IR) technologies. Over the last several years, I have been involved with such AI/IR research; it offers novel opportunities both for automatic learning, and for building systems that have immediate practical value.

Series of experiments and discoveries led researchers at Thinking Machines, most notably Craig Stanfill and Brewster Kahle, to devise a document retrieval system that works in parallel on the Connection Machine (Stanfill & Kahle, 1986; Stanfill, 1988). The resulting system, now a commercial product, provides a high quality search through a clever interface that can be used effectively by a computer-naïve person after only about 5 minutes of training. The basic idea is this: A database of documents (e.g., news articles, abstracts, books, etc.) is distributed to each of the many processors of a Connection Machine (if documents are 2K bytes long, each processor can hold about 12 documents). The user types a few words (a question, description, or list of terms will do) and a carriage return; the terms are broadcast to all the processors in parallel along with a numerical "weight" indicating the importance of each term.[5] Each processor compares the terms with the contents of its documents, and adds the "weight" to the score for each document in which the term occurs. The headlines for the documents with the highest total scores are then displayed to the user. The user can view the text of each of these documents by clicking a mouse button while pointing to the headline. When a user sees a document (or paragraph of a document)

---

[3]Commercially available natural language systems include INTELLECT (Harris, 1977), a product of Artificial Intelligence Corp., which allows users to get information from a database by typing, questions in English; NL Menu (Tennant, 1983), a product of Texas Instruments, that lets users build natural language "front ends" for programs—one uses a mouse to select the words for each sentence from a set of menu choices, insuring that the system will "understand" any user input; Q and A, a natural language database front end from Semantic Inc., and EPISTLE, a grammar correcting system from IBM.

[4]DARPA, the Defense Advanced Research Projects Agency, expects to spend only about $1.4 million in fiscal 1989 on natural language processing, compared to over $7 million the previous year. Much of funding has been switched to support speech processing research.

[5]Term weights are assigned automatically by a program that pre-processes the text and updates the database. The number of occurrences of each term is saved, and weights computed proportional to the negative log of the probability of occurrences of each term.

that answers their request, the user can mark the document "good" by pointing and clicking the mouse. The system collects all the terms from all the documents marked "good" along with the initial words the user typed, and repeats the search process described above, but now with many more terms (often several hundred). Each search requires less than a second, even on databases up to 10 GBytes. This method, called "relevance feedback," generally produces substantially better search than is possible with Boolean search systems (Blair & Maron, 1985).[6]

This system offers two interesting opportunities to extend natural language processing systems:

1. It is highly desirable to add natural language pre- and post-processing to the existing system, to improve its performance, and to extend its capabilities. For example, we are building recognizers that can find, label, and store lists of terms that refer to company names, geographic locations, names of persons, etc. Ultimately, this will help users to ask and obtain answers to questions that would be very difficult to phrase as Boolean queries. For example: Typing "Earnings reports for New England utility companies" would expand to "Earnings reports for Maine, New Hampshire, Vermont, Massachusetts, Connecticut, Rhode Island utilities, power companies, electric companies, Edison, power, light. . . ." In addition, natural language processing systems will allow us to post-process retrieved documents, to filter out irrelevant articles, and thus improve the performance of the system from the user's point of view.

2. The retrieval system itself can be adapted to extract phrase sentence and paragraph "templates" or patterns, in order to aid the building of recognizers for particular topics or types of stories. Such processing can provide empirical data on language usage that would be very difficult to find or invent any other way, leading to "dictionaries" of multi-word and multi-sentence language patterns and to FRUMP-like systems (De-Jong, 1982) with broad subject coverage.[7]

---

[6]A commercial software system based on these ideas has been developed at Thinking Machines and purchased by Dow Jones, Inc.

[7]FRUMP recognized about 70 types of stylized or "scriptal" newspaper articles: auto accidents, diplomatic visits, burglaries, etc. Frump contained quite specific, hand-coded sets of patterns to match each of the types of information needed to fill in the values in its scripts for each story-type.

The most attractive part of this effort is that our system is immediately useful, and thus can pay for the research on its own augmentation.

Other related research, using dictionaries or thesauruses, has become popular in recent years. Some striking successes have been achieved by Ken Church and coworkers at AT&T Bell Laboratories (Church, 1988; Ejerhed, 1988) using the augmented "Brown Corpus" (Kucera & Francis, 1982). The Brown Corpus consists of one million words of text, chosen to represent a wide range of text types and styles (newspaper and magazine articles, books on history, economics, etc.). It was "augmented" by Kucera and Francis by assigning each word in the corpus to one of about 450 classes, covering standard grammatical categories (noun, verb, adjective) but also including substantially finer distinctions (e.g., noun–agent of sentence; verb–complements of particular types). Church collected statistics on the probabilities that various words would follow particular other word (or category) combinations. This system has been used to judge the most likely categories for words in novel text taken from newswire sources. Success rates for Church's system are in the range of 98–99%, much higher than for the best syntactic parsers (in the range of 33% [Salton, 1988, personal communication]).

All these current lines of research emphasize *breadth* of coverage, rather than *depth* of coverage, and are thus complementary to the goals of traditional AI NL processing research. All present attractive alternatives to hand-coding (Lenat, et al, 1986). And all can be used to accelerate the research into deep processing. I believe these general approaches will have great importance in the ultimate story of the achieving of truly intelligent systems.

REFERENCES

Blair, D., & Maron, M. (1985). An evaluation of retrieval effectiveness for a full-text document retrieval system. *Communications of the ACM, 28,* 289–299.

Bookman, L. (1988). A connectionist scheme for modeling context. In D. Touretzky, G. Hinton, & T. Sejnowski (Eds.), *Proceedings of the 1988 Connectionist Models Summer School.* Los Altos, CA: Morgan-Kaufmann.

Brachman, R., & Levesque, H. (1983). *Readings in knowledge representation.* Los Alto, CA: Morgan Kaufman Publishers.

Brewer, W.F., & Lichtenstein, E.H. (1982). Stories are to entertain: a structural-affect theory of stories. *Journal of Pragmatics, 6,* 473–486.

Church, K. (1988). A stochastic parts program and noun phrase parser for unrestricted text. Unpublished manuscript, AT&T Bell Labs, Murray Hill, NJ.

Dorfman, M. (1985). A model for understanding the points of stories. *Proceedings of the 7th Annual Conference of the Cognitive Science Society*, (pp. 262–63). Irvine, CA.

DeJong, G. (1982). An Overview of the FRUMP System. In W. Lehnert & M. Ringle (Eds.), *Strategies for natural language processing*, Hillsdale, NJ: Lawrence Erlbaum Associates.

Ejerhed, E. (1988). Finding clauses in unrestricted text by stochastic and finitary methods. Unpublished manuscript, AT&T Bell Labs, Murray Hill, NJ.

Harris, L. (1977). Robot: A full performance natural language data base query system, *Proceedings of the Fifth International Joint Conference on Artificial Intelligence* (pp. 903–904).

Herskovits, A. (1985). Semantics and pragmatics of locative expression. *Cognitive Science, 9,* 341–378.

Hillis, D. (1985). *The connection machine.* Cambridge, MA: MIT Press.

Hillis, D. (1988). Intelligence as an emergent behavior; or, The songs of eden. *Daedalus, (Journal of the American Academy of Arts and Sciences),* 175–189.

Hopfield, J. (1988). Remarks to AAAI workshop on how slow components can think so fast. Stanford University, March 22–24.

Jackendoff, R. (1983). *Semantics and cognition.* Cambridge, MA: MIT Press.

Jackendoff, R. (1976). Toward an explanatory semantic representation. *Linguitic Inquiry, 7,* 89–150.

Kucera, H., & Frances, W. (1982). *Frequency analysis of english usage,* Boston: Houghton Mifflin Company.

Langacker, R.W. (1986). An introduction to cognitive grammar. *Cognitive Science, 10,* 1–40.

Lenat, G., Prakash, M., & Shepherd, M. (1986). CYC: Using common sense knowledge to overcome brittleness and knowledge acquisition bottleneck. *AI Magazine, 4,* 65–85.

Minsky, M. (1975). A framework for representing knowledge. In P. Winston (Ed.), *The psychology of computer vision* (pp. 211–277). New York: McGraw-Hill.

Maddox, A.B. (1988). Perceptual interpretation and the transformation of events into language. Doctoral dissertation, University of Illinois, Urbana, Illinois.

Miller, G.A., & Johson-Laird, P. (1976). *Language and perception.* Cambridge, MA: Harvard University Press.

Minsky, M. (1987). *The society of mind.* New York: Simon & Schuster.

Minsky, M., & Papert, S. (1969). *Perceptrons: An introduction to computational geometry.* Cambridge, MA: MIT Press.

Newell, R. (1981). The knowledge level. *AI Magazine, 2,* 1–20.

Norman, D.A., Rumelhart, D.E., & LNR Research Group (1975). *Explorations in cognition.* San Francisco: W.H. Freeman.

Pustejovsky, J. (in press). *Semantics and the lexicon.* Dordrecht, Holland: Klumer.

Rosenblatt, F. (1962). Strategic approaches to the study of brain models. In

H. von Foerster (Ed.), *Principles of Self Organization*. Elmsford, NY: Pergamon Press.

Rumelhart, D., & McClelland, J., et al. (1986). *Parallel distributed processing*. Cambridge, MA: MIT Press.

Selman, B., & Hirst, G. (1985). A rule-based connectionist parsing system. *Proceedings of the Seventh Annual Conference of the Cognitive Science Society* (pp. 212–219). Irvine, CA.

Schank, R.C. (1986). *Explanation patterns: understanding mechanically and creatively*. Hillsdale, NJ: Lawrence Erlbaum Associates.

Schank, R. (1975). *Conceptual information processing*. Amsterdam: North Holland.

Simon, H. (1965). *The sciences of the artificial*. Cambridge, MA: MIT Press.

Small, S. (1983). *Word expert parsing: A theory of distributed word-based natural language understanding*, Technical Report 954. Department of Computer Science, University of Maryland.

Sowa, J. (1984). *Conceptual structures*. Reading, MA: Addison-Wesley.

Stanfill, C. (1988). Parallel computing for information retrieval: recent developments. Thinking Machines Corporation Technical Report #DR88-1.

Stanfill, C., & Kahle, B. (1986). Parallel free text search on the connection machine system. *Communications of the ACM, 29*, 12.

Stein, J.M., & Urdang, L. (1981). *The Random House dictionary of the English language*. NY: Random House.

Talmy, L. (1988). Force dynamics in language and cognition. *Cognitive Science, 12*, 49–100.

Tennant, H. (1984). Menu-based natural language understanding, *AFIPS Proceedings of the National Computer Conference*, Las Vegas, NV, 629–635.

Waltz, D., & Feldman, J. (Eds.) (1988). *Connectionist models and their implementations*. Norwood, NJ: Ablex.

Waltz, D.L. (1982). Event shape diagrams. *Proceedings of the National Conference on Artificial Intelligence* (pp. 84–87). Pittsburgh, PA.

Waltz, D.L. (1981a). Toward a detailed model of processing for language describing the physical world. *Proceedings of International Joint Conference on Artificial Intelligence, 81*, (pp. 1–6). Vancouver, B.C.

Waltz, D.L. (1981b). Generating and understanding scene descriptions. In Joshi, Sag, & Webber (Eds.), *Elements of discourse understanding* (pp. 266–282). Cambridge, UK: Cambridge University Press.

Waltz, D.L., & Boggess, L. (1979). Visual analog representations for natural language understanding. *Proceedings 6th International Joint Conference on Artificial Intelligence* (pp. 926–934). Tokyo, Japan.

Waltz, D.L., & Dorfman, M. (1983). The holes in points. *The Behavioral and Brain Sciences, 6*, 612–613.

Waltz, D.L. & Pollack, J.B. (1985). Massively parallel parsing: a strongly interactive model of natural language interpretation, *Cognitive Science 9*, 1, 51–74. Also in Waltz & Feldman (1988), 181–204.

Wilensky, R., (1983). Story grammars versus story points. *The Behavioral and Brain Sciences, 6*, 579–623.

Wilks, Y.A. (1975). An intelligent analyzer and understander of English. *Communications of the ACM, 18*, 264–274.

Winograd, T. (1978). On primitives, prototypes, and other semantic anomalies. In D. Waltz (Ed.), *TINLAP-2: Theoretical Issues in Natural Language Processing-2* (pp. 25–32). NY: Association for Computational Machinery.

Woods, W.A. (1975). What's in a link: foundations for semantic networks. In D. Bobrow & A. Collins, *Representation and Understanding: Studies in Cognitive Science*, NY: Academic Press, 35–82. Also in Brachman & Levesque (1983), 217–241.

CHAPTER 1

Knowledge Interactions and Integrated Parsing for Narrative Comprehension

MICHAEL G. DYER
Computer Science Department
University of California, Los Angeles

INTRODUCTION

This chapter describes some of the major theoretical aspects of BORIS, a story-understanding and question-answering computer program developed by the author while at Yale University (Dyer, 1983a). BORIS is designed to read stories involving complicated interpersonal and social situations, specifically those that arise in a divorce. The following is a story that BORIS received as verbatim input, followed by sample questions and their answers as generated by BORIS.

DIVORCE–1

D1-pgh1: Richard hadn't heard from his college roommate Paul for years. Richard had borrowed money from Paul which was never paid back, but now he had no idea where to find his old friend. When a letter finally arrived from San Francisco, Richard was anxious to find out how Paul was.

D1-pgh2: Unfortunately, the news was not good. Paul's wife Sarah wanted a divorce. She also wanted the car, the house, the children,

1

and alimony. Paul wanted the divorce, but he didn't want to see Sarah walk off with everything he had. His salary from the state school system was very small. Not knowing who to turn to, he was hoping for a favor from the only lawyer he knew. Paul gave his home phone number in case Richard felt he could help.

D1-pgh3: Richard eagerly picked up the phone and dialed. After a brief conversation, Paul agreed to have lunch with him the next day. He sounded extremely relieved and grateful.

D1-pgh4: The next day, as Richard was driving to the restaurant he barely avoided hitting an old man on the street. He felt extremely upset by the incident, and had three drinks at the restaurant. When Paul arrived Richard was fairly drunk. After the food came, Richard spilled a cup of coffee on Paul. Paul seemed very annoyed by this so Richard offered to drive him home for a change of clothes.

D1-pgh5: When Paul walked into the bedroom and found Sarah with another man he nearly had a heart attack. Then he realized what a blessing it was. With Richard there as a witness, Sarah's divorce case was shot. Richard congratulated Paul and suggested that they celebrate at dinner. Paul was eager to comply.

> What happened to Richard at home?
> RICHARD GOT A LETTER FROM PAUL.
>
> Did Richard want to see Paul?
> YES, RICHARD WANTED TO KNOW HOW PAUL WAS.
>
> Had Paul helped Richard?
> YES, PAUL LENT MONEY TO RICHARD.
>
> Why didn't Richard pay Paul back?
> RICHARD DID NOT KNOW WHERE PAUL WAS.
>
> What was the letter about?
> PAUL AND SARAH WERE GETTING A DIVORCE.
>
> Did Paul write Sarah?
> NO, IT WASN'T SARAH, IT WAS RICHARD
> WHO GOT THE LETTER.
>
> Why was Paul upset about the divorce?
> PAUL AND SARAH WERE FIGHTING OVER
> THE FAMILY POSSESSIONS.
>
> What did Paul do for a living?
> PAUL WAS A TEACHER.
>
> What did Sarah want?
> SARAH WANTED TO HAVE THE CAR AND THE HOUSE AND
> THE KIDS AND THE ALIMONY.

Why did Paul write to Richard?
PAUL WANTED RICHARD TO BE HIS LAWYER.

How did Richard contact Paul?
BY PHONE.

Why did Richard call Paul?
RICHARD WANTED TO ARRANGE A MEETING WITH PAUL.

How did Paul feel when Richard called?
PAUL WAS HAPPY BECAUSE RICHARD AGREED TO BE
PAUL'S LAWYER.

Why did Richard eat out with Paul?
RICHARD WANTED TO DISCUSS THE DIVORCE CASE
WITH PAUL.

What happened to Richard on the way
to the restaurant?
RICHARD ALMOST RAN OVER AN OLD MAN.

Why did Richard get drunk?
RICHARD WAS UPSET ABOUT ALMOST RUNNING OVER
THE OLD MAN.

What happened at the restaurant?
RICHARD SPILLED COFFEE ON PAUL.

Why did Richard spill the coffee?
RICHARD WAS DRUNK.

Why did Richard drive Paul home?
SO PAUL COULD CHANGE HIS CLOTHES.

What happened to Paul at home?
PAUL CAUGHT SARAH COMMITTING ADULTERY.

Why was Paul surprised when he got home?
PAUL CAUGHT SARAH COMMITTING ADULTERY.

Why did Sarah lose her divorce case?
SARAH COMMITTED ADULTERY.

Why did Richard congratulate Paul?
PAUL WON THE DIVORCE CASE.

The process of narrative comprehension involves extracting the conceptual content of natural language statements in order to construct an episodic memory that represents the causal and conceptual relationships between the actions and motivations of narrative characters. The resulting episodic memory is then accessed and searched by retrieval processes during question answering. However, the task of narrative comprehension is complex. We can see why this is the case by briefly examining the stories read by BORIS. Consider some of the problems that DIVORCE–1 poses for computer comprehension:

> D1-pgh1: Richard hadn't heard from . . . which was never paid back . . . no idea where to find . . . When a letter arrived . . . Richard was anxious to find out how Paul was.

In the first paragraph we are presented with three nonevents. But what is BORIS supposed to do when told that something did not happen? Nonevents are meaningful only in the context of expectations for their occurrence.

BORIS must contain a theory of expectation failures to properly process such negatives. Notice also that the text never explicitly states that the letter is from Paul. BORIS must infer this fact from knowledge of letters and interpersonal goals.

> D1-pgh2: . . . Paul's wife wanted a divorce . . . he didn't want to see Sarah walk off with everything he had . . . he was hoping for a favor from the only lawyer he knew.

What is a "divorce" in computer memory? Why does Paul need a lawyer? To understand what is going on here, BORIS must have knowledge of both the legal and interpersonal aspects of marriage. What does "everything" refer to? "Walk off" here does not refer simply to a physical action of the legs. Notice also that the text never explicitly states that Richard is a lawyer. This also must be inferred from character goals and plans. In addition, this entire paragraph is actually an embedded narration within the context of the letter. Yet, we are never explicitly told that we are entering or leaving the content of this letter.

> D1-pgh3: . . . Paul agreed to have lunch with him the next day. He sounded very relieved and grateful.

Who does "he" refer to here, Paul or Richard? What are the conceptual representations for "relieved" and "grateful" and how do they help resolve this reference?

> D1-pgh4: . . . barely avoided hitting an old man . . . When Paul arrived . . . Richard spilled coffee . . . offered to drive . . .

Again we have a nonevent (i.e., an accident never occurred), but it has an effect on Richard nonetheless. Why? When Paul arrives we are not surprised. Why not? Why are we expecting Paul here? What does spilled coffee have to do with clothing and an offer to drive someone home? All of these events have to be connected up in a causally meaningful way.

> D1-pgh5: . . . Paul walked into the bedroom and found Sarah with another man he nearly had a heart attack . . . Sarah's divorce case was shot . . . Richard congratulated Paul . . .

Here, "heart attack" does not really refer to cardiac arrest, but to an emotional reaction. But why is Paul surprised? Notice that the text never explicitly states that Sarah was having a sexual encounter. This inference must be made based on knowledge of settings. The phrase, "case was shot" does not refer to a container being hit by bullets. Context must be used to correctly disambiguate word meanings. What is the representation of "congratulated" and why is Paul congratulated? We are not told that Paul has won. This must be inferred from the fact that Sarah has lost.

These problems are not unique to DIVORCE–1, but occur naturally in almost any narrative text. To test the generality of BORIS, a second story, DIVORCE–2, was created. This story is presented here, along with questions and answers generated by BORIS.

DIVORCE–2

D2-pgh1: George was having lunch with another teacher and grading homework assignments when the waitress accidentally knocked a glass of coke on him. George was very annoyed and left, refusing to pay the check. He decided to drive home to get out of his wet clothes.

D2-pgh2: When he got there, he found his wife Ann and another man in bed. George became extremely upset and felt like going out and getting plastered.

D2-pgh3: At the bar he ran into an old college roommate David, who he hadn't seen in years. David offered to buy him a few drinks and soon they were both pretty drunk. When George found out that David was a lawyer, he told him all about his troubles and asked David to represent him in court. Since David owed George money he had never returned, he felt obligated to help out.

D2-pgh4: Later, David wrote to Ann, informing her that George wanted a divorce. Her lawyer called back and told David that she intended to get the house, the children, and a lot of alimony. When George heard this, he was very worried. He didn't earn much at the junior high school. David told him not to worry, since the judge would award the case to George once he learned that Ann had been cheating on him.

D2-pgh5: When they got to court, David presented George's case, but without a witness they had no proof and Ann won. George almost had a fit. David could only offer George his condolences.

D2-pgh6: A week later, George received a large bill in the mail from David. Was he furious!

What did George do for a living?
GEORGE WAS A TEACHER.

What happened at the restaurant?
THE WAITRESS SPILLED COKE ON GEORGE
AND HE REFUSED TO PAY THE CHECK.

How did George feel at the restaurant?
GEORGE WAS ANGRY BECAUSE THE WAITRESS
SPILLED COKE ON HIM.

How did the waitress feel at the restaurant?
THE WAITRESS REGRETTED THAT SHE SPILLED COKE
ON GEORGE.

Why did George go home?
GEORGE WANTED TO CHANGE CLOTHES.

Why didn't George pay the check?
BECAUSE THE WAITRESS SPILLED COKE ON GEORGE.

How did Ann feel when George caught her
cheating on him?
SHE WAS SURPRISED.

Why did George want to get drunk?
HE WAS UPSET BECAUSE HIS WIFE WAS CHEATING ON HIM.

Why did David buy George drinks?
BECAUSE THEY WERE FRIENDS.

What did David do for a living?
HE WAS A LAWYER.

Did George borrow money from David?
NO. IT WASN'T GEORGE WHO BORROWED MONEY,
IT WAS DAVID.

Why did George tell David his troubles?
GEORGE WANTED DAVID TO BE HIS LAYWER.

Why did David feel obligated to help out George?
HE WANTED TO RETURN A FAVOR BECAUSE HE OWED
GEORGE MONEY.

Why did Ann's lawyer phone David?
HE WANTED TO INFORM DAVID THAT ANN WANTED
THE HOUSE, THE CHILDREN, AND ALIMONY.

Why did David reassure George?
DAVID BELIEVED THAT THE JUDGE WOULD AWARD

THE CASE TO GEORGE BECAUSE ANN HAD BROKEN
THE MARRIAGE CONTRACT.

What happened at court?
THE JUDGE AWARDED THE CASE TO ANN.

How did George feel about the verdict?
GEORGE WAS SURPRISED BECAUSE ANN WON.

Why did George lose the case?
GEORGE DID NOT HAVE A WITNESS TO
THE VIOLATION.

How did David feel about the verdict?
DAVID FELT GUILTY BECAUSE HE HAD TOLD
GEORGE THAT HE WOULD WIN.

Why did David console George?
BECAUSE GEORGE LOST THE FAMILY POSSESSIONS.

Why did David send George a bill?
DAVID REPRESENTED HIM IN COURT.

How did George feel when he received the bill?
GEORGE WAS ANGRY AT DAVID.

Why?
BECAUSE THE BILL WAS TOO LARGE.

DIVORCE–2 differs extensively from DIVORCE–1 in terms of lexical phrases, grammatical constructs, sequence of events, and final outcomes. However, BORIS applies the same world knowledge to understand both divorce stories, and similar problems of comprehension arise in DIVORCE–2. The problems are discussed here.

The Ambiguity Problem

Natural language statements contain words that mean different things depending on the meanings of the words surrounding them. For instance, in D2-pgh2, "getting plastered" means becoming intoxicated, rather than being covered with a composition of lime, sand, and water. In D2-pgh3, "ran into" does not mean the physical act of running, nor does it refer to a vehicle accident, as in "the car ran into a telephone pole."

The Reference Problem

Natural languages contain many forms of reference, which often cannot be resolved syntactically. Consider this sentence in paragraph 4:

D2-pgh4: David told him not to worry, since the judge would award
the case to George once *he* learned that Ann had been cheating on *him*.

People know immediately that "he" refers to the judge, whereas
"him" refers to George. The resolution of these references cannot be
obtained by recourse to syntactic structure or word position. Consider the following alternate sentence:

David told him not to worry, since the judge would award the case to
George once *he* revealed in court that Ann had been cheating on *him*.

Here, "he" refers to George. In each case, knowing who "he" and
"him" refer to requires applying knowledge about judges, witnesses,
and the roles they play.

D2-pgh5: David could only offer George *his* condolences.

Here, the closest referent to "his" is George. However, people correctly resolve "his" to David. How is this resolution accomplished?

D2-pgh6: A week later, George received a large bill in the mail from
David. Was *he* furious!

Who is furious, David or George? Resolving this reference requires
knowledge of social violations and emotional responses.

The Syntax/Semantics Problem

In formal languages, each syntactic construct has a semantic construct associated with it. As a result, semantic analysis can be syntax
directed. In natural languages, however, the syntactic structure of a
sentence often is subservient to the meaning being conveyed. Consider these two sentences:

S1: George was eating lunch with a teacher.
S2: George was eating lunch with a spoon.

In the first sentence, the prepositional phrase "with a teacher" modifies the noun "lunch." In the second sentence, however, the phrase
"with a spoon" modifies the verb phrase "was eating" and indicates
the instrument used in the act of eating. It is the fact that we know
conceptually about the social and physical aspects of eating lunch

that allows us to determine the syntactic structure of these sentences.

The Paraphrase Problem

There are many different ways of conveying the same information and ideas in everyday communication. Consider these pairs of text.

DIVORCE–1:	. . . hadn't heard from his college roommate Paul for years.
DIVORCE–2:	. . . an old college roommmate David, who he hadn't seen in years.
DIVORCE–1:	. . . drive him home for a change of clothes
DIVORCE–2:	. . . drive home to get out of his wet clothes.
DIVORCE–1:	His salary from the state school was very small.
DIVORCE–2:	He didn't earn much at the junior high school.

In each case, BORIS must be able to create the same internal conceptualizations although the input varies both syntactically and lexically.

The Inference Problem

Natural language statements are highly abbreviated and fragmentary at the semantic level. For instance, in DIVORCE–2 we are told:

D2-pgh3: . . . David offered to buy him a few drinks and soon they were both pretty drunk . . .

The text does not explicitly state that David bought drinks, nor that they drank anything, nor where the drinks came from. It is left to the reader to automatically access knowledge about bars, money, chairs, bartenders, swallowing, and the effects of liquor in order to fill in this fragmentary description. Inferences must be applied throughout. Why are George's clothes wet? Why does George refuse to pay the waitress? Why does George want to "get plastered"? Why does David decide to help George? The information needed to answer these questions must be inferred by the reader. If we examine the text of DIVORCE–2, we see that the information needed to answer these questions are not directly supplied in the text. Instead, they must be inferred from knowledge about interpersonal relationships, social obligations, and the physical world of actions and events. A key problem, then, is representing and indexing this knowledge so that the appropriate inferences are applied at the appropriate moment during comprehension.

The Representation Problem

If we are to build a computer program that can understand natural language, we must first have a way of representing the concepts, thoughts, and ideas that sentences in natural languages convey. For instance, how do we represent the concepts conveyed here?

> . . . accidentally knocked a glass of coke . . .
> . . . he told him all about his troubles . . .
> . . . he felt obligated to help out . . .
> . . . Ann had been cheating on him . . .
> . . . without a witness they had no proof . . .
> . . . could only offer George his condolences.

How are these phrases to be conceptually parsed, and what should the result of the parsing process yield? A major task facing any researcher interested in modeling processes of language comprehension is that of representing in a computer the thoughts conveyed in everyday utterances.

FOUNDATIONS IN COMPREHENSION

BORIS is an outgrowth of more than a decade of research in natural language processing. Each of the language-understanding systems and corresponding theoretical constructs described in this section have been incorporated into the BORIS program. As a result, these earlier systems serve as a necessary foundation and context for discussing the advances and novel theoretical extensions that were developed in BORIS and that are discussed in the sections that follow.

Conceptual Dependency Theory

The problem of representing the conceptualizations expressed in everyday natural language utterances was addressed in (Schank, 1973). Schank developed a system of Conceptual Dependencies (CD) based on a small number of semantic primitives that were used to organize shared concepts and inferences in a language-independent way. For example, consider the word "walked," as in:

S3: Henry walked home.

After being told S3 we can conclude that Henry is now at home. To draw such a conclusion, the computer could access a rule, such as:

If a person P1 walks to a location L1
Then P1 will end up at L1

However, in each of the following situations the same conclusion holds:

Henry ran home.
Henry drove home.
Henry took a bus home.
Henry took a train home.
Henry got a ride home.
Frank gave Henry a lift home.

In order for the computer to draw the same conclusion, it appears that many inference rules might be required, including:

If a person P1 runs to a location L1
Then P1 will end up at L1
If a person P1 takes a train to location L1
Then P1 will end up at L1
If a person P1 drives to location L1 . . .

Clearly, the problem with this approach is that the conclusion being drawn has been associated with specific lexical items, such as "walk," "run," and "take a train," instead of being associated with a single concept (i.e., the concept of movement through space). In CD theory, this concept is represented by the semantic primitive PTRANS, which stands for physical transfer. Associated with each semantic primitive are a number of cases, which indicate the object being transferred, the source location, the destination, and the means used to achieve the transfer.

```
PTRANS ACTOR  X
       OBJECT  O
       FROM   L1
       TO  L2
       INSTRUMENT  I
```

This conceptualization is independent of any particular language. For instance, the conceptualizations built by the English words "went," "left," "flew" or the Spanish words "viajar" (travel), "llegar" (arive), all have PTRANS as an integral part of their meaning. One inference associated with the semantic primitive PTRANS is:

> If x PTRANS o from location L1 to L2
> Then both x and o will be at 12.

Now, when the computer analyzes the sentence:

> Henry drove Betty to Los Angeles.

it can access a PTRANS conceptualization as one aspect of the meaning of "drive," execute the corresponding rule, and draw the conclusion that, at some given time, both Henry and Betty were in Los Angeles.

Clearly there are other semantic elements associated with the concept of driving (the use of a car, for instance) and these other components must be represented by other conceptualizations. What we end up with is a conceptual memory where knowledge is factored out, not according to the language being used, but according to shared cultural knowledge and common sense inferences people make about the world. For instance, another CD primitive is ATRANS, which stands for transfer of possession. The English word "buy" is represented in terms of two ATRANSes:

```
ATRANS ACTOR  P1              ATRANS ACTOR  P2
       OBJECT money                  OBJECT o
       FROM  P1          &           FROM  P2
       TO    P2                      TO    P1
```

That is, person P1 transfers possession of money to P2 in exchange for possession of some object. For instance, BORIS constructs conceptualizations involving ATRANS when reading the following texts:

> D1-pgh1: . . . Richard had borrowed money from Paul which was never paid back . . .
> D2-pgh1: . . . George . . . left refusing to pay the check . . .
> D2-pgh3: . . . David offered to buy him a few drinks . . .

Each lexical item may have associations with more than one concept structure. For instance, the concepts of "fly" and "take a train" include, in addition to PTRANS, connections to an ATRANS conceptualization because each of these activities involves the payment of money. One inference rule associated with ATRANS is:

> If actor P1 ATRANS object o to P2
> Then P2 will have possession of o
> and P1 will no longer possess o.

The theory of Conceptual Dependency served as the foundation of the MARGIE system (Schank, 1975). MARGIE demonstrated its understanding of English sentences by generating paraphrases. For instance, given the input sentence:

> S4: Henry paid 2 dollars to the bartender for some wine.

MARGIE could generate numerous paraphrases, including:

Henry paid the bartender 2 dollars for some wine.
The bartender sold Henry some wine for 2 dollars.
Henry paid the bartender 2 dollars to give him some wine.
The bartender gave Henry some wine and he gave him 2 dollars.
Henry bought some wine from the bartender for 2 dollars.
The bartender traded Henry some wine for 2 dollars.

The MARGIE (Schank, 1975) system was composed of three modules: (a) ELI, a natural language sentence understander (Riesbeck & Schank, 1976), (b) MEMORY, a memory and inferencing module (Rieger, 1975), and (c) a natural-language generator called BABEL (Goldman, 1975). Given a sentence as input, ELI mapped it into a language independent conceptualization in CD. Given a CD structure as input, BABEL would generate one or more equivalent expressions in English. Now we can see how MARGIE generated the paraphrases above for sentence S4. First, the ELI module analyzed the sentence to produce the conceptualization:

ATRANS ACTOR Henry		ATRANS ACTOR bartender
FROM Henry		FROM bartender
OBJECT money	&	OBJECT wine
TO bartender		TO Henry

where Henry, money, wine, and bartender are themselves represented as conceptual objects. The BABEL generator took this conceptualization as input. BABEL knew various ways of expressing ATRANS concepts in English. For example, the word "trade" expresses a pair of ATRANSes. The word "buy" indicates that one of the objects involved is money and that the focus of the sentence is on whichever actor ATRANSed the money. The word "sell" focuses on the actor who ATRANSes an object in exchange for the money, and so on.

In addition to generating paraphrases, MARGIE also demonstrated its understanding by generating inferences. Rieger's MEMORY model was organized around 16 classes of inferences. Here are examples of 4 classes of inference that the MEMORY module generated.

1. Specification Inferences
     Henry picked up a brick and hit Frank.
     ⟨Infer: Henry hit Frank with the brick.⟩
2. Functional Inferences
     Henry wants a hamburger.
     ⟨Infer: Henry probably wants to eat it.⟩
3. Feature Inferences
     Pete's diaper is wet.
     ⟨Infer: Pete is probably a baby.⟩
4. Action Prediction Inferences
     Henry wants a new lawn mower.
     ⟨Infer: Henry will probably go to a hardware store.⟩

Although MARGIE was not really designed to handle connected text, the hope was to generate enough inferences so that a chain of conceptualizations could always be found between one sentence and the next. However, there were two problems. For one thing, a great many inferences were generated. For example, consider the sentence:

S5: Henry told Betty that Frank wants a hamburger.

Some of the possible inferences are:

- Henry believes that Frank wants a hamburger.
- Betty now knows that Frank wants a hamburger.
- Frank wants a hamburger.
- Frank wants to come to possess a hamburger.
- Frank probably wants to eat the hamburger after gaining possession of it.

- Frank might get the hamburger himself.
- Henry might get Frank a hamburger.
- Betty might get Frank a hamburger.
- Henry may want Betty to get Frank a hamburger.
- Henry and Betty may have been together recently.

As each new conceptualization was created, many new inferences were generated, leading to an explosion of inferences. In many cases, the chains of inferences produced were extremely implausible. For example,

Henry hit Betty.
|
Betty was hurt.
|
Betty went to the hospital.
|
Betty got better.
|
Betty met a doctor and got married.

Inference: Henry hit Betty so that she would get married.

At the time MARGIE was designed, nobody could see any way around the problem of inference explosion. Rieger argued that massive parallelism would ultimately be needed to make all of these inferences computationally feasible. However, this did not solve the fundamental problem of deciding which particular inference chains made sense, and which did not.

Scripts

Schank noticed that people did not seem to be overwhelmed by irrelevant inferences. In contrast, people have the ability to make just the right inferences in the appropriate situations. Schank postulated that people use cultural knowledge of recurring social situations to control the inferencing process. He called this knowledge a *script*.

Scripts (Schank & Abelson, 1977) contain prepackaged chains of causal inferences that connect conceptualizations representing stereotypic action sequences. For example, a common script is $RESTAU-RANT, which contains the roles of diner, waiter (or waitress), cashier, cook, and the following sequence of CD structures:

```
diner PTRANS to restaurant
diner PTRANS to table
waiter PTRANS to diner
diner ORDER food
waiter PTRANS from table to kitchen
waiter PTRANS food from kitchen to table
waiter ATRANS food from waiter to diner
diner INGEST food
diner PTRANS from table to cashier
diner ATRANS money from diner to cashier
diner PTRANS from restaurant
```

This description specifies a default sequence of actions. A script may contain alternate "paths." For example, the diner may pay the waiter instead of paying the cashier, or the diner may wait for the waiter to seat the diner. Scripts also have internal structure. For example, the restaurant script is broken up into various scenes. The ORDER scene has its own internal structure, including examining a menu, conversing with the waiter, and so on. Also, some scenes are more important than others. For example, the eating scene is the main scene in $RESTAURANT. Finally, scripts have a standard setting. For example, $RESTAURANT occurs in a restaurant, $MOVIE occurs inside a theater, $WEDDING at a church, $GROCERY-SHOPPING at a grocery store, $FOOTBALL at a playing field, and so on.

The theory of scripts was tested computationally in a story-understanding program named SAM (Cullingford, 1978). SAM used scripts to understand stories about stereotypic activities. Consider the following story fragment SAM read:

STORY 1: John went to the restaurant. The waiter brought John a menu. John ordered lobster. Later, John left a big tip.

What did John eat? Clearly, the answer is "lobster." However, we were never told this fact explicitly. This can only be inferred from cultural knowledge about what goes on in restaurant (i.e., that people usually eat what they order).

SAM operated as follows: SAM's conceptual analyzer would parse each sentence into a Conceptual Dependency structure. When SAM noticed a PTRANS to a restaurant setting it would activate the script $RESTAURANT. After each subsequent sentence was parsed, $RESTAURANT would be applied and if a match were found, then the corresponding event in $RESTAURANT would be instantiated. Unmentioned, intervening events within the script would also be instantiated. Thus, SAM knew that John must have INGESTED the lobster even though this event was never mentioned. SAM also knew that John probably read a menu, that the waiter brought the food, and that John paid for the food.

In BORIS, for instance, knowledge of the restaurant script is used to understand the text:

> D1-pgh4: . . . After the food came, Richard spilled a cup of coffee . . .

Of course, food cannot arrive on its own power. BORIS uses scriptal knowledge to infer that Richard and Paul had previously ordered food, and that this food was being brought to them by a waitress. Similarly, the mention of "a cup of coffee" is not surprising to BORIS because coffee is a standard *prop* in the restaurant script.

Scripts gave SAM cultural knowledge about human behavior and social interactions. Because scripts contain prepackaged inference chains, by activating the correct script SAM could avoid the combinatoric explosion of irrelevant inferences that had plagued MARGIE. In addition, scripts provide a social and linguistic context that aids the process of comprehension. For example, scripts can be used to handle pronoun references, as in STORY 2:

> STORY 2: John entered the restaurant and the waiter seated *him*. Then *he* gave *him* a menu. After *he* read *it* *he* decided to order lobster. After *he* brought *it* to *him* *he* ate *it*. Later, *he* left *him* a big tip.

STORY 2 is not a very clearly written story; however, people have little trouble understanding it. The pronouns in this story cannot be resolved by syntactic or semantic information. The only way they can be resolved is at the cultural level. We must know what goes on in a restaurant and apply this knowledge before we can make sense of these references. Such pronoun references were easy for SAM. For instance, "he ate it" would be parsed into:

INGEST ACTOR (ANIMATE
GENDER MALE)
OBJECT (PHYSICAL-OBJECT)

Because $RESTAURANT was active, this script would be applied. That is, this conceptualization would be analyzed in the context of what happens in a restaurant. At this point, a match would be found with the INGEST event in $RESTAURANT. Thus, the "he" would end up being bound to the diner and the "it" to the food.

Goals and Plans

Scripts are useful for understanding stereotypic behavior, such as throwing rice at a wedding or saying "hello" when answering the phone. However, not all human behavior can be captured by scripts. Consider the following text:

> The vice-president wanted to become president.
> He went to the drug store and bought some poison.

When people read this text they draw the conclusion that the vice-president plans to poison the president. However, it is rather far-fetched to postulate a script called VICE-DRUG-STORE-POISON-PRES in order to understand this text. Instead, people use more general knowledge about people's goals and the kinds of plans available for achieving them. In this case we know:

> Poisoning a person is a way of killing that person.
> Poison can be obtained at a drug store.
> When a president dies the vice-president becomes president.

Because we know the vice-president's goal, we understand his action of buying poison as part of a plan to achieve his goal.

PAM was a story understanding system that used goal/plan information to handle stories dealing with character motivations and actions that are nonstereotypic (Wilensky, 1978). Some of the classes of goals (Schank & Abelson, 1977) used in PAM were:

> satisfaction goals: (i.e., recurring bodily needs)
>   S-HUNGER, S-THIRST, S-SLEEP, S-SEX
> delta-goals: (i.e., goals to achieve a change in state)
>   D-PROX (change in proximity to a location)
>   D-CONT (change in control of an object)
>   D-KNOW (change in knowledge state)
>   D-AGENT (acquire/change agent)
> preservation goals: (i.e., goals activated only when threatened)
>   P-HEALTH, P-FINANCES, P-FRIENDSHIP
> achievement goals: (i.e., long-term aspirations)
>   A-GOOD-JOB, A-POWER, A-SKILL, A-STATUS
> entertainment goals:
>   E-TRAVEL, E-EXERCISE, E-EATING, E-COMPETITION

For each goal, PAM knew several ways of achieving it. For example,

PAM knew that the goal of gaining control of an object (i.e., D-CONT) could be achieved by the following plans:

1. Ask the owner to give it to you.
2. Talk the owner into giving it to you by explaining why it would be to his advantage.
3. Bargain with the owner, offering to buy or exchange some other object for it.
4. Threaten the owner with harm if he doesn't give it to you.
5. Overpower the owner and take it from him by force.
6. Steal the object when the owner is unaware.

For example, PAM used knowledge of goals and plans to understand the following story:

STORY 3: John wanted money. He got a gun and walked into the liquor store. He told the owner he wanted some money. The owner gave John the money and John left.

and to answer the following goal-oriented questions:

Q: Why did John get the gun?
A: Because John wanted to rob the liquor store.
Q: Why did John threaten the shopkeeper?
A: Because John needed some money.
Q: Why did the shopkeeper give John the money?
A: Because the shopkeeper didn't want to get hurt.

Basically, whenever PAM was told about a character's goal, followed subsequently by a character action, PAM would try to match that action against possible plans available for achieving that goal. PAM used its knowledge of goals and plans in STORY 3 to realize that John was threatening to violate the shopkeeper's goal of preservation of health by shooting the shopkeeper with the gun, and that is why the shopkeeper gave John the money.

BORIS uses goals and plans to represent the motivations and actions of its narrative characters. For example, the spilling of liquid on Paul in DIVORCE–1, and on George in DIVORCE–2, caused each a violation of P-COMFORT and P-APPEARANCE goals. One way to satisfy these goals is to execute the plan of CHANGE-CLOTHES. An enablement condition on this plan is the delta-goal of D-PROX(HOME). One plan for achieving D-PROX(HOME) is to PTRANS with a VEHICLE (i.e., "drive"). The ACTOR of this PTRANS may be an AGENT, as in the case of Richard driving Paul home in DIVORCE–1. As a result of this goal/plan analysis, BORIS can connect up the sequence of acts and states (i.e., spill, wet, drive, home, change, clothes) into a causally connected conceptual structure that is then traversed during question answering.

Object Primitives

The theory of Conceptual Dependency originally developed by Schank was best suited for representing knowledge about physical actions. As we have seen, this theory was later extended by Schank and Abelson, Cullingford, and Wilensky to handle stereotypic social situations and human intentionality through the creation of scripts, plans, and goals. Conceptual Dependency theory was further extended by Lehnert, who developed a system of Object Primitives (Lehnert, 1978). These primitives correspond with the primitives of CD theory, but are designed to capture knowledge about physical objects. These primitives include: CONNECTOR, SEPARATOR, SOURCE, CONSUMER, GESTALT, and RELATIONAL. Object Primitives are used to organize inferences around the meaning of physical objects. For example:

```
faucet = SOURCE for water
            enablement: turn handle
ballpoint pen = SOURCE for ink
            enablement: contact with paper
window (closed) = SEPARATOR for sound
                    CONNECTOR for vision
door (open) = CONNECTOR for PTRANS from room1 to room2
umbrella (open) = SEPARATOR
                    disenables: rain PTRANS to head
radio = SOURCE for music
            enablement: turn knob clockwise
table setting = GESTALT
                    parts: plate, glass, bowl, silverware, napkin
                    configuration: radial with plate at center
                        silverware on-top-of napkin glass at one o'clock,
                        etc.
```

Consider the following story, taken from (Lehnert, 1978):

STORY 4: John picked up a newspaper. He went in from the hall into the kitchen and got some milk. But the milk carton was empty, and so he threw it out. He turned on the light and radio. Then he listened to music and read.

Understanding this story requires knowledge of physical objects. Without such knowledge, the following questions cannot be answered, because none of this information is explicitly given.

> Q: Where did the milk come from?
> A: The refrigerator.
> Q: Where did the milk carton go?
> A: The garbage bag.
> Q: What did John read?
> A: The newspaper.
> Q: Why did John turn on the radio?
> A: So he could hear the music.

Lehnert and Burstein (1979) developed a program, OPUS, that could read stories like STORY 4 and answer such questions. For example, when asked where the milk carton went, OPUS used its knowledge of objects to realize that the question referred to a CONSUMER of empty cartons. It then accessed its knowledge of physical objects to draw the conclusion that John probably threw the milk carton into a garbage bag.

BORIS must know about physical objects and their roles. Just some of the physical objects mentioned in DIVORCE−1 and DIVORCE−2 are: phone, money, alcohol, bed, house, car, and glass. In BORIS, physical objects are understood in terms of enablement conditions and social use. For instance, ALCOHOL is LIQUID, therefore it can be INGESTed. Furthermore, ALCOHOL enables the mental state of INTOXI-CATION. BORIS applies this knowledge to understand:

> D1-pgh3: . . . had three drinks at the restaurant. When Paul arrived Richard was fairly drunk . . .
> D2-pgh2: . . . offered to buy him a few drinks and soon they were both pretty drunk . . .

Skimming with Sketchy Scripts

Both SAM and PAM received CD conceptualizations as input. They relied on ELI to perform the task of conceptual analysis. Thus, parsing was performed first, followed by either goal/plan or script application. However, there are two major problems with this approach:

1. This approach lacks psychological validity. Recent experiments indicate that people do not first build a concept for a sentence, and then apply general knowledge afterwards. Instead, it appears that people apply many forms of knowledge, on a word-to-word basis, as the sentence is being understood (Marslen-Wilson, Tyler, & Seidenberg, 1978).
2. Isolating parsing from knowledge application makes parsing more difficult. In both SAM and PAM, the parser had to understand each sentence first. This meant that the knowledge available in the script applier and goal/plan applier were not available at parsing time to aid in the parsing process.

As an experiment in integrated partial understanding, FRUMP (DeJong, 1979) was developed. FRUMP was a text skimmer, "sketchy script" applier, and UPI news wire summary generator. That is, FRUMP had many shallow scripts in memory and would try to understand just enough of a given story to instantiate one of its scripts. FRUMP then used its instantiated script as the basis for generating a sparse, one-to-two sentence summary of each news story read.

What was novel about FRUMP was that script application was no longer separate from conceptual analysis. In FRUMP, the active script directed the parsing process. For example, once the script $FIGHTING was selected, the script applier would direct the parser to look for an instance of shooting. If the word "shot" were encountered, the parser would immediate interpret it as an instance of firing a weapon. Other potential meanings, such as taking a picture (as in "the cameramen shot the love scene") would never even be considered.

This top-down approach made FRUMP a very fast and robust text skimmer. However, FRUMP had fundamental limitations. First, FRUMP was unable to deal with knowledge interactions. Whenever several scripts occurred in a news story, FRUMP could only activate the first script it encountered. Second, FRUMP's top-down approach meant that any text that did not conform to FRUMP's scriptal expectations would not be understood. Thus, many unusual and interesting events were completely ignored. FRUMP could only understand texts that fit, in some sense, what it already expected to hear.

In contrast, BORIS attempts to understand everything it reads, relying on bottom-up information available in the text. Unlike FRUMP, BORIS must integrate many distinct sources of knowledge.

MULTIPLE KNOWLEDGE SOURCES IN BORIS

As we have seen, SAM applied scripts; PAM accessed goal- and plan-based knowledge; OPUS used Object Primitives, whereas FRUMP integrated parsing processes with script-based processing. After experience with these programs, it became clear that an important next step in narrative comprehension required designing a program able to integrate all of these knowledge structures into a coherent whole in order to understand more complicated stories.

To understand DIVORCE−1 and DIVORCE−2, BORIS must access and integrate many disparate sources of knowledge, including:

Knowledge	Examples
scripts	restaurant, bar, phoning
plans	deciding to go home
	deciding to meet for lunch
goals	wanting to win the case
	wanting help from a friend
general situations	favors, service contracts
relationships	friendship, roommates, marriage
social roles	lawyer, waitress, teacher
settings	home, restaurant, road, bedroom
physical objects	phone, liquor, money, food, letter
physical actions	eating, talking, walking
beliefs & legal	that Sarah would lose her case
reasoning	that Paul would win his case
	and how the judge would rule
emotions	gratitude, anger, surprise, worry
expectation	
failures	spilled liquid, overcharged bill,
	cheating wife

The resulting theory of narrative comprehension is embodied in BORIS (Better Organized Reading and Inference System). BORIS (Dyer, 1983a, Dyer & Lehnert, 1982) contains a number of advances over previous story understanding systems developed at Yale. These include:

1. Extensions in knowledge representation: BORIS accounts for knowledge interactions and comprehension with multiple perspectives.
2. A theory of integrated, bottom-up parsing: BORIS integrates parsing processes with episodic memory search processes. This integration has novel effects on both question comprehension and answer retrieval.
3. A system of AFFECT primitives: BORIS uses these primitives for representing and understanding the significance of emotional responses and interpersonal relationships on the part of narrative characters.
4. A theory of in-depth understanding, cross-contextual remindings, and abstract planning through the representation and recognition of abstract themes.

Each of these advances are discussed in turn.

GENERALIZING SCRIPTS WITH MULTIPLE PERSPECTIVES

The notion of script was extended and generalized in BORIS through the use of MOPs (Memory Organization Packets). MOPs were originally postulated in (Schank, 1982a) to account for memory confusions in human recall. For example, in memory and reading experiments, subjects would confuse visits to doctors with visits to dentists (Bower, Black, & Turner, 1979). In script theory, however, $DENTIST-VISIT and $DOCTOR-VISIT were two distinct scripts, so no memory confusions were possible. The theory of MOPs was proposed to account for these memory confusions by capturing those elements shared among scripts. In BORIS, MOPs are used to relate different types of knowledge so that only relevant knowledge constructs are activated during comprehension. MOPs serve three purposes in BORIS:

1. They are used during processing as one way of representing a single event from more than one *perspective*.
2. MOPs represent knowledge that is more abstract and general than scripts.
3. MOPs hold goal and plan information lacking in earlier script structures.

Events in each MOP are related to events in other MOPs by way of *strands* (i.e., associations across MOPs that indicate relations between goals, plans, and roles). The use of strands is depicted in Figure 1.1. As we can see in Figure 1.1., BORIS not only knows about specific activities performed by waiters in a restaurant, it also knows that these activities are part of a more general situation (i.e., a contract for service). M-SERVICE also functions as a perspective on M-REPRESENT-CLIENT, and accounts for one of several perspectives on the goals of the lawyer. From the perspectives of M-LEGAL-DISPUTE, a lawyer represents a client in order to win the case for his client by convincing the judge to side with his client. From the perspective of M-SERVICE, however, a lawyer has the goal of representing a client in order to obtain money in payment for services rendered. M-SERVICE holds very general information about service contracts. Figure 1.2 depicts graphically part of the internal structure of M-SERVICE.

Plans appear in the middle of Figure 1.2, whereas the goals of the server and the client are depicted on either side. Goals and plans are connected by a series of intentional links (I-links), which are abbreviated in the diagram as "a," "i," and "m." These I-links stand for "achievement," "intention," and "motivation," respectively.

I-link	semantics
a	If plan P is executed, then it will result in the achievement of goal G
i	If a character x has goal G active, then x may intend to use plan P.
m	If plan P is followed, then its realization may motivate new goals on the part of characters affected by P

```
                    M-SERVICE              M-LEGAL-DISPUTE
                 +----------------+      +--------------------+
                 |              |        |                  |
              * * * *  *WANT-SERVICE* * * |                  |
                 *    |          | *      |    PETITION- * * |
          * * * * * * * * DO-SERVICE  | *  |    JUDGE     * |
          *      *    |        *     | *   |             * |
          *      *    +-------*--------+ * +--------------*-+
          *  * * *         *       *                      *
          *  *          * * *      *                      *
          *  *  M-RESTAURANT    *    *  M-REPRESENT-CLIENT  *
          *  * +--------------+   *    * +--------------------+ *
          *  * |            |   *    * |                  | *
          *  * * *WANT-FOOD  |   *    * * * * NEED-LAWYER  | *
          *    |            |   *    * |                  | *
          *    |            | * * * * * * * PRESENT-* * * * *
          * * * * BRING-FOOD  |        |    EVIDENCE     |
               |            |        |                  |
               +--------------+      +--------------------+
```

Figure 1.1.

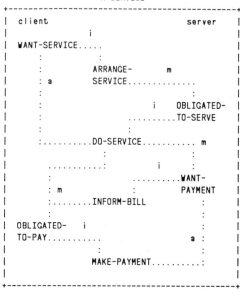

Figure 1.2.

M-SERVICE captures the following common sense knowledge about service contracts: If a client has a goal (WANT-SERVICE) that requires an agent, then the client can negotiate (ARRANGE-SERVICE) with the server for service. If the server agrees, then the server will now have the goal (OGLIGATED-TO-SERVE) of performing the service. This goal can only be satisfied by performing the service (DO-SERVICE). Once the service has been performed, the client's goal is achieved. Furthermore, the realization of the service will motivate the client (OBLIGATED-TO-PAY) to pay the server for his service (MAKE-PAYMENT). If the client has not yet paid the server, then the server may remind the client (INFORM-BILL) of this fact. Once the client has paid the server, the server's goal for having performed the service (WANT-PAYMENT) is then achieved. Each goal and plan has its own internal conceptualizations. For example, WANT-PAYMENT contains a CD structure with as D-CONT goal as its conceptualization:

D-CONT ACTOR server
OBJECT money
FROM client

Notice that the goals and events in M-SERVICE are very abstract. Any activity might constitute a service. So the specific content of M-

SERVICE depends on the way in which it is instantiated during processing.

The use of multiple perspectives (Dyer, 1981a) increases the ability of BORIS to deal with the unexpected. Whenever an unexpected event occurs, BORIS searches MOP strands in an attempt to find a knowledge construct that can deal with the expectation failure. For example, consider the following story:

> STORY 5: John left his car at the garage to be fixed. When John came back, the car was leaking oil. John refused to pay the mechanic.

For SAM to understand this story, SAM would have to have a special path built into $GARAGE containing the event sequence of not paying after encountering something wrong. A similar path was also required in $RESTAURANT for SAM to understand any story in which the diner did not pay because his food was burnt. Basically, SAM could only handle those scriptal deviations that had already been incorporated into the script as an alternate path. Unfortunately, the approach of building each deviant path into each script lead to a proliferation of paths. In SAM each service-related script had to contain numerous alternate paths. In BORIS, however, there is only one M-SERVICE where this information is contained. When any service-related script is violated, strands are traversed to M-SERVICE, and the violation is then understood in terms of this more general perspective.

Consider how BORIS processes the following fragment from DIVORCE−2:

> Pgh-1: George was having lunch . . . when the waitress accidentally knocked a glass of coke on him. George . . . left refusing to pay the check . . .

Briefly, an analysis of "having lunch" activates M-MEAL. When "waitress" occurs, the MOPs associated with this role are examined. If a MOP being examined has a strand to an active MOP, then it is also activated. Because there are strands from M-RESTAURANT to M-MEAL, and because M-MEAL is already active, M-RESTAURANT is activated also. (In this way, BORIS avoids activating M-RESTAURANT in cases such as: "George is in love with a waitress.") An interpretation of "accidentally" indicates that a violation may follow. This heuristic is based on the assumption that unintended actions usually violate scriptal expectations.

"Knocked a glass of coke on him" is analyzed in terms of the Conceptual Dependency primitive PROPEL (Object = Liquid). Given this event, BORIS tries to match it against the events expected in M-RESTAURANT. This match would normally fail, because M-RESTAURANT does not expect waitresses to PROPEL foodstuffs. However, "accidentally" has warned BORIS of a possible violation, so a violation match is attempted and succeeds. At this point, BORIS realizes that the PROPEL event is a violation of the event BRING-FOOD in M-RESTAURANT, rather than some event totally unrelated to M-RESTAURANT.

Now what is BORIS to do? In previous systems, there would be a path in the script for such a deviation. However, this is not the case here. When BORIS encounters a deviation, it searches the strands connected to the event where the deviation occurred. This leads to the DO-SERVICE event in M-SERVICE. Associated with M-SERVICE is general knowledge about how things may "go wrong" for each event in M-SERVICE. There are several events, such as: ARRANGE-SERVICE, DO-SERVICE, INFORM-BILL, MAKE-PAYMENT, and so on. For example, the sentence:

> The waitress overcharged George

constitutes a violation of INFORM-BILL in M-SERVICE. In addition, there is knowledge about how violations may be related to one another. This knowledge is represented by these rules:

> sr1: If SERVER has done SERVICE
>   badly (or not at all),
>   Then SERVER should either not BILL
>   CONTRACTOR or BILL for amount < NORM.
> sr2: If SERVER has done SERVICE badly
>   or BILLs CONTRACTOR for amount > NORM,
>   Then CONTRACTOR may REFUSE PAYMENT.

BORIS uses this knowledge to recognize the connection between the waitress' PROPEL LIQUID and George's refusal to pay a check.

Left to consider is how BORIS realizes that the violation of BRING-FOOD actually constitutes POOR-SERVICE. This is accomplished by tracking the goals of the characters. The PROPEL LIQUID on George is understood to cause a P-COMFORT goal for George. This goal is examined by M-SERVICE, which applies the following heuristic:

> sr3: If SERVER causes a PERSERVATION
>   GOAL for CONTRACTOR while
>   performing SERVICE,
>   Then it is probably POOR-SERVICE.

Thus, BORIS uses several sources of knowledge to understand what has happened. M-RESTAURANT supplies expectations for what the waitress should have done. Knowledge about PROPEL and LIQUIDS supplies goal information, whereas M-SERVICE (between waitress and diner) provides very general knowledge about how contractors will respond to poor service.

M-SERVICE is also used in processing the last paragraph in DIVORCE −2:

> A week later, George received a large bill in the mail from David. Was he furious!

Who does "he" refer to in "Was he furious!"? When BORIS reads about the receipt of a bill, it matches the billing event expected in M-SERVICE. The mention of "large" indicates that the AMOUNT of the bill is greater than the norm. This constitutes a violation. In both cases:

1. Refusing to pay the waitress.
2. Receiving a large bill from the lawyer.

the processing and memory instantiations are very similar.

In BORIS, more than one perspective can be active for the same event. For example, people often give two answers to the following question:

> Q: Why did Richard meet Paul at the restaurant?
> A1: Richard wanted to renew an old friendship with old college roomate.
> A2: Richard wanted to discuss Paul's divorce case with him.

These two answers come from two different perspectives active for the meeting. One is a legal perspective, whereas the other is interpersonal. Similarly, when people are asked:

> Q: How did Paul feel when he caught his wife committing adultery?

they often provide more than one answer.

> A1: Surprised and happy.
> A2: Shocked and angry.

Again, each response comes from a different perspective. From the point of view of M-LEGAL-DISPUTE, Paul should feel happy. From a marital point of view, Paul should be angry.

PROCESSES OF COMPREHENSION

As we have seen, the parser used by SAM and PAM operated in isolation from script and goal/plan application. FRUMP achieved a level of parsing integration; however, the parser in FRUMP was totally directed by the script applier. As a result, FRUMP was insensitive to unexpected information available from the text itself. Consider the following story:

> STORY 6: John went into the restaurant, pulled out a gun and ordered the waitress to go to the cash register.

Once FRUMP selected $RESTAURANT as the active script, the word "ordered" would be interpreted as the ordering scene in $RESTAURANT. Bottom-up information, available directly from the text, would be ignored in favor of preexisting expectations.

To understand STORY 6, two problems must be solved: (a) bottom-up and top-down information must be applied in an effective manner, and (b) different sources of knowledge must interact coherently. For instance, in STORY 6 the gun and the ordering should be understood in terms of a robbery; the waitress in terms of the restaurant script, and the cash register in terms of both knowledge sources.

Knowledge interactions occur throughout both divorce stories. For example, in DIVORCE–2 George refuses to pay after having liquid spilled on him. In DIVORCE–1, Paul also has liquid spilled on him. However, in this case it would be very strange for Paul to refuse to pay the waitress. Why is this so? Clearly, the reactions of the characters not only depend on the goal that has been violated, but also on the relationship existing between the characters involved. Consequently, BORIS cannot have a simple rule, such as:

> If x spills liquid on y in a restaurant
> They y can refuse to pay the check.

Instead, BORIS must monitor the relationship between the characters. In the case of a contractual violation, payment may be refused. Among friends, however, the following rule applies:

> If x causes a goal failure for y
> and x and y are friends
> Then x may offer to help y recover from the failure

Thus, Richard's offer to drive Paul home makes sense.[1]

In both DIVORCE–1 and DIVORCE–2, the husbands find their wives with another man. Again, BORIS combines different sources of knowledge in order to infer sexual activity. This inference is made on the basis of knowledge about settings. BORIS interprets the phrase "with another man" in terms of a social activity. When BORIS fails to instantiate this activity it then tries to infer it, using the following rule:

> If the social activity between x and y
> is unknown, but the setting is known
> and there is a social activity SA
> associated with this setting
> Then instantiate SA as the social activity

This rule works in many situations. For instance:

> John and Mary were at a discotheque.

Here we assume that John and Mary are dancing. In BORIS, the bedroom setting has three activities associated with it: sleeping, having sex, and changing clothes. Because having sex is the only social activity of the three, BORIS assumes that the wife and the other man were engaged in sex. As in the case of the spilled liquid, BORIS again monitors the relationship between the characters involved. In DIVORCE–2, the phrase "his wife Ann" has just caused BORIS to instantiate a marriage construct in episodic memory. Marriage has both interpersonal and contractual aspects. When BORIS compares Ann's sexual act against their marriage contract, BORIS finds a violation. At this point, BORIS realizes that Ann has committed adultery. As a result, when George later asks David to "represent him in court," BORIS will be able to infer that George has the goal of terminating the marriage contract.

Demon-Based Parsing

In BORIS, script, goal, plan, and all other knowledge-application processes occur as an integrated part of parsing. BORIS does not wait

---

[1]Paul could have decided not to hire Richard as his lawyer because of the spilling. This situation would have to be understood in terms of the lawyer/client M-SERVICE contract.

first to parse an entire sentence into its conceptual representation before knowledge sources are applied. All inference and memory processes occur at the word-by-word level. In BORIS, all processes of language analysis, knowledge application, and knowledge interactions are implemented as *demons*. Demons fall within the class of production systems (Anderson, 1976; Davis & King, 1977; Newell, 1973; Schank & Riesbeck, 1981; Waterman & Hayes-Roth, 1978) and are a generalization of Riesbeck's requests (Riesbeck & Schank, 1976). Demons implement a form of delayed processing. Demons wait until their test conditions are satisfied, at which point they fire and execute their actions. Each live (active) demon is in charge of its own life cycle, deciding how long to stay alive and when to die. A demon usually kills itself whenever one of the following situations occurs: (a) the demon has performed its task, (b) the demon notices that some other demon has already accomplished the same task, or (c) the demon decides that its test condition no longer has any chance of being satisfied.

Several demons may be assigned the same task, with each one attempting to accomplish it by different heuristic methods. In this way, even if one demon fails another may still succeed, resulting in a more robust system. Once one demon has succeeded, competing demons notice this and kill themselves. As a result, the number of demons active at any time remains small, and this results in efficient processing.

Demons may also "spawn" other demons, thus forming more complicated processing structures, such as a "discrimination tree" of demons. Finally, demons take arguments, which are bound to corresponding demon parameters at the time the demons are spawned. As a result, processing code is easily shared between demons and many variant instantiations of the same demon, each containing different arguments, may be active at the same time.[2]

BORIS reads each narrative sentence (or narrative question) word by word in a left-to-right order. Entries in the lexicon may be words, phrases, roots, or suffixes. Associated with each lexical item are conceptualizations and attached demons. When a lexical item is recognized, the associated conceptualization is placed into a working memory and its attached demons are spawned.

As a result, processing in BORIS occurs in a bottom-up fashion with each lexical item generating one of more demons. When de-

---

[2]BORIS demons are not to be confused with demons in (Charniak, 1972). Problems with Charniak-style demons are cogently discussed in (Charniak, 1975). For more detail on BORIS demons, see (Dyer, 1983a).

mons "fire," they bind together conceptual structures in working memory and instantiate long-term conceptual structures in episodic memory. These conceptual structures are then accessed by other demons. Thus, both episodic and working memory serves as a context for parsing. Consider the phrase "picked up the phone and dialed" in DIVORCE–1. In the lexicon, "pick up" is defined in terms of the CD conceptualization GRASP. Associated with this conceptualization are demons that fill in cases associated with GRASP.

Lexical Entry
pick up   (GRASP ACTOR * <==(EXPECT 'HUMAN 'BEFORE)
             OBJECT * <==(EXPECT 'PHYS-OBJ 'AFTER)
             INSTAN * <==(APPLY-KS))
phone   (PHYS-OBJ TYPE (PHONE))
associated demons:
EXPECT [Pattern, Direction]
    Search Working Memory for Pattern
    in the Direction specified
    When found, bind to role
APPLY-KS [ACT]
    If a primitive CD ACT is encountered
    Then examine the OBJECT of the ACT
        and If the OBJECT has an associated script or MOP
        Then apply that script of MOP to the ACT
        If MOP found which is uninstantiated,
        Then create an instance in episodic memory

Associated with each unambiguous lexical entry is a single conceptualization. Each unfilled role is followed by a star (*) that acts as a placeholder for a binding. Demons whose task it is to fill these roles appear after the arrow <==. Each arrow indicates where to bind the return values of the demons. Several demons may try to fill the same role. This is indicated by more than one demon following the same arrow. Demons that take parameters are enclosed within parentheses, followed by the arguments passed to them.

When BORIS reads "picked up," the GRASP conceptualization is placed in working memory and the associated demons are spawned. Immediately, one of the demons fires and binds George as the ACTOR of the GRASP. When "phone" is encountered, another instantiation of the same EXPECT demon fires and binds PHONE as the OBJECT of the GRASP. At this point, APPLY-KS fires. It is the task of this demon to reinterpret the GRASP in terms of a larger knowledge structure. APPLY-KS contains several heuristics. One heuristic is to search BORIS'

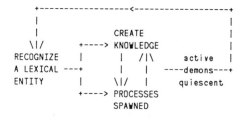

Figure 1.3.

object primitive knowledge of whatever is bound in the OBJECT slot. Through the physical object of PHONE, BORIS accesses the MOP M-PHONE, which holds information about how to answer and make calls. APPLY-KS then applies M-PHONE to the GRASP conceptualization. Because GRASP (phone) is an act in M-PHONE, the match succeeds. Because this is the first instance of a phone call with Richard as the caller, BORIS creates an instantiation of this event in episodic memory with Richard as CALLER. When "dialed" is read, the demon associated with dialing will immediately find M-PHONE instantiated in working memory with a pointer to a corresponding event in episodic memory. As a result, the dialing action will simply update this instance of M-PHONE. Meanwhile, demons associated with M-PHONE have been spawned. These demons look for the recipient of the call, the message being conveyed, and whatever goal Richard plans to achieve by making this call.

This process is depicted in Figure 1.3. Thus, the process of comprehension may be abstractly characterized as a cycle of knowledge structures spawning processes that build new knowledge structures, where both demons and knowledge structures arise from lexical input.

The Role of Language Structure

The approach to language comprehension in BORIS is highly knowledge based. Language is not viewed as a phenomenon isolated from general cognitive processes. On the contrary, processes of memory search, memory indexing, inference generation, inference control, knowledge representation, and knowledge application are viewed as more central to language processing than that of syntactic analysis or construction. People do not retain a memory of the syntactic structure of a sentence in episodic memory. Only conceptual content and causally significant inferences are remembered. In addition, there are an enormous number of English sentences that conform to any given structural pattern, such as "subject verb object." However, each of these grammatically identical sentences will mean something completely different at the conceptual level. Consequently, syntactic structure is not very predictive of meaning. On the other hand, a little knowledge can go a long way in aiding comprehension. Consider the following texts:

> The waitress spilled coke on George. She was very embarrassed.
> The waitress, who spilled coke on George, felt very embarrassed.
> After spilling coke on George, the waitress was very embarrassed.
> The waitress felt very embarrassed because she had spilled coke on George.
> The waitress was embarrassed for spilling coke on George.
> * Waitress embarrassed. On George she spill coke.

These sentences vary enormously in syntactic structure. Some have relative clauses; some contain conjunctions; some differ in word/sentence order; the last one is even ungrammatical. The conceptual significance of each of these sentences is not conveyed by syntactic structure or by the function words "because," "after," or "for." Such words simply indicate that motivational or causal connections should be sought. However, the sentences just given that lack these explicit connectives are still comprehensible. What is most useful for comprehension is the application of preexisting knowledge about what spilling *is*, and the social and emotional consequences it entails.

Very difficult linguistic problems can be solved sometimes by simply bypassing them in favor of a more basic conceptual approach. We have already seen this happen with the problem of pronoun reference in STORY 2. That is, by addressing language comprehension as a process of script application, a class of pronoun references that had heretofore been very difficult, suddenly became a trivial part of a larger process of knowledge application. This result leads us to believe that the classic linguistic problem of pronoun reference (Hirst, 1981) will not be solved by building an isolated "pronoun reference module."

It is also likely that all other structural aspects of language are best treated as integrated with other intelligent cognitive processes. Linguistic knowledge should be treated as only one of many knowledge sources that must be integrated to produce intelligent comprehension.

BORIS has no explicit knowledge of strictly syntactic constructs, nor does BORIS maintain any isolated grammatical component. Items in the lexicon are not categorized according to whether they are nouns, verbs, adjectives, and so on. In the earlier example of how BORIS processes "picked up the phone" there was no notion of the grammatical constructs of "verb," "verb phrase," or "direct object." Instead, lexical items directly cause conceptual structures to be created, along with demons that will perform necessary search and inferencing to connect these conceptual components into larger conceptualizations.

Although all demons are semantics oriented, there are a number of cases where demons must know about language structure in order to find an appropriate conceptual structure. For instance, a demon that binds the TO slot in a PTRANS conceptualization will know to search for a LOCATION that follows the word "to" or "toward," as in "John drove to the store." Because demons take parameters, the same demon can be invoked to fill the instrumental slot in an INGEST by searching for a utensil that follows the word "with" as in "With a fork John ate his ice cream." In this way, purely linguistic knowledge can be shared among semantics-oriented demons.

In BORIS, linguistic knowledge simply provides clues to semantics-directed processes. For instance, when BORIS encounters the pattern "x because y," BORIS builds a conceptual structure of the form (LEADTO ANTE y CONSE x). This simply captures the fact the there is a causal connection between x and y without saying what it is. BORIS must still rely on demons associated with both x and y to properly understand this causal connection. Because demons associated with x and y are spawned anyway, often the word "because" is superfluous. Thus, the sentence can still be understood when such connectives are omitted.

Many kinds of purely linguistic knowledge, however, are essential. For instance, demons that bind case slots in CD conceptualizations must know about word order, clause boundaries, and active/passive voice. All other demons, however, operate in a language-independent manner. (For more parsing details, see Dyer, 1983a.)

MEMORY MODIFICATION
DURING QUESTION ANSWERING

We have argued that parsing processes cannot be isolated from other knowledge sources. In BORIS, parsing is a process of memory search and instantiation. Thus, the lexicon is viewed as an indexing scheme into episodic memory. Understanding an event means building or retrieving an appropriate episode from memory. In addition to applying general world knowledge during comprehension, the parser must also have access to instantiated events in episodic memory. Consider the following stories:

STORY 7: Fred owed Harry money from college and wanted to pay Harry back. But Fred didn't know where Harry was.

STORY 8: Harry had set Fred's house on fire and run off with Harry's wife. Fred vowed to pay Harry back, but Fred didn't know where Harry was.

For both stories, the answer to the question below is the same.

Q: Why hadn't Fred paid Harry back?
A: Fred didn't know where Harry was.

However, for STORY 7 the question is understood to mean: "Why hasn't Fred returned the borrowed money?" For STORY 8 it means: "Why hasn't Fred gotten his revenge yet?"

In each case it is important to parse the question to the correct conceptualization. If the question for STORY 8 were understood as referring to a loan, then an inappropriate index for search would be used and a sensible answer would never be found. The only way to understand the question correctly is to access episodic (i.e., story) memory during question understanding. This is what BORIS does (Dyer, 1981b). In fact, BORIS applies the same understanding processes during question comprehension that it uses during narrative understanding. In SAM and PAM, the process of question answering was treated as an isolated component, and is depicted in Figure 1.4. Notice that questions are parsed without access to episodic memory. In contrast, BORIS applies the same parsing processes used at story understanding time to parse questions, as diagrammed in Figure 1.5. Whether BORIS builds a new episode in memory or retrieves an old episode depends on whichever demons are activated during parsing. In the question–answering case, retrieval demons are associated with such words as "why," "what," "how," and so on. These demons must decide whether a question is being asked or not, and if so, then determine which retrieval strategy to execute.

This integrated approach to question understanding has two interesting consequences:

1. BORIS often knows the answer to a question before it has finished parsing the question.
2. Parsing certain questions leads BORIS to alter its episodic memory.

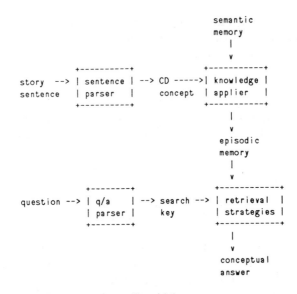

```
                                          semantic
                                          memory
                                             |
                                             v
          +----------+               +-----------+
story  -->| sentence | --> CD ----->| knowledge |
sentence  | parser   |     concept  | applier   |
          +----------+               +-----------+
                                             |
                                             v
                                          episodic
                                          memory
                                             |
                                             v
          +--------+                +------------+
question -->| q/a   | --> search --> | retrieval  |
          | parser |      key       | strategies |
          +--------+                +------------+
                                             |
                                             v
                                          conceptual
                                          answer
```

Figure 1.4.

Both these phenomena are exhibited in human protocols. Consider the following story:

> STORY 9: Jessie James robbed the bank and stole a million dollars. He shot and killed several guards while leaving the scene of the crime.

When people are asked:

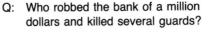

Q: Who robbed the bank of a million
    dollars and killed several guards?

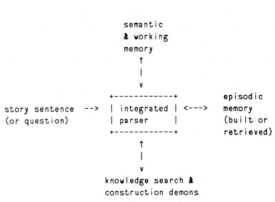

```
                          semantic
                          & working
                          memory
                             ↑
                             |
                             v
                          +------------+
story sentence   -->      | integrated | <--->   episodic
(or question)             | parser     |         memory
                          +------------+         (built or
                             ↑                   retrieved)
                             |
                             v
                          knowledge search &
                          construction demons
```

Figure 1.5.

they usually access "Jessie James" as the answer before they have reached the word "million." Because BORIS is searching episodic memory as each word is parsed, it often retrieves the final answer before parsing is completed. In general, this more integrated scheme has an advantage insofar as once an episode in memory has been found, the information within it can become available to aid the understanding process.

The second phenomenon has been documented in human protocols and is called the "Loftus effect." Loftus noticed that certain questions could permanently alter episodic memory (Loftus, 1979). For example, people who had seen a film (or read a story) about a car going through a red light would later be asked how fast the car had been going when it went through "the stop sign." Afterward, people would recall that the car had gone through a stop sign. All traces of the actual red light would be missing from the subjects' memories. This effect occurs in BORIS because the parser that builds episodic memories during text comprehension is essentially the same parser that reads questions about the story. Thus, if BORIS is given a presupposition in a question that supplies new information without causing any expectation failures,[3] new memories will be constructed just as they are during story-understanding time. For instance, right after reading D1-pgh4:

> . . . Paul seemed very annoyed by this, so Richard offered to drive him home for a change of clothes.

if BORIS is asked:

> Q: Why did Richard drive Paul home?

BORIS will assume at this point that Richard has actually driven Paul home and will update episodic memory with this event. However, the text at this point only states that Richard "offered to" drive Paul, so before the question was presented, episodic memory contained only an instantiation of Paul's *goal* to drive Richard home.

At first, this unforeseen behavior was viewed as a program "bug." Upon reflection, however, it was nice result, because it provided a computational explanation for the "Loftus effect," which until now had been treated as an isolated psychological fact (almost aberration) concerning human memory. We argue that memory modification

---

[3]Expectation failures are discussed in the next section, Thematic Abstraction Units.

during question—answering is a natural consequence of using the same integrated parser to understand both the story itself and questions about the story.

THEORY OF AFFECT

Previous stories read by SAM and PAM were action oriented. In contrast, the stories read by BORIS are more oriented around interpersonal relationships and emotional reactions. As a result, a theory of AFFECT (Dyer, 1983b) and interpersonal feelings was required. Although BORIS is incapable of "feeling" any emotion, BORIS does have knowledge about the causes and consequences of emotional reactions on the part of narrative characters. This includes such emotions as: anger, sadness, happiness, fear, hope, eagerness, disappointment, surprise, gratitude, relief, guilt, envy, pride, and regret. Thus, BORIS can understand and answer questions about why characters feel the way they do, or make inferences and predictions about what characters will feel in various situations.

In BORIS, emotions are represented in terms of *affect primitives,* which hold information about abstract goal situations. A portion of the BORIS affect lexicon is given here:

BORIS Affect Lexicon

lexicon	affect info.	goal situation

happy
joyous
glad
	(AFFECT
	  STATE (POS)
	  CHAR x
	  G-SITU (a))
		(a) Goal of x
		    achieved

unhappy
upset
sad
	(AFFECT
	  STATE (NEG)
	  CHAR x
	  G-SITU (b))
		(b) Goal of x
		    thwarted or
		    suspended or
		    preservation
		    goal active

grateful
thankful
	(AFFECT
	  STATE (POS)
	  CHAR x
	  G-SITU (c)
	  TOWARD y)
		(c) y caused goal
		    situation (a)
		    to occur

annoyed
angry
furious
	(AFFECT
	  STATE (NEG)
	  CHAR x
		(d) y caused goal
		    situation (b)
		    to occur

	G-SITU (d) TOWARD y)	
hopeful	(AFFECT STATE (POS) CHAR x G-SITU (e) E-MODE (EXPECTED))	(e) Goal of x is active
fearful worried	(AFFECT STATE (NEG) CHAR x G-SITU (f) E-MODE (EXPECTED))	(f) P-goal (i.e. preservation goal) is active
surprised shocked	(AFFECT STATE pos/neg CHAR x G-SITU (g) E-MODE (UNEXPECTED))	(g) A goal is achieved or thwarted
relieved allayed	(AFFECT STATE (POS) CHAR x G-SITU (h))	(h) Situation (f) was active but p-goal failure avoided
disappointed	(AFFECT STATE (NEG) CHAR x G-SITU (i)	(i) Situation (e) was active but goal is now thwarted
proud smug	(AFFECT STATE (POS) CHAR x G-SITU (j) TOWARD y)	(j) goal of y achieved by x
guilty ashamed embarrassed regretful	(AFFECT STATE (NEG) CHAR x G-SITU (k) TOWARD y)	(k) goal of y thwarted by x

AFFECT STATES are either positive (POS) or negative (NEG). In general, POS indicates goal success, whereas NEG indicates goal failure. AFFECTS can also be directed TOWARD another character by CHAR (i.e., the character feeling the emotion). For example, the emotion of anger is often directed by one character at another. The most important

AFFECT component is G-SITU, which holds information about an *abstract goal situation*. For example, when BORIS reads that a character x is "angry at y," BORIS assumes that x believes that y was instrumental in violating one of x's goals. The specific goal, or the specific way in which it has been violated, is not revealed by the word "angry." Therefore, BORIS must search episodic memory to find a concrete instance of this abstract situation. If no event is found, then BORIS creates an expectation for such an event to be mentioned. Consider the following story fragment read by BORIS:

> DIVORCE–2: George was having lunch . . . when the waitress accidentally knocked a glass of coke on him. George was very annoyed . . .

When BORIS reads that George is annoyed, it searches for a goal failure on George's part. At this point BORIS recalls that George's preservation goals of P-APPEARANCE AND P-COMFORT goals were violated by the waitress, so BORIS builds a connection between George's AFFECT and these goal violations. Later, these connections will be used to answer the question:

> Q: Why was George angry at the waitress?

even though the text never explicitly mentioned toward whom George's anger was directed.

AFFECTs also contain E-MODE and SCALE components. E-MODEs hold character expectations. These expectations are compared against goal outcomes and are used to represent such emotional reactions as disappointment and relief. For instance, disappointment is represented as an abstract situation in which a character expected a goal success, but instead experienced a goal failure.

The SCALE component is used to represent the intensity of an emotional reaction. For example, the term *ecstatic* is represented as joy with SCALE > NORM. AFFECT SCALE is used by BORIS to determine the importance of a goal situation for a character. If a character is "very" upset or "extremely" grateful, then BORIS can infer that the goal thwarted (or achieved) was an important goal for that character. This is useful in connecting up goal situations when more than one goal is active for a given character.

Emotional reactions occur frequently in DIVORCE–1:

> . . . Richard was *anxious* to find out how Paul was . . . *Unfortunately* . . . Richard *eagerly* picked up the phone . . . He felt *extremely upset* by the incident . . . Paul seemed *very annoyed* by this . . . he near-

ly had a heart attack . . . Richard *congratulated* Paul . . . *celebrate* at dinner . . . *eager* to comply.

BORIS uses its AFFECT knowledge both to aid in parsing and to generate inferences. For example, BORIS infers that Richard will take Paul's case even though this is never explicitly stated. BORIS infers this from the phrase: "Richard eagerly picked up the phone." Eagerness is understood as a positive AFFECT coupled with a desire to achieve a goal. BORIS uses the following AFFECT interpretation rule:

If x ASK y to serve as agent for x
and y has POS AFFECT
Then y has goal of being x's agent.

to generate an expectation that Richard wants to help Paul. Later, when BORIS encounters the sentence: "He was extremely relieved and grateful." BORIS searches episodic memory for an active preservation goal that is to be achieved by another character. Because it is Paul who is in trouble and who needs Richard's help, BORIS correctly identifies "he" as referring to Paul.

Sometimes narrative characters respond emotionally to the goal situations of other characters. Why should a character have a positive or negative AFFECT when it is not his own goal that was achieved or thwarted? BORIS interprets these situations as expressions of *empathy* and uses such situations to monitor interpersonal relationships. In BORIS, long-term feelings, such as love and hate, are distinguished from short-term emotional reactions. Love and hate are represented as *interpersonal themes*, such as IPT-FRIENDS, IPT-LOVERS, and IPT-ENEMIES. For example, BORIS knows that if x and y are lovers, then they will empathize with each other's goal successes and failures.

Part of BORIS' empathetic knowledge can be summed up in the following table:

Empathy Table

Y has a goal FAILURE	Y has a goal SUCCESS	interpersonal theme
X feels NEG	X feels POS	IPT-FRIENDS(X,Y) (goal accord)
X feels POS	X feels NEG	IPT-ENEMIES(X,Y) (goal conflict)

The Empathy Table encodes, among others, the following rules:

> em1: If x and y are friends,
>   and y has a goal failure
>   Then x will experience a NEG AFFECT
>
> em2: If y has a goal failure
>   and x experiences a POS AFFECT
>   Then either x and y are enemies
>   or they are in conflict over this goal
>
> em3: If x and y are enemies
>   and x causes y a goal failure
>   Then x may feel "smug"
>   rather than "guilty"

This empathetic knowledge is used to represent and process such phrases in DIVORCE-1 as "unfortunately" and "congratulate." In BORIS, "unfortunately" means that x feels a NEG AFFECT because y has experienced a threatened or failed goal, and x and y have a positive interpersonal theme. In DIVORCE-1, BORIS interprets "unfortunately" to mean that Richard feels badly because Paul is having marital troubles and because Richard is Paul's friend. For BORIS, "x congratulate y" means that x has communicated to y that x feels a POS AFFECT as a result of y achieving a goal success. BORIS uses this knowledge to connect Richard's congratulations with Paul's winning his case.

THEMATIC ABSTRACTION UNITS

In addition to answering questions about character reactions and causal motivations, people are also able to recognize recurring narrative themes. One class of themes is based on abstract planning situations that people often characterize in terms of common sayings, or adages (Dyer, 1981c). Consider the following story:

> STORY 10: Cathy was in love with David, but David kept dating other girls. Cathy became angry with David and wanted revenge. Cathy decided to commit suicide in order to make David feel bad. So one night Cathy took a bottle of sleeping pills. David later married a woman he met at work.

We could imagine a story understanding program able to answer questions of fact and causality, such as:

Q: Who was Cathy in love with?
A: David.
Q: Why did Cathy decide to commit suicide?
A: To make David feel guilty.
Q: How did Cathy kill herself?
A: She took a bottle of sleeping pills.

Somehow, these questions fail to get at the point of the story (i.e., what makes the story memorable and worth telling). There is a theme in STORY 10 that these questions have not captured. But this story can be characterized by the adage:

Adg-1: Cutting off one's nose to spite one's face.

After people read this story, they often forget the names of the characters, but still remember the story as "that ironic one about a woman who killed herself to spite her lover." So STORY 10 is indexed in episodic memory in terms of its irony. How is this done? Why does Adg-1 characterize an important element of STORY 10 and how does such an adage come to mind?

Recognizing such *abstract themes* in narratives constitutes a level of understanding that goes deeper than previous story understanding systems. This deeper level involves recognizing what is memorable about a story at the thematic level. In DIVORCE-1, for example, people often commented on the irony of Paul catching Sarah committing adultery because it was Sarah who was demanding a lot of alimony from Paul. How can we get a computer program to recognize this irony?

In BORIS, this level of understanding is achieved through another knowledge construct, called a TAU (Thematic Abstraction Unit). TAUs hold information about *abstract planning errors*. For example, the abstract planning error in STORY 10 is represented by TAU-GREATER-HARM, which contains the following information:

y has violated a goal G of x
x counterplanning against y
x wants to violate y's goal G1
x executes plan P designed to thwart G1
a necessary side-effect of P thwarts a goal G2
of x where G2 is a more serious goal failure
than that of G

This is exactly the abstract situation and planning failure expressed by the adage "Cutting off your nose to spite your face." This adage is associated with TAU-GREATER-HARM and is one way this planning failure is expressed in our culture.

When we examine adages, we discover that a great many of them actually contain advice in planning, usually by describing situations to avoid. Consider the adages here:

Adg-2: Burning bridges behind you.
Adg-3: Throwing rocks when you live in a glass house.
Adg-4: Stalking a rhino with a pea shooter.
Adg-5: Shooting a fly with an elephant gun.

Each adage emphasizes a different aspect of planning that must be considered to avoid failure. For instance, Adg-2 gives advice on having alternative plans if the current plan fails. Adg-3 describes a situation similar to TAU-GREATER-HARM, except that in this case, it advises one to avoid thwarting an opponent's goal when one is vulnerable to a similar attack. Both Adg-4 and Adg-5 point out the error of using plans that are inappropriate for a given goal. In the cases of Adg-4, the plan is too weak, and in Adg-5, too powerful, expensive, and risky in relation to the importance of the goal. There are many other aspects of planning which are must be considered, and for each aspect there tends to be one or more adages which contain relevant advice at an abstract level. For instance, timing is important to plan success:

Adg-6: A stitch in time saves nine.
Adg-7: Strike while the iron is hot.
Adg-8: The early bird gets the worm.

The selection of legitimate versus illegitimate plans is another aspect of planning that must be considered:

Adg-9: The pot calling the kettle black.
Adg-10: Who live by the sword die by the sword.

The irony noticed by people in DIVORCE–1 is related to Adg-9, which is captured by TAU-HYPOCRISY. This TAU holds information about one planner accusing the other of unethical behavior while at the same time performing similar behavior. The situation in DIVORCE–1 is a variation of TAU-HYPOCRISY. That is, Sarah has demanded that Paul give Sarah all the possessions of the marriage even though it is Sarah who has been secretly breaking the marriage contract. This plan is only effective as long as the other individual is unaware of the illegitimate behavior. In DIVORCE–1, once Sarah is caught, she loses the case.

Recognizing Narrative Themes

TAUs are more difficult to recognize than scripts, goals, and plans. For instance, not every reader of DIVORCE–1 notices the irony in Sarah's demands in the context of her affair. It is possible to understand the facts and basic causal relationships between story episodes without recognizing these more abstract themes. One reason TAUs are difficult to recognize is that they are more abstract in nature than specific scripts, plans, or goals.

Consider the way scripts are recognized. Script activation in BORIS is based on the occurrence of concrete settings, roles, props, or events associated with a given script. Here are two script activation strategies:

> sa1: If a character enters a setting that has a
>   script associated with it
>   Then activate that script
> sa2: If a role or prop from script S is mentioned
>   and an action matches an event in S
>   Then activate S and instantiate that event

For instance, these rules would activate $RESTAURANT in the following cases:

situation	rule	mentioned
John went to the restaurant.	sa1	concrete setting
John picked up the menu.	sa2	concrete prop
The waiter brought the food.	sa2	concrete role

Similarly, goals and plans are connected up by examining specific goal-enablement conditions. In contrast, TAUs do not have specific settings, goals or roles. For instance, the abstract situation characterized by Adg-3, "Throwing rocks when you live in a glass house," could occur in any setting and with any number of active goals.

Thus, BORIS recognizes TAUs by monitoring plans and expectation failures. Whenever a plan is used, BORIS checks the appropriateness of the plan according to various *planning metrics*. A planning metric is an aspect of planning that must be considered for a plan to succeed. There are 11 planning metrics:

1. *Enablement.* Necessary preconditions before a plan can or should be executed. This includes such things as a) when a plan should be executed, and b) the correct order in which various sub-portions of a plan must be executed before proceeding to the next sub-portion.

2. *Cost.* Resources used during plan execution, including time, money, physical and mental effort, etc.

3. *Efficacy.* The perceived capability of a plan to achieve a particular goal. This is usually based on the past performance of a plan under various circumstances and in the service of differing goals.

4. *Risk.* The potential of negative side-effects during plan execution, or the dangers involved in using a particular plan if something goes wrong.

5. *Coordination.* The ability to successfully divide a single plan between multiple planners to achieve a common goal.

6. *Availability.* The number of plans which are currently available for achieving a current goal, including the flexibility of altering a current plan or selecting a new plan in the face of a potential planning failure.

7. *Legitimacy.* The perceived judgment by any important party concerning the correct ethical use of a given plan in a given situation.

8. *Affect.* Emotional responses to plan failure (or success) and its effect on subsequent planning.

9. *Skill.* The ability of a planner to correctly execute a known plan, based on a "scorecard" of past use.

10. *Vulnerability.* In counterplanning situations, the planner must be able to take into account the potential of retaliation from his opponents.

11. *Liability.* In alliance situations, the planner must take into account the obligations created by accepting help from his allies.

Whenever a nonstandard plan is chosen to achieve a given goal, the planning metrics are analyzed. Associated with each metric is implicit advice on planning. For instance, whenever possible, the planner should choose safe, cost-effective plans over risky, expensive ones. If a planning metric is violated, then an associated TAU is accessed which matches the abstract goal/plan that is active.

Consider how story STORY 10 might be analyzed in terms of planning metrics. First, David has caused a goal failure for Cathy by terminating their social relationship. Next, Cathy seeks revenge. Consequently, we expect her to choose a counterplan that will violate a social goal of David's. Instead, Cathy executes the unusual plan of suicide. This plan violates the planning metric of RISK since it has the side-effect of causing Cathy a larger goal failure for herself (i.e., complete failure of P-LIFE) than the goal failure she plans to cause David. The abstract pattern in this case is represented in BORIS as TAU-GREATER-HARM:

    y causes goal failure for x
    x counterplans against y
    x chooses inappropriate
    plan (in terms of risk, cost,
    or vulnerability)
    x causes greater goal failure for x

Associated with this TAU is the adage: "cutting off one's nose to spite one's face." Once TAU-GREATER-HARM has been recognized, this adage becomes accessible and can be used during generation to characterize this abstract theme in English.

The task of TAU recognition differs from computer planners and problem solvers in an important way. Many current planning systems are given the best known plans available for achieving each goal. The system then applies each plan that is appropriate for the given goal or intervening enablement condition. The problem of TAU recognition, however, is that of examining the *poor* planning of others, recognizing this fact, and realizing how it can be corrected. Unlike computer systems, with the best planning methods already programmed into them by their designers, human beings must learn how to plan through a process of repeated planning attempts and plan failures.[4] By the time one is an adult, a large body of planning failures and planning advice has been accumulated and organized in episodic memory. This memory organization can then be used to recognize poor planning in others and to avoid it in oneself. The most common, recurrent forms of planning advice become incorporated into the adages and common stories of one's culture.

---

[4]Much human planning knowledge is learned vicariously (i.e., by witnessing, hearing, or reading about the errors of others).

FUTURE RESEARCH

There a numerous directions for future research. Much work is needed to augment each knowledge source used in BORIS. In this section, I mention only two areas of future research on TAUs.

TAU Generation and Translation

People often use adages when giving general advice. Why is this the case? For one thing, an adage is easier to produce, remember, and understand than a description of abstract planning. For instance, it is easier to hear

Adg-3: Don't throw rocks when you live in a glass house.

than to be told:

"When you're retaliating against a foe, don't choose a plan to violate a goal of his when you have the very same goal and he can violate it by retaliating against you with a similar counterplan."

However, it is invalid to generate an adage by printing it out as a canned expression directly associated with a given TAU. Adages must actually make sense. This means that components of an adage must correspond in some meaningful way with components in the associated TAU. For example, Figure 1.6 shows how Adg-3 corresponds with elements in TAU-VULNERABLE. Thus, Adg-3 itself represents a little episode that matches the planning situation in TAU-VULNERABLE. Whenever TAU-VULNERABLE has to be generated, this prototypic episode becomes available.

This view of generation has an interesting consequence for machine translation of adages. Clearly, many adages cannot be trans-

```
throw rock    <----->   x chooses counterplan P
                        against opponent y


living in     <----->   x has active preservation
                        goal G to maintain


glass house   <----->   G itself is vulnerable
                        to the same counterplan P
                        by y against x
```

Figure 1.6.

lated on a word-by-word basis. It appears also that a direct interpretation of the semantic content of an adage may also be insufficient to produce an appropriate translation. Consider the following adages and their translations in Chinese:

TAU-INCOMPETENT-AGENT

    English: The blind leading the blind.
                (A blind man can't see where he's going.)
    Chinese: Swimming across the river on a clay buddha.
                (The clay buddha will dissolve in the water.)

TAU-SELF-DECEPTION

    English: Don't ignore a problem by hiding your head in the sand. (The ostrich thinks he's safe since he can't see his attacker.)
    Chinese: Don't cover your ears while stealing the town bell. (The thief holds his ears when the bell begins to ring. He thinks he won't be caught since he can't hear the bell ring.)

Each adage pair describes the same planning failure, yet the situations described at the concrete level are completely different. As a result, the only way to successfully translate these adages into their corresponding sayings in Chinese is:

1. Recognize the abstract planning failure being described and access the appropriate TAU.
2. Retrieve the prototypic episode of the target culture which is associated with this TAU and generate the corresponding adage.

TAUs and Cross-Contextual Remindings

TAUs are also very useful in accounting for cross-contextual remindings. Consider story STORY 11:

> STORY 11: The Black residents were angry with the rich White bankers, who had failed to invest in their community. So to show their displeasure they rioted and ended up burning down the few Black-owned businesses in their own neighborhood.

People who read STORY 11 are sometimes reminded of STORY 10, even though one story is about ghetto riots while the other story concerns a love affair gone wrong. This reminding can be explained by the fact that both stories were understood in terms of the same TAU. If both stories are understood in terms of the same abstract planning error, then they will be indexed under the same TAU in episodic memory. As a result, reading one story will give cause the related story to be recalled.

As argued in (Schank, 1980) and (Schank, 1982b), the reminding process is useful for the following reason: Once a situation has caused one to be reminded of an episode, all of the expectations associated with that episode become available for use in making predictions about what will occur next. In the case of TAUs, their associated expectations include advice on either how to avoid making the error predicted by the TAU, or on what alternative plan can be used to recover from the error once it has been made. The ability to store cross-contextual episodes make TAUs very general and powerful mechanisms. Once an episode has been indexed under a TAU, its recovery/avoidance heuristics become available for use in completely different situations. Thus, planning advice learned in one context can help processing in other contexts, if the experience was recognized in terms of an appropriate TAU in the first place.

CONCLUSIONS

The advantage of building computer programs to read, answer questions, and generate stories is that they provide a medium for testing theories of knowledge representation and application for supporting everyday intelligent comprehension. As each representational construct is invented, its scope and limitations can be experimented with. These experiments point out new directions for research. For example, after Conceptual Dependency theory was developed, attempts were made to represent the concept of "kiss." An initial attempt was:

x kiss y = x PTRANS lips of x to cheek of y

This allowed a computer program to draw the conclusion:

lips of x are at location of cheek of y

Clearly, something is missing in a representation that can only capture the physical aspect of kissing. This kind of limitation helps lead to continuing development in representations for human motivations, relationships, and emotions.

BORIS offers several theoretical advances over previous story understanding and question answering systems. These advances include extensions both in representing human knowledge structures and in coordinating their application during comprehension. Experiments in integrated parsing has lead to a reexamination of the "Loftus effect" that heretofore had been viewed as an isolated psychological phenomenon. This effect can now be explored as a natural consequence of parsing integration. Research on knowledge interactions has lead both to a system of *affect* representation and to a model of *in-depth* understanding through the recognition of abstract themes based on expectation failures and planning errors.

The research described here is based on the premise that comprehension is a process of intelligent inference, memory access and knowledge application. The key to understanding lies in computational insight into *human knowledge and memory structures:* their representation, application, instantiation, interaction, control, coordination, indexing, access, search, and retrieval.

One reason language understanding is so difficult is that many different sources of knowledge must be manipulated. These knowledge constructs differ in their representations, interconnections, effects on inferencing, and strategies for retrieval. For instance, people find that recalling all the restaurants they have recently been to is a distinct task from recalling times they felt "gratitutde" or "disappointment." Similarly, retrieving events that occurred in a given physical setting requires different strategies from recalling events where a planning failure occurred. Again, remembering all of one's relatives or roommates is different from remembering times someone performed a favor for you, or cheated you.

The ability of computers to process narrative text is limited by our understanding of these human cognitive processes. For instance, descriptive passages cannot be handled until more is known about how to represent visual images. Comprehension of science fiction stories and fairy tales require computational insight into the cognitive processes of human imagination. Handling a medium-length literary story, let alone a full-length novel, is currently impracticable. At the very least, more must first be known about human episodic memory organization, and what people tend to remember and forget about what they read and experience.

Narrative comprehension is at the center of intelligence. Narratives serve as both a communication medium for, and reflection of, the processes of human reasoning, planning, motivations, and ideas. To understand natural language, those thought processes evoked during communication must be explored through building computer models of human cognitive processing. BORIS offers an opportunity for such computational experimentation and exploration into human cognition.

ACKNOWLEDGMENTS

I want to thank Peter Johnson and Thomas Wolf for their contributions to the design and implementation of BORIS. The work described here was supported in part by the Advanced Research Projects Agency under contract N0014-75-C-1111 and in part by the National Science Foundation under contract IST7918463.

REFERENCES

Anderson, J. R. (1976). *Language, memory and thought.* Hillsdale, NJ: Lawrence Erlbaum Associated.

Bower, G. H., Black, J. B., & Turner, T. J. (1979). Scripts in memory for text. *Cognitive Psychology, 11,* 177–220.

Charniak, E. (1972). Toward a model of children's story comprehension. Unpublished doctoral dissertation, Artificial Intelligence Lab, MIT, Cambridge, MA.

Charniak, E. (1975). Organization and inference in a frame-like system of common sense knowledge. In R. Schank & B. Nash-Webber (eds.), *TIN-LAP-1: Theoretical.issues in natural language processing* (pp. 46–55). ACL.

Cullingford, R. E. Unpublished doctoral (1978). Script application: Computer understanding of newspaper stories dissertation, Yale University, Department of Computer Science, New Haven, CT.

Davis, R., & King, J. (1977). An overview of productive systems. *Machine Intelligence, 8,* 300–331.

DeJong, G. F. II (1979). Skimming stories in real time: An experiment in integrated understanding. Unpublished doctoral dissertation, Yale University, Department of Computer Science, New Haven, CT.

Dyer, M. G. (1981a, August). $RESTAURANT revisited or 'lunch with BORIS'. Proceedings of the 7th International Joint Conference on Artificial Intelligence, (pp. 234–236) Vancouver, BC.

Dyer, M. G. (1981b). *Integration, unification, reconstruction, modification: An eternal parsing braid.* Proceedings of the 7th International Joint Conference on Artificial Intelligence, (pp. 37–42) Vancouver, BC.

Dyer, M. G. (1981c, August). *The role of TAUs in narratives.* Proceedings of the 3rd Annual Conference of the Cognitive Science Society, (pp. 225–227). Berkeley, CA.

Dyer, M. G. (1983a). *In-depth understanding.* Cambridge, MA: M.I.T. Press.

Dyer, M. G. (1983b). The role of affect in narratives. *Cognitive Science, 7,* 3. (pp. 211–242).

Dyer, M. G., & Lehnert, W. G. (1982). Question answering for narrative memory. In J. F. Le Ny and W. Kintsch (Eds.), *Language and comprehension,* (pp. 239–258). Amsterdam: North-Holland.

Goldman, N. (1975). Conceptual generation. In R. Schank (Ed.), *Conceptual information processing* (pp. 289–371). New York: American Elsevier.

Hirst, G. (1981). *Anaphora in natural language understanding: A survey.* New York: Springer-Verlag.

Lehnert, W. G. (1978). *The process of question answering.* Hillsdale, NJ: Lawrence Erlbaum Associates.

Lehnert, W. G., & Burstein, M. H. (1979). *The role of object primitives in natural language processing.* Proceedings of the 6th International Joint Conference on Artificial Intelligence, (pp. 522–524). Tokyo, Japan.

Loftus, E. F. (1979). *Eyewitness testimony.* Cambridge, MA: Harvard University Press.

Marslen-Wilson, W., Tyler, L., & Seidenberg, M. (1978). Sentence processing and the clause boundary. In W. Levelt & G. Flores d'Arcais (eds), *Studies in the perception of language.* New York: Wiley.

Newell, A. (1973). Production systems: Models of control structures. In W. C. Chase (Ed.), *Visual information processing,* New York: Academic Press.

Rieger, C. J., III (1975). Conceptual memory and inference. In R. Schank (ed.), *Conceptual information processing* (pp. 157–288). New York: American Elsevier.

Riesbeck, C. K., & Schank, R. C. (1976). Comprehension by computer: Expectation-based analysis of sentences in context (Tech Rep. No. 78). New Haven, CT: Yale University. Department of Computer Science.

Schank, R. C. (1973). Identification of conceptualizations underlying natural language. In R. C. Schank & K. M. Colby (Eds.), *Computer models of thought and language* (pp. 187–247). San Francisco: Freeman.

Schank, R. C. (Ed.). (1975). *Conceptual information processing, fundamental studies in computer science* (Vol. 3). New York: American Elsevier.

Schank, R. C. (1980). Language and memory. *Cognitive Science, 4*(3). (pp. 243–284).

Schank, R. C. (1982a). Reminding and memory organization: An introduction to MOPs. In W. Lehnert & M. Ringle (Eds.), *Strategies for natural language processing* (pp. 455–493). Hillsdale, NJ: Lawrence Erlbaum Associates.

Schank, R. C. (1982b). *Dynamic memory: A theory of reminding and learning in computers and people.* New York: Cambridge University Press.

Schank, R., & Abelson, R. (1977). *Scripts, plans, goals, and understanding.* Hillsdale, NJ: Lawrence Erlbaum Associates.

Schank, R. C., & C. K. Riesbeck (Eds.). (1981). *Inside computer understand-*

ing: *Five programs plus miniatures.* Hillsdale, NJ: Lawrence Erlbaum Associates.

Waterman, D. A., & Hayes-Roth, F. (Eds.). (1978). *Pattern-directed inference systems.* New York: Academic Press.

Wilensky, R. (1978). Understanding goal-based stories. Unpublished doctoral dissertation, Department of Computer Science. Yale University, New Haven, CT.

CHAPTER 2

Event Concept
Coherence

RICHARD ALTERMAN
Computer Science Division
University of California, Berkeley

INTRODUCTION

Consider the following text from *The Clever Peasant and the Czar's General* (Protter, 1961):

> A peasant was digging in his garden one day when his spade unexpectedly hit a hard object. (p. 97)

There are several kinds of representation schemes that can be devised to account for the connectivity of the preceding text. Some examples are: the connectivity can be represented by its causal/intentional structures, by its conformity to narrative form, by its referential connectivity, by its rhetorical coherence. In each case the representation scheme is emphasizing a different feature of the text. In each case the computational requirements vary.

This chapter presents a theory for capturing one aspect of the connectivity of text, its *event concept coherence* (ECC). An ECC representation represents the text in a manner that brings the relatedness of the events to the forefront. It characterizes dependencies amongst the events in a causally neutral, but causally relevant, form.

It acts as a sort of way station, organizing the text for determinations that are more contextually dependent.

The construction of an ECC representation makes the following assumption: Two event descriptions in a piece of text are event concept coherent if the positions of the concepts they invoke are proximal to one another in the underlying conceptual network. An ECC interpretation captures the connectivity of a piece of text by essentially copying out the relevant portion of the network (by the mesh of concept relations that are invoked).

In the previous example, the concepts 'digging' and 'hitting' are interrelated via the concepts 'pushing' and 'moving'. Because the peasant was 'digging' he 'pushed' the spade into the ground. Because he 'pushed' the spade, it 'moved', which is a necessary condition of 'hitting'. Some of the same nexus of concepts are invoked by the following piece of text:

The batter swung the bat. It hit the ball.

Because the batter *swung* the bat, the bat was *moving* and it *hit* the ball. An ECC analysis can capture the commonality of both of the pieces of text just given, even though in one case the *hitting* is intentional and in the other case it is not.

This chapter is a series of papers that develops the theme of event concept coherence. An earlier paper (Alterman, 1985) described in great detail a program called NEXUS, which constructs this type of representation in a spreading activation fashion. Another paper (Alterman, 1986) explored the relationship between ECC and the narrative stream, demonstrating some techniques for summarization that can be effectively applied using an associative level representation. Recently, these techniques have been expanded to an entire page-and-a-half length folktale (Alterman & Bookman, 1988).

This chapter is intended to explore the way-station status of the ECC representation scheme. After giving an overview of the NEXUS program, it embarks on a tour of various other representation schemes in the literature. In each case, a piece of text, used in the description of some other representation scheme, is represented from an ECC perspective. The intended effect of these representational exercises is twofold: First, it demonstrates the breadth of the ECC scheme. Second, and perhaps more importantly, each representation serves to better focus not only the ECC scheme, but also the nature of these other representations. Included in this survey are discourse coherence, conceptual dependency, plan-based interpretations, story schemas, causal interpretations, speech acts, and scripts.

HOW NEXUS WORKS

Overview

NEXUS' basic procedure is to match text against its network. The descriptions of the text are event concept coherent if the positions of the concepts they invoke are proximal to one another in the knowledge network. If the concepts are event concept coherent, NEXUS copies out the relevant portion of the network as a representation of the connectivity of the text. The input to NEXUS are the clauses of the text in case notation form. The event descriptions of the text act as indices into NEXUS' knowledge network. The representations that NEXUS constructs are intended as a way station in a process that gradually enriches the interpretations of the text.

The NEXUS knowledge base is a semantic network that contains approximately 150 concepts and some of the interrelationships amongst those concepts. Relationships between concepts in the knowledge base are represented using one of the seven concept coherence relations. Relationships between the event descriptions of the text also use the concept coherence relations. The knowledge base and the text's representation reflect one another's structure: The text instantiates the nexus of concepts in the knowledge base that are invoked by the text's event descriptions.

The knowledge base is represented in terms of semantic nets. Semantic nets are dealt with as abstractions at the conceptual level (cf. Brachman, 1979). Cases are incorporated into the net (cf. Simmons, 1973); cases were chosen over roles because they simplify processing problems (cf. Charniak, 1981). Associated with each relation in the network are constraints on the corresponding cases of the related concepts. Because the knowledge base and the representations of the text share the same structure, the knowledge base could be constructed from an analysis of text.

The coherence building process works in a spreading activation fashion (see Charniak, 1983, and Norvig, 1987, for other models of text comprehension using spreading activation like mechanisms). NEXUS has two stages. In stage one, bi-directional search is used to find a connecting path between invoked event/state concepts. In stage two, constraints on the corresponding cases of related concepts are used to test connections and resolve references.

NEXUS is programmed in procedural logic using HCPRVR (Chester 1980a, 1980b), a horn clause theorem prover embedded in LISP. Procedural logic was chosen as a programming language because it both separates the logic component from the control component (cf. Kowalski, 1979) and provides automatic backtracking and unification, thus tending to focus the programming task on the larger research issues.

Seven Relations

NEXUS supports seven event/state concept coherence relations (see Figure 2.1). One of the relations is taxonomic, two are partonomic,[1] and four are temporal. The taxonomic relation is used to indicate property inheritance. The partonomic relations capture the intuition that event/state concepts can be borken out into identifiable components. The temporal relations can be used to string together event/state types whose instances co-occur with regularity in the world.

Class/Subclass (sc) is the property inheritance relationship. Two event/state concepts are in a class/subclass relationship if one concept inherits properties and relationships from the other. For example, 'falling' inherits properties and relationships from 'moving': it is a kind of 'moving.' One of the relationships that 'moving' participates in is a relationship with 'hitting'; if two objects 'hit' one of them had to be 'moving.' So if a dish 'falls' then it 'moves' and because it was 'moving', in principle, it could 'hit' the floor.

A subclass concept frequently adds properties to its parent concept. 'Falling' adds a directional component to 'moving': If an elevator 'falls' then it is 'moving downwards.' 'Falling' also directly participates in interevent relationships that 'moving' does not. For example, if an object is 'dropped' then it will 'fall'; there is a necessary direct relationship between 'dropping' and 'falling' that does not exist between 'dropping' and 'moving.' The relationship between 'dropping' and 'moving' is mediated by the concept 'falling'.

One of the major advantages of having a property inheritance relation is that it supports inferencing. Because a subclass concept inherits properties from its parent class certain kinds of inferences are implicit in that relationship. Because 'falling' is a subclass of 'moving' it is not necessary to directly relate 'falling' and 'hitting',

---

[1]The term *partonomic* refers to the part hierarchy. For example, parts of a hand are fingers and the palm, and parts of a finger are knuckles and a nail.

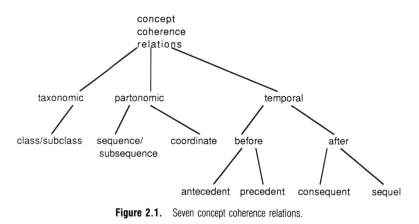

Figure 2.1. Seven concept coherence relations.

that relationship is implicit in the net via the class/subclass relationship between 'falling' and 'moving.'

Given the text:
John dropped the dish.
It hit the floor.

it is the class/subclass relation between 'falling' and 'moving' that is the key to connecting the event/state terms used in the text (see Figure 2.2). 'Dropping' has a co-definitional relationship to 'falling.' 'Falling' is a subclass of 'moving' and inherits from that relationship a relation to the event/state concept 'hitting'.

NEXUS supports two partonomic relations. *Sequence/Subsequence* (*subseq*) and *coordination* (*coord*) can be distinguished by their time intervals. A subsequence concept lasts for a subinterval of time of its supersequence. 'Soaking' is a subsequence of 'washing',

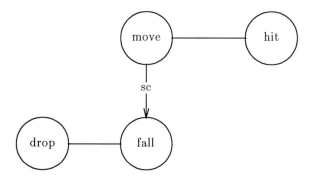

Figure 2.2. Dropping a dish.

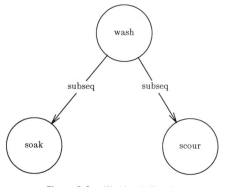

Figure 2.3. Washing the laundry.

another is 'scouring'. A coordinate lasts for the same interval of its parent concept. One coordinate of 'carrying' is 'traveling' another is 'holding'.

In order to expand the description of a particular event, text will frequently describe the subsequences of an event/state concept as opposed to the encompassing event/state concept. So, for example, given the text:

John soaked and scoured his laundry.

NEXUS could use its dictionary to construct a representation of the relationship between 'soaking' and 'scouring'. 'Soaking' and 'scouring' are both parts (subsequences) of 'washing' (see Figure 2.3).

Sometimes two event/state descriptions are related because a co-

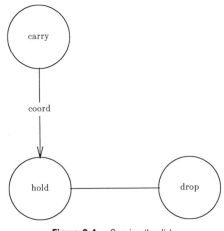

Figure 2.4. Carrying the dish.

TABLE 2.1.
Differences Among Four Temporal Relations

	Before	After
Plausible	precedent	sequel
Necessary	antecedent	consequent

ordinate of one of the associated event/state concepts is related to the other associated event/state concept. Consider the text:

John carried the dish.
He dropped it.

A coordinate of 'carrying' is 'holding'. If something is 'dropped' it first must have been 'held'. Because 'holding' is an implicit part (coordinate) of 'carrying' NEXUS can construct a representation of the relationship between 'carrying' and 'dropping' (see Figure 2.4).

The four temporal relations can be differentiated along two dimensions: before/after and plausible/necessary (alternately default/definitional). Table 2.1 summarizes the differences among these four relations.

If one event with some regularity occurs before another event then NEXUS uses the *precedent* relation (prec) to represent the relationship between the concepts associated with them. It is plausible that before I 'eat' I am 'hungry.'
Given the text:

John was hungry
He ate.

NEXUS uses the temporal relation precedent to connect the two event/state descriptions (see Figure 2.5). Given the text:

John was hungry.
He gorged on pasta.

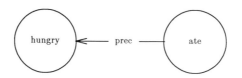

Figure 2.5. John is hungry.

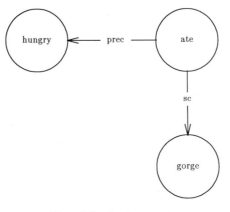

Figure 2.6. Gorging on pasta.

NEXUS would use a combination of temporal and class/subclass relations to represent the text (see Figure 2.6). Plausibly it is the case that because John was 'hungry' he 'ate.' One way of 'eating' is 'gorging.'

If one event necessarily occurs before another event then NEXUS uses the *antecedent* relation (*ante*) to represent the relationship between the concepts associated with them. It is necessarily the case that before I can 'eat food' I must 'have food.' Given the text:

John bought some food.
He ate it.

the descriptions are related because as a result of 'buying food' John 'had food' and 'having food' is an antecedent of 'eating food' (see Figure 2.7).

If one event with some regularity occurs after another event then NEXUS uses the *sequel* relation (*seq*) to represent the relationship between the concepts associated with them. It is plausibly the case that if a horse is 'reined' it will 'stop'. Given the text:

John reined the horse.
It stopped.

Figure 2.7. Buying some food.

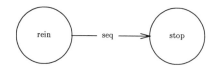

Figure 2.8. Reining a horse.

NEXUS could use the sequel relationship between 'reining' and 'stopping' as a basis for representing the text (see Figure 2.8).

If one event necessarily follows another event then NEXUS uses the *consequent* relation (*conseq*) to represent the relationship between the concepts associated with them. It is necessarily the case that if John 'gathers' something then he 'has' it. Given the text:

John gathered flowers
He carried them home.

NEXUS can use a consequent relation to help connect the two event/state descriptions in the text (see Figure 2.9). Because John 'gathered' flowers he 'had' flowers. Because he 'had' the flowers he could 'carry' the flowers.

The Knowledge Network

NEXUS' knowledge base is a dictionary of event/state concepts represented in the form of a network. Relationships between concepts are represented using one of the seven coherence relations described in the preceding section. The net is oriented toward event/state concepts. Concepts in the net are structured (i.e., cases are incorporated into the net). The cases are mainly derived from Simmons (1984), but also include pieces of the case system of de Beaugrande (1980). In NEXUS the cases are included into the net in two different ways: Associated with each of the event/state concepts are default values for its cases, and attached to each of the relationships in the net are constraints on the matching of cases between the related concepts. NEXUS processes the net at the level of coherence relations among event/state concepts, and the associated cases are mainly used for filling default arguments and constraint checking.

Figure 2.9. Gathering flowers.

NEXUS' network represents the relationship between concepts at the conceptual, as opposed to epistemic, level (cf. Brachman, 1979). Since Woods (1975) raised issue about the logical adequacy of semantic nets, there have been an increasing number of papers on the epistemological status of nets. NEXUS does not represent a theory of semantic nets at the epistemic level. This research uses semantic nets as a conceptual tool (abstraction); it does not investigate their foundations. The method has been to separate semantic nets, the abstract data type, from semantic nets, the concrete representation. It matters little to its concerns which of the epistemologically sounder nets its representations are eventually translated into. It is to NEXUS' advantage that many of the difficult issues dealt with at the epistemic level are hidden by an abstraction (cf. Parnas, 1972).

NEXUS' network was compiled by analzying parts of 10 folktales. Because the knowledge network and the representations of the text were intended to reflect one another, it was possible to compile the knowledge base by analyzing parts of 10 folktales. After creating the representations for the text, the dictionary of concepts was extracted from the representations. In particular, the coherence relations between the event concepts designated by the text's descriptions were extracted.

The folktales come from *A Children's Treasury of Folk and Fairy Tales* and were adapted by Protter (1961). Folktales were chosen for three reasons: They include a diverse range of event/state concepts, the prose style is relatively simple, and the researcher enjoyed reading them. A useful tool was Webster's *New World Dictionary* (1958), but it was not sufficient because a normal dictionary leaves out many important conceptual relationships that are presumed to be understood.

The analysis consisted of converting each event/state description into case notation and then trying to connect them using concept coherence relations. For example, given the text:

John dropped the ball. It fell.

the analysis would produce something like:

[DROP (agent JOHN) (object BALL)
   (consequent (FALL (object BALL)))]

The words of the text are capitalized and the case and coherence relation names appear in lower case letters. Roughly this representation reads: John is the *agent* of dropping, and the *object* he dropped is a ball, a *consequent* of the 'dropping' is a 'falling' and the ball is the *object* that falls.

Piece by piece, the representations generated during the analysis phase were considered and coherence relations were extracted. Before each relationship was added to the dictionary, it was necessary to determine how the new relationships would interact with the relationships previously established between concepts. In particular, several questions needed to be answered. Was the new relationship consistent with previous ones? Was it an improvement? Was it redundant? (i.e., already in the net because of property inheritance). What constraints and default values should be added to prevent erroneous inferences? For the example of 'dropping the ball' the coherence relation extracted would be:

A *consequent* of 'dropping' is 'falling.'

An example of an extracted constraint would be:

In the *consequent* relationship between 'dropping' and 'falling' the *objects* of the 'dropping' and 'falling' must match.

An example of a default value extracted would be:

The default value of the *object* of a 'dropping' is 'physical-object.'

The compilation of the dictionary resulted in a network of approximately 150 event/state concepts.

Figure 2.10 shows, at the level of coherence amongst event/state concepts, a piece of network concerning the concepts: 'move,' 'fall,'

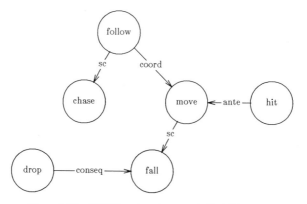

Figure 2.10. NEXUS' version of some mutually defining concepts.

'chase,' 'hit,' 'drop,' and 'follow.' A subclass of 'moving' is 'falling.' An antecedent of 'hitting' is 'moving.' A coordinate of 'following' is 'moving.' A subclass of 'following' is 'chasing.'

The internal form of the network is a set of four-tuples that represent the relationships between event/state concepts, and a set of three tuples for defining the default case values of a concept. Tuples are particularly easy to manipulate in procedural logic since parameters are passed via unification. Each four tuple is of the form:

[relation event/state event/state list-of-constraints]

The constraints describe how the case arguments of the two event/state concepts should match. So, for example, the relationship between the concepts 'moving' and 'falling' would be represented:

[subclass move fall ((match object object) (match location location)..)]

Roughly that reads: a subclass of 'move' is 'fall,' and constraints on that relationship are that the object that is 'falling' must match the object that is 'moving,' the location of the 'falling' must match the location of the 'moving,' and so on. NEXUS uses several different match functions. In the case of *match*, two cases *match* if they are identical, or if one is a pronoun form of the other, or if one is a taxonomic descendant of the other, or if one is a partonomic descendant of the other. For example, the following pairs would *match*: axe-axe, axe-it, axe-tool, axe-handle.

Each three tuple is of the form:
[template event/state list-of-default-values]

The default values for the concept 'fall' would be stored as:

[template fall ((object physical-object)...)]

So the default value for the object case is 'physical-object.'

The Representation Building Process

NEXUS' processing of an event description works in two stages. Consider the prototypical case of determining the concept coherence between two event descriptions. In the first stage, NEXUS uses a bi-directional breadth-first search to find a path in its knowledge net between the event/state concepts designated by the two event descriptions. In the second stage, NEXUS propagates the constraints along the path, simultaneously testing validity and performing reference resolution. NEXUS' scheme for connecting text is similar to the spreading activation scheme originally proposed by Quillian (1968, 1969). Instead of a fan of activation, it uses bi-directional breadth-first search. It differs in its orientation toward event concepts. Another difference is that concepts are related using coherence relations. Also, it incorporates cases into the net, using them to constrain the coherence building process. Finally, it handles larger pieces of text.

To see how this two stage process works, consider the text:

The cup fell. It hit the floor.

The input to NEXUS would look like:

[FALL (object CUP (determiner THE))]
[HIT (object1 IT) (object2 (FLOOR (determiner THE)))]

In the first stage of processing, using the event concepts designated by the text, NEXUS finds the coherence path fall-move-hit (see Figure 2.10), that is,

[subclass MOVE FALL ((match object object) ...)]
[antecedent HIT MOVE (match object1 object) . ..)]

During the constraint checking phase, NEXUS determines the resolution of the 'it' reference because the *object* of the 'fall' must match the *object* of the 'move,' and the *object* of the 'move' must match one of the *objects* of the 'hitting.' Thus 'it' is resolved to be the 'cup,' and the following representation is eventually produced:

[HIT (object1 (CUP (determiner THE)))
    (object2 (FLOOR (determiner THE)))
    antecedent (MOVE (object1 (CUP (determiner THE)))
        subclass (FALL (object1 (CUP (determiner THE)))))))]

Notice that the representation NEXUS constructs is essentially a copy of the structure of its network (again see Figure 2.10). The major difference is that the case arguments are filled with the objects described in the text.

For pieces of text larger than the prototypical two event descriptions the story is only slightly more complicated (see Figure 2.11). The text is processed in order, one event description at a time. Pre-

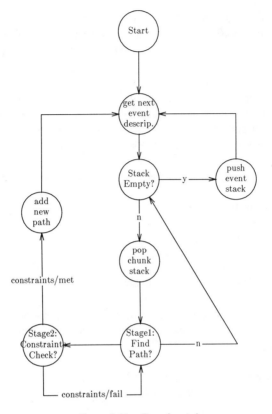

Figure 2.11. Flow of control

viously built concept coherence representations are kept on a stack in order of recency. Initially, there are no event concept coherence chunks on the stack, so the first description is pushed onto the stack. Thereafter, each description is compared against the representations on the stack one at a time until a path of coherence is found between the new description and one of the chunks of preceding coherence representations. The new description is compared to a chunk by treating it as the source of the bi-directional search and the chunk as the goal and then preceeding with the two-stage process previously described. During the second stage of processing all the constraints in the chunk, as well as the ones along the new path, are checked, thus allowing the propagation of references. When a coherence path is successfully found the new path of coherence is added into the chunk. If NEXUS fails to find a path between the current description and any of the chunks on the stack, NEXUS pushes it on the top of the stack and continues processing with the next description.

IN THE CONTEXT OF SOME OTHER
REPRESENTATION SCHEMES

Discourse Coherence

Hobbs (1979) has suggested a theory of *discourse coherence*. His coherence relations *"correspond to the coherent continuation move he {the speaker} can make"* (p. 68). To represent the connection between two segments of discourse Hobbs establishes a rhetorical coherence relation. His coherence relations can be categorized by their communicative function (Hobbs, 1978). Some examples of discourse relations are 'contrast,' 'elaboration,' and 'example.'

An example for which the 'elaboration' discourse relation holds is suggested in Hobbs' paper (1979) on coherence and coreference:

John can **open** Bill's safe.
He **knows** the combination.

The second sentence embellishes the description of the first sentence. Rhetorically the first sentence describes a situation and the second one a "procedural detail" of that situation. When this discourse was produced 'elaborating on a topic' was a rule of production that was applied.

To represent this text using the coherence of event concepts it is necessary to find a small portion of the network that the text invokes. Figure 2.12 depicts an ECC representation of the text. In an attempt to make the correspondence between the text and the event concept

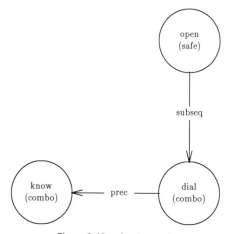

Figure 2.12. Opening a safe

coherence graphs more readable, the figures in this section of the chapter include within parentheses some instantiated values for cases. A subsequence of 'opening a safe' is 'dialing the combination.' 'Dialing the combination' is normally preceded by 'knowing it.'

The representations produced by these two theories are radically different. The first representation rhetorically classifies the text. The second representation conceptually organizes the events. The first representation captures the communicative relationship between the two sentences. The second shows the concept coherence of the event descriptions. For the discourse coherence scheme, the author has 'elaborated.' For the ECC scheme, the author has copied out and used, in a reduced form, a subnet of the dictionary of concepts. In short, the basic difference is that event concept coherence reflects the coherence of concepts that are described in the text as opposed to discourse coherence that captures the rhetorical intentions of the speaker.

Conceptual Dependency

Conceptual Dependency (CD) theory (Schank, 1973) was intended as a representation system for actions. Some outstanding features of CD are: it uses semantic primitives, subscribes to a theory of canonicalization, and claims that by reducing actions to primitives similar inferences on similar actions can be made.

The most outstanding difference between an event concept coherence representation and a CD representation is that the former represents concepts by their relationships to other concepts, and the latter attempts to reduce concepts to a small set of primitives. For example, consider the concepts 'release' and 'drop.' In CD the concepts 'release' and 'drop' would both be collapsed to the concept 'grasp.' Figure 2.13 shows a NEXUS-style representation of these concepts. A subclass of 'releasing' is 'dropping.' 'Grasp' is an antecedent of 'release,' and 'hold' a subclass of 'grasp.' A consequent of 'drop' is 'fall.'

Both theories are able to account for text like:

1. The dog held the bone. He dropped it.

For NEXUS the relationship is the path through the network shown in Figure 2.13. Now consider following pairs of sentences.

2. John dropped the pencil. It fell.
3. John released the door handle. It fell.

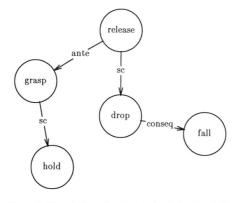

Figure 2.13. A piece of net concerning 'release' and 'drop'

For CD theory there are two possible interpretations of how it handles texts like 2 and 3. One interpretation is that the move to semantic primitives loses the distinction between 'release' and 'drop,' and
consequently CD theory cannot account for the fact that for the first
pair of sentences 'falling' is necessary and expected and in the second pair it is neither necessary nor expected. The other interpretation is that the representation in terms of semantic primitives does
account for the differences in meaning, but then the claim of canonicalization turns out to be only partial canonicalization (cf.
Woods, 1975; also Wilensky, 1987). But then the claims of reducing
the set of inferences to inferences on primitives is lost because different inferences have to be made on two concepts (i.e., 'drop' and
'release') that have the same partial canonicalization. In which case
it appears that CD front loads all the inferencing, whereas a network
semantic system, such as event concept coherence, unfolds the
meaning of concepts on a 'need to' basis. So for semantic primitives
the difference between 'drop' and 'release' are always realized,
whereas in event concept coherence the differences and similarities
are implicitly realized, by the process of finding the coherence of
concepts, when required by the text.

Plans and Causal Chains

Robbing a Liquor Store.   For Schank and Abelson (1977; Wilensky,
1978) plans are made up of information about how actors achieve
goals. In planned behavior, there is associated with every kind of
goal a list of planboxes and scripts that can achieve that goal. Suppose an actor wants to have control of a bicycle, he or she can

achieve this goal by stealing it. Stealing is a planbox associated with the goal of controlling an object. In NEXUS, text that invokes a planbox associated with a goal takes the form of event concept-coherence chains that includes the goal concept. In NEXUS, 'having' and 'stealing' are in a consequent relationship: A consequent of 'stealing' is 'having.' The relationships between these two concepts is not separated out as a special type, but instead enmeshed in with the rest of the relationships contained in the network. The concept of 'stealing' is in part defined by its relationship to the concept of 'having the stolen object' after it is 'stolen.'

There is a crucial difference in how the plan and event concept coherence interpretations are produced. The plan-based interpretation of text is based on the recognition of goals. The event concept coherence representation is based on the coherence of the mutually defining relationships of the event concepts invoked by the text.

Wilensky (1978) provided an example of text for which a plan analysis applies.

> John **wanted** money. He **got** a gun and **walked** into a liquor store. He **told** the owner he **wanted** some money. The owner **gave** John the money and John **left**.

John's goal is that he 'wants money.' His plan is to threaten somebody in order to get the money; his plan is to rob somebody. There is a *goal competition* between John's goal and the liquor store owner's goal of preserving money. The liquor store owner has two goals in conflict: one is to preserve money, the other is to preserve his health. Preserving health is more important so he gives John the money. Goal competitions and goal conflicts are among the metagoals discussed by Wilensky (1983).

Figure 2.14 shows the representation produced by NEXUS. Again with NEXUS the representation takes the form of the relevant portion of its dictionary of concepts. In order to 'rob' the 'robber' needs a 'have a weapon,' in this case a 'gun.' Part of 'robbing' is 'asking for valuables.' The NEXUS representation displays the interrelationships of concepts associated with 'robbing' that are invoked by the event/state descriptions of the text.[2]

To summarize: a plan-based analysis of text applies when there are actors attempting to achieve well-defined goals. Such a representation is produced by recognizing a character's goals and attaching to it the sequences of actions that attempts to achieve that goal. Text

---

[2]The theme case relation is explained in the section on speech acts.

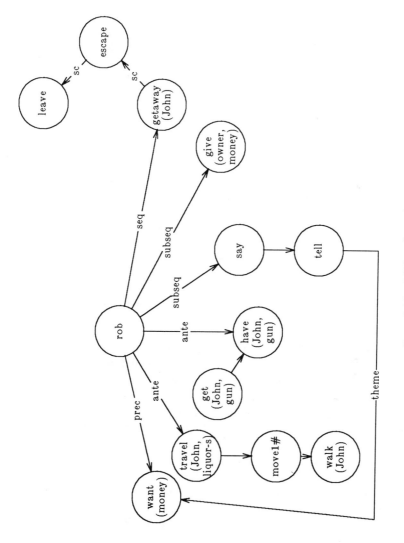

Figure 2.14. Robbing a liquor store

that is plan-based is also event concept coherent (i.e., the event descriptions invoke concepts that are coherent in a co-definitional network). The plan-based interpretation represents a deeper understanding of the text, but is more difficult to establish because it requires the recognition of goals and intentions. Moreover, a plan-based interpretation only applies to text involving intended actions. The ECC representation of a piece of text is independent of an intentional analysis: hence easier to establish and more widely applicable. The next section expands on this latter point.

Margie's Story. This example was originally discussed by Rumelhart (1975) in his paper on story grammars. Rumelhart's story grammar produces two different trees: One tree represents the syntactic organization of a story, the other a form of semantic organization. The story tree it produces for a piece of text represents the overall structure of the story by dividing it into categories like setting and episode. Whereas the story grammar is intended to capture the syntactic structure of narrative text, the NEXUS produced representation captures the coherence of the event concepts used in the text. The "Margie Story" goes as follows:

> Margie was **holding** tightly to the string of her beautiful new balloon. Suddenly, a gust of wind **caught** it. The wind **carried** it into a tree. The balloon **hit** a branch and **burst**. . .

Figure 2.15 shows the ECC representation of this text. The event/state concepts implicit in the text mutually define one another in NEXUS' dictionary of concepts. The wind 'takes' the balloon by 'catching' it. Because its 'taken' the balloon it 'has' the balloon. To 'move' the balloon the wind must 'have' the balloon. One way of 'moving' a balloon is 'carrying' it. If the balloon is being 'carried' then the balloon is 'moving.' If two objects 'hit' one of them must have been 'moving.' The conceptual structure that adheres to the event/state descriptions of the text is fairly rich. From these descriptions it is possible to reconstruct, using the dictionary of concepts, the coherence of their associated concepts.

This example shows that NEXUS can represent causal text that does not involve actors attempting to achieve well-defined goals. The representation that NEXUS produces for the "Margie Story" connects the event concepts 'carrying' and 'bursting.' This shows NEXUS' capability for structuring events beyond what can be accounted for by plans; the relationships between 'carrying' and 'bursting' is not a plan-based attempt to achieve a goal. The text

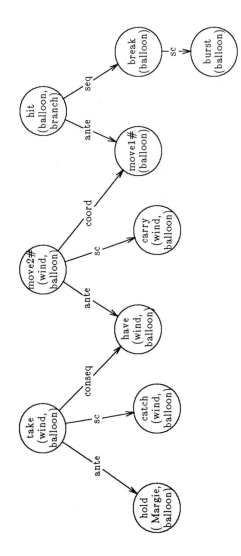

Figure 2.15. The Margie story

invokes event/state concepts that imply one another independent of whether the events are actually intended actions.

Also notice how vastly different the ECC representation is from a representation that characterizes the text by its syntactic organization. In some ways, story grammars and rhetorical coherence are similar projects. They both use the semantics of the text to construct a syntactic structure: For rhetorical coherence it is the discourse moves of the author, and for story grammars the syntactic structure of narrative text. An ECC representation captures the conceptual connectivity of the text. For entire stories this takes the form of a narrative stream (Alterman, 1986); in the case of Margie's story the stream is a fairly simple one, temporal sequence. Each concept tree represents an expansion of an event concept, and a connection between two trees in the stream occur when they share a concept in their expansion. The sense of movement and direction that is suggested by the narrative stream emerges from the temporal connections between the trees.

A Rock Fell Off the Cliff. In an attempt to deal with causality in narrative text, Wilks (1977) simplified the problem by dividing event chains into two types *causal* and *goal*. A sequence of events is a causal chain if the events are causally related. A sequence of events is a goal chain if the causal chain is directed toward the achievement of some character's goal. So the types of text that a plan-based analysis applies to are goal chains, and chains such as those described in the "Margie Story" are causal. In narrative text, goal chains are the preferred interpretation. Consider an example provided by Wilks.

The rock **fell** off the cliff and **crushed** John's lunch. Peter **pushed** it.

According to Wilks, the preferred interpretation of this text is that it is a goal chain (i.e., it was Peter's intention to push the rock off the cliff and crush John's lunch). But could be either one. If Peter was angry at John it is indeed a goal chain, but if Peter was clearing a spot to pitch a tent it is instead a causal chain. A plan-based representation system could represent the text if it is a goal chain and either misrepresent, or not represent at all, the text if it is causal.

Figure 2.16 shows the NEXUS representation of this text. Again, the event/state descriptions invoke a mesh of event/state concepts. Because Peter 'pushed' the rock it was 'propelled,' it 'moved' by 'falling.' Because it was 'falling' it was 'moving.' In order for two things to 'hit' one of the must have been 'moving.'

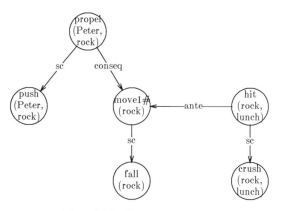

Figure 2.16. The rock fell off the cliff.

NEXUS makes no commitment to the type of the event chain associated with this text; it is neutral with regard to the causal nature of this chain. The NEXUS representation captures the concept coherence of the event descriptions. Depending on the context the same pattern of event concept coherence can turn out to be either causal or goal. For example, the relationship between 'move1#' and 'hitting' also occurred in the "Margie Story." For that story the chain was causal, whereas in this case it could be either a causal or goal chain.

Can You Reach the Salt?   Recent approaches (Allen, 1983; Cohen, 1979; Cohen, Perrault, & Allen, 1981) to question-answering have attempted to treat the interactions between man and machine as speech acts (Austin, 1969; Searle, 1969): Utterances are purposeful actions. For a computer system to engage successfully in a useful dialogue with a human it must have the capability to go beyond the surface meaning of the user's utterance and infer implicit plans and goals (i.e., it must be able to deal with *indirect speech acts*). Allen (1979) wrote a dialogue system that provided gate information for train travelers. It took a speech act approach to recognizing the traveler's intentions when he or she makes a request for information. For a request like

When does the Montreal train leave?

it would produce the answer:

3:15 at gate 7

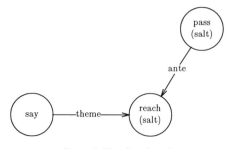

Figure 2.17. Pass the salt

Notice that the system infers that the traveler not only wants to know the time that the train is scheduled to leave, but also the location of its departure.

Indirect speech acts also occur in narrative test. A modified example from Allen's dissertation is:

John **asked** Mary, "Can you **reach** the salt?" She **passed** the salt.

From the NEXUS perspective there is an event concept coherence structure that would encompass both John's request and Mary's action: NEXUS has to find a connection between the *theme* of John's utterance and Mary's action.[3] The connection it should find is that 'reaching the salt' is an antecedent of 'passing the salt': 'reaching' and 'passing' lie in proximity in NEXUS' knowledge-net. Figure 2.17 shows the ECC representation of this text.

From a speech act point of view a number of things about mutual beliefs has been left out of the representation. For example, neither John's belief that Mary can reach the salt, nor Mary's belief that John believes that Mary can reach the salt, are represented in the ECC representation. The point here is that a text's description of an indirect speech act and the hearer's response to an indirect speech act

---

[3]For NEXUS these kinds of coherent chunks, where one is embedded in another, are linked by a **THEME** case relation (Simmons, 1973) and can also occur for mental events, conversations, and continuous perceptions. The following piece of text (Protter, 1961) includes a continuous perception.

The prince **spied** the pig *carrying* her laundry to the stream.
He **watched** her *soak* and *scour* it.

Notice that there is an embedding context (e.g., spying and watching) that forms a coherent chunk (ways of seeing the pigs activities). Embedded in it is another coherent chunk (cleaning the laundry). The perceptions of the princes are linked via a *theme* relation to the activities of the pig.

can be understood to be coherent without an explicit analysis of the speaker's goals or intentions. The ECC representation shows the coherence of John's request and Mary's action, but does not commit itself to an interpretation of John's intention or plan.

In conjunction with the rest of the discussion on plans and causal chains, it should become clear at this point what I mean when I say that the ECC representation is a sort of way station. There is a correlation between computational ease and representational complexity: The more detailed the representation, the more difficult the computation. When the representation attempts to differentiate between intended and unintended actions, or capture the mutual beliefs of communicating agents, the corresponding burden for the system that produces such a representation becomes more difficult. The ECC representation attempts to collect and connect the various event descriptions of the text by mitigating the effects of context—it avoids making the determinations that are most likely to involve problem solving. The deeper question here is: To what extent is it necessary, or cognitively feasible, for an 'understander' to make such detailed determinations on a regular basis? In the case of a habitual situation, like the one at the train station, it is hard to imagine that any of the mutual belief analysis is occurring with regularity; a coherence model, that captures the coherence between the user's request and the system's knowledge of specific travel plans, might be sufficient for this kind of task. Moreover, Alterman (1986) demonstrated that a certain kind of summarization of text, summarization-in-the-small, can be performed given the ECC level analysis.

A Restaurant Story

A script (Cullingford, 1978; Schank & Abelson, 1977) is a culturally stereotypical situation. It is a sequence of events that is strongly coupled with a particular context. For example, a restaurant script includes: props (e.g., tables), roles (e.g., waiter), entry conditions (e.g., hunger), and exit conditions (e.g., not hungry). The sequence of events coupled to the restaurant context include: ordering, eating, and tipping. In one sense, comparing an ECC representation to a script is like comparing apples and oranges. Where for ECC theory the underlying network and the representation produced for the text have essentially the same structure, scripts are intended as a knowledge structure and not as a representation form for the text; the text is represented by a causal chain. For the purposes of this discussion, I assume that the structure of the script is used to structure the text.

Schank and Abelson provided an example of text for which a restaurant script applies:

John **went** to a restaurant. The hostess **seated** John. The hostess **gave** John a menu. The waiter **came** to the table. John **ordered** a lobster. He was **served** quickly. He **left** a large tip. He **left** the restaurant.

Figure 2.18 shows NEXUS' handling of this text. When NEXUS was applied to the example it gathered the text into a single instance of the concept of eating: NEXUS produces a single concept tree. The events in the story can be subsumed under the banner of an 'eating' event, and consequently, NEXUS, in case notation form, summarizes this story: "John ate lobster at a restaurant."

For NEXUS, all of the event/state concepts invoked by the text mutually define one another. Some are interrelated because of the co-definitional relationships associated with the general concept 'eating' (e.g., 'serving'), others due to relationships that only occur in a restaurant context (e.g., 'tipping'). Relationships that occur only in specialized contexts are controlled by attaching constraints to those relationships. The relationship between 'eating' and 'tipping' only occurs in a restaurant. NEXUS controls this inference by specifying that the locations of 'eating' and 'tipping' must be a restaurant in order for this relationship to exist.

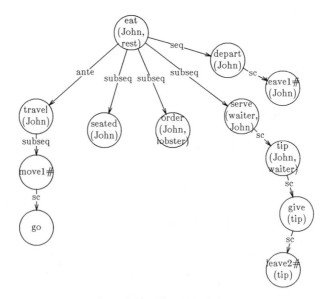

Figure 2.18. The restaurant story

Because scripts are situationalized events separated out from other types of event connections, unexpected events are treated separately. For example, suppose, within a restaurant story, the reader is informed "While carrying the food to the table, the waiter dropped the tray." For a restaurant script this is an exceptional event: It is not part of the normal restaurant script. NEXUS handles the connection between these two concepts in the normal course of its processing; implicit in the concept 'carrying' is 'holding' and an *antecedent* of 'dropping' is 'holding.'

SUMMARY AND CONCLUSIONS

This chapter presents a theory for capturing one aspect of the connectivity of text, its event concept coherence. An ECC representation represents the text in a manner that brings the relatedness of the events to the forefront. It characterizes dependencies among the events in a causally neutral, but causally relevant, form. It acts as a sort of way station, organizing the text for determinations that are more contextually dependent. The construction of an ECC representation makes the following assumption: The representation of the event descriptions of the text are a reflection of the relationships of the event/state concepts invoked by the text.

This theory has been implemented in a system called NEXUS. NEXUS' knowledge base is a semantic network containing interrelationships among event/state concepts. The event concept coherence representation NEXUS produces is essentially a copy of the connections that are contained in the knowledge net and invoked by the text.

Because a representation of a piece of text reflects the structure of the knowledge net, the knowledge base could be constructed by an analysis of text. NEXUS' knowledge net was constructed from an analysis of parts of 10 folktales. Associated with each concept in the knowledge net are constraints on the matching of case arguments. In addition to controlling inferencing the constraints enable reference resolution to occur as a by-product of building a representation for a piece of text.

There are seven event/state concept coherence relations. There is one taxonomic relation (class/subclass) and two partonomic relations (sequence/subsequence and coordinate). The four temporal relations (antecedent, precedent, consequent, sequel) are differentiated by their time and likelihood of occurrence.

NEXUS' basic procedure works in two stages. In the first stage, NEXUS uses a bi-directional breadth-first search to find a connecting path among the concepts invoked in its knowledge net. In the second stage, NEXUS propagates the constraints associated with each relationship in the path, simultaneously testing validity and performing reference resolution.

The paper analyzed several pieces of text from the literature from the ECC vantage point. The first example was used to point out the difference between discourse coherence and concept coherence. Discourse coherence relations characterize the continuation moves made by the speaker (writer). Event concept coherence captured the mesh of mutually defining event/state concept interrelationships that are invoked by the descriptions of the text. Event concept coherence reflects the coherence of concepts described in the text as opposed to discourse coherence which captures the rhetorical intentions of the speaker.

The second comparison concerned conceptual dependency. The major contrasting point was that CD represents a concept by reducing it to primitives and event concept coherence represents a concept by its position in a network of mutually defining concepts. The gist of the discussion was that the property of partial canonicalization that is exhibited by primitives is also attributable to semantic networks.

There were four examples discussed concerning plans and causal chains. The thematic point throughout all these examples is that there is a correlation between computational ease and representational complexity: The more detailed the representation, the more difficult the computation. When the representation attempts to differentiate between intended and unintended actions, or to capture the mutual beliefs of communicating agents, the corresponding burden for the system that produces such a representation becomes more difficult. The ECC representation attempts to collect and connect the various event descriptions of the text by mitigating the effects of context—it avoids making the determinations that are most likely to involve problem solving. The question that begins to emerge from these considerations is: To what extent is it necessary, or, for that matter, cognitively feasible, for an 'understander' to make, on a regular basis, such detailed determinations concerning the subtle problems of intentionality and mutual belief?

There were several observations included in the section on the plan-based example. One observation was that plan-based text is also event concept coherent. A second is that plan-based interpretations are more difficult to establish. A third is that plan-based interpretations are limited to text concerning intended actions, whereas event concept coherence interpretations are not.

The "Margie Story" demonstrated more clearly the last of these points. An analysis showed that this story included text that was event concept coherent but not plan based. Moreover, the metaphor of narrative stream, which emerges from conceptual connectivity, was contrasted to the notion of story schema that characterizes the syntactic form of the text. In the discussion of text concerning 'the rock that fell off the cliff' it was pointed out that although ECC can represent both plan-based and nonplan-based text, it does not differentiate between the two kinds of chain.

The plan and causal chain discussion concluded with some text involving an indirect speech act. The point of this example was that a representation of the connectivity of an indirect speech act could be built without an explicit analysis of the speaker's goals or intentions. The event concept coherence representation showed the coherence of the text without committing itself to an interpretation of mutual beliefs.

A piece of text involving the restaurant script was the basis of the last comparison. Where a script serves only as a knowledge structure, the knowledge network associated with NEXUS also structures the representation of the text. Some of the concept coherent terms in the text were related regardless of the restaurant context. Others required a restaurant context and in NEXUS are constrained through the matching of case arguments. It was pointed out that what was an exception for a restaurant script would be exceptionless for a representation based on event concept coherence.

ACKNOWLEDGMENTS

I would like to thank David Waltz, Bob Simmons, and an anonymous reviewer for their detailed reading and commenting on earlier versions of this chapter.

This research is not without its context. Much of the original work was done at the University of Texas. I am deeply indebted to Bob Simmons. I would also like to thank Michael K. Smith and Elaine Rich for a number of interactions. At UC Berkeley this work has benefited from some discussion with Bob Wilensky. Two of his graduate student have participated in a number of useful conversations: Peter Norvig and James H. Martin.

Since arriving at UC Berkeley, this research was sponsored in part by the Defense Advance Research Projects Agency (DOD), Arpa Order No. 4031, Monitored by Naval Electronic system command under Contract No. N00039-C-0235.

REFERENCES

Allen, J. (1983). Recognizing intentions from natural language utterances. In R. C. Berwick & M. Brady (Eds.), *Computational models of discourse* (pp. 107–166). MIT Press.

Allen, J. (1979). *A plan-based approach to speech act recognition.* Unpublished doctoral dissertation, University of Toronto.

Alterman, R., & Bookman, L. (1988). How to summarize thick text (and represent it too). Proceedings of the 10th annual conference of the Cognitive Science Society (pp. 69–75). Hillsdale, NJ: Lawrence Erlbaum Associates.

Alterman, R. (1986). Summarization in the small. In N. Sharkey (Ed.), *Advances in cognitive science 1* (pp. 72–93). Ellis Harwood.

Alterman, R. (1985). A dictionary based on concept coherence. *Artificial Intelligence, 25,* 153–186.

Alterman, R. (1982). *A system of seven coherence relations for hierarchically organizing event concepts in narrative text* (Technical Report TR-209). University of Texas at Austin.

Austin, J. L. (1986). *How to do things with words.* Oxford University Press.

Brachman, R. J. (1979). On the epistemological status of semantic networks. In N. Findler (Ed.), *Associative networks: The representation and use of knowledge in computers,* (pp. 3–49). New York: Academic Press.

Charniak, E. (1983). Passing markers: A theory of contextual influences in language comprehension. *Cognitive Science 7,* 171–190.

Charniak, E. (1981). The case-slot identity theory. *Cognitive Science, 5,* (3), 285–292.

Chester, D. (1980a). *Using HCPRVR* (Technical Report). University of Texas at Austin.

Chester, D. (1980b). HCPRVR: A logic program interpreter in lisp. *Proceedings of AAAI.* Los Altos, CA: Morgan Kaufman.

Cohen, P. R., Perrault, C. R., & Allen, J. F. (1981). *Beyond question-answering* (Technical Report No. 4644). Cambridge, MA: Bolt Beranek and Newman.

Cohen, P. R., & Perrault, R. S. (1979). Elements of a plan-based theory of speech acts. *Cognitive Science, 3,*(4), 177–202.

Cullingford, R. (1978). *Script application: Computer understanding of newspaper stories.* Unpublished doctoral dissertation, Yale University.

de Beaugrande, R. (1980). Discourse and process: Toward a multidisciplinary science of texts. In *Advances in discourse processes, Vol. 4.* Norwood, N.J.: Ablex.

Hobbs, J. (1979). Coherence and coreference. *Cognitive Science, 3*(1), 67–90.

Hobbs, J. (1978). *Why is discourse coherent?* (Technical Note 176). Menlo Park, CA: SRI.

Kowalski, R. (1979). Algortihm = logic + control, *Communications of the ACM, 22*(7), 424–436.

Norvig, P. (1987). *Inference processes and knowledge representation for text understanding.* Unpublished doctoral dissertation, University of California at Berkeley.

Parnas, D. L. (1972). On the criteria to be used in decomposing system into modules. *Communications of the ACM, 15*(12), 1053–1058.

Protter, E. (1961). *A children's treasury of folk and fairy tales.* Great Neck: NY: Channel Press.

Quillian, R. (1969). The teachable language comprehender: A simulation program and theory of language. *Communications of the ACM, 12*(8), 459–476.

Quillian, R. (1968). Semantic memory. In M. Minsky (Ed.), *Semantic information processing.* MIT Press.

Rumelhart, D. E. (1975). Notes on a schema for stories. In D. G. Bobrow & A. Collins (Eds.), *Representation and understanding.* New York: Academic Press.

Schank, R. C., & Abelson, R. P. (1977). Scripts, plans, goals, and understanding. Hillsdale, NJ: Lawrence Erlbaum Associates.

Schank, R. C. (1973). Identification of conceptualizations underlying natural language. In R. Schank & K. Colby (Eds.), *Computer models of thought and language.* San Francisco: W. H. Freeman and Company.

Searle, J. R. (1969). *Speech acts.* Cambridge University Press.

Simmons, R. F. (1984). Computations from the English. Englewood Cliff, NJ: Prentice-Hall.

Simmons, R. F. (1973). Semantic networks: Their computation and use for understanding English sentence. In R. Schank & K. Colby (Eds.), *Computer Models of Thought and Language.* W. H. Freeman and Company.

Wilensky, R. (1987). *Some problems and proposals for knowledge representation* (Report No. UCB.CSD 86/294). Computer Science Division, University of California at Berkeley.

Wilensky, R. (1983). *Planning and understanding.* Reading, MA: Addison-Wesley Publishing Company.

Wilensky, R. (1978). *Understanding goal-based stories.* Unpublished doctoral dissertation, Yale University.

Wilks, Y. (1977). What sort of taxonomy of causation do we need? *Cognitive Science, 1,* 235–264.

Woods, W. A. (1975). What's in a link: Foundations for semantic networks. In D. G. Bobrow & A. Collins (Eds.), *Representation and Understanding* (pp. 35–82). New York: Academic Press.

CHAPTER 3

Learning Word Meanings from Examples

ROBERT C. BERWICK
Artificial Intelligence Laboratory
Massachusetts Institute of Technology

INTRODUCTION

This chapter describes an experimental computer program that de-
duces the meaning of novel verbs from the context of story descriptions. The key idea is a variation on Winston's (Winston, 1975)
program that learned the structural descriptions of block world
scenes. Instead of learning descriptions of toy block assemblies like
ARCH and TOWER, the word-learning program acquires frame-based
descriptions of English verbs like MURDER or DONATE. The program
works by assuming that similar verbs will play similar causal roles
in common story plots. For example, ASSASSINATE is like MURDER
because both MURDER and ASSASSINATE cause similar things to happen and are caused by similar patterns and events. Intuitively, we
learn about a new verb like ASSASSINATE as a kind of family resemblance variation on a core verb like MURDER. The program works
in a similar way. Syntactic constraints derived from the parsing of
story plots are used to drive an analogical matching procedure. Analogical matching gives a way to compare descriptions of known
words to unknown words. The "meaning" of a new verb is learned
by matching part of the causal network description of a story précis

containing the unknown word to a set of such descriptions derived from similar stories that contain only known words. The best match forges an assignment between objects and relations such that the unknown verb is matched to a known verb. The causal network surrounding the unknown item is then used as a scaffolding to construct a network representing the meaning of the novel word in a particular context. In some ways, the model is similar in spirit to that of Granger (1977), who also extracted context-based descriptions to acquire meaning descriptions of novel words. As we see, this way of describing word meaning has several advantages over definitional approaches.

A second aim of this research is to explore the interaction between syntax and semantics in learning. The word-learning program is embedded into a larger system that can acquire new syntactic rules for English, as described in Berwick (1979, 1980, 1982, 1985). The word-learning component uses the larger system's determination of the syntactic category of a new word and its predicate-argument structure. These last two abilities are based on the $\bar{X}$ theory of Jackendoff (1977) and a theory of syntax that assumes a strong principle of lexical transparency (roughly, that the semantic argument structure of a verb appears at all levels of representation). Here, *syntax* means simply the grammatical *form* of sentences, whereas *semantics* refers to such notions as case relationships (Agent, Affected Object), as well as the causal description language used for word matching itself. Although some have emphasized either syntax or semantics as a key to word learning, the position taken here is that either may serve as a constraint on the other. It is the interaction between syntax and semantics that drives word leaning. In some cases, syntax helps semantics. We see several examples of this here, where prior knowledge of sentence structure plays a vital role in figuring out the candidate words for a causally based match. Recently, Landau and Gleitman (1985) have independently confirmed this theoretical finding by studying a blind child's acquisition of verb meanings. They found that syntactic constraints were crucial for successful acquisition of verbs such as *look at* or *see*. Language acquisition involves the complex interplay between these two sources of constraint.

Third, this chapter suggests a concrete computational model for the acquisition of word *protoypes* from positive examples. In addition, it also suggests a way of automatically generating A K O ("a-kind-of") hierarchies from positive examples. Importantly, this method follows a natural formal and empirically justified constraint on the evolution of categorizations first explored by Keil (1979).

The moral of this chapter is that *constraints* make learning possible. A learning theory can be built only if one has a good representation of what it is that is learned, and some idea of the constraints on that target state. For our theory, the constraints include a restricted vocabulary of *thematic relations* (a "case system") plus a causal description language. The hardest part of constructing a theory of word learning is figuring out just how to represent the "meaning" of a word. Fortunately, a variety of linguistic constraints can help us here. The second moral is that learning does not seem possible unless one almost already knows what is to be learned—a principle of "incremental learning." Whether all learning abides by these principles is not certain, but it seems true that so far all successful artificial intelligence (AI) learning programs have followed them.

Our first job, then, is to describe the representation for word meaning to be used by the learning program. Before we do so, however, it would be best to give an example of the kind of competence we want our word-learning system to display. As mentioned, a key underlying assumption is that the meaning of a word is determined by the role it plays in a causal network description of an event, and that similar words are those that play similar roles in the description of similar events. Consider the following scenario:

> Suppose we are given two versions of the story of Macbeth, one reporting that "Macbeth murders Duncan" and the other that "Macbeth assassinates Duncan." Further suppose that MURDER is a known word but not ASSASSINATE. We should conclude that ASSASSINATE is most like MURDER, because, comparing stories, it seems to us that ASSASSINATE plays the same role that MURDER does in the Macbeth plot. We should also conclude that ASSASSINATE has political overtones, because we note that the Macbeth story includes such relations as *Macbeth wants to be king* and *Macbeth becomes king*. Probing further, later stories should inform us that the uses of ASSASSINATE and MURDER are slightly different, because MURDER need not carry that political connotations that ASSASSINATE does. We should also be able to use the story of Hamlet to deduce the same kind of relationship between MURDER and ASSASSINATE.

Here is the actual input for the Macbeth story:

> MA is a story about Macbeth Lady-macbeth Duncan and Macduff.
>   Macbeth is an evil noble. Lady-macbeth is a greedy ambitious woman. Duncan is a king. Macduff is a noble.
>   Lady-macbeth persuades Macbeth to want to be king because she wants him to be king. She wants him to be king because she is greedy.

She can convince him because Macbeth loves her and also because Macbeth is wimpy.

Macbeth assassinates Duncan with a knife. Macbeth assassinates Duncan because Macbeth wants to be king. Lady-macbeth becomes insane. She kills herself because she is insane.

Macduff becomes angry because the king was assassinated. Macduff kills Macbeth because Macbeth assassinated Duncan and because Macduff is loyal to Duncan.

Remember MA.

Using the techniques described in Winston (1980) and Katz and Winston (1982) the system builds a causal network description of the story, as shown in Figure 3.1. This network is basically an object-oriented semantic network, with objects, agents, and qualities (and sometimes propositional attitudes like beliefs or desires) serving as the nodes in the network, and verbs serving as the links between nodes.

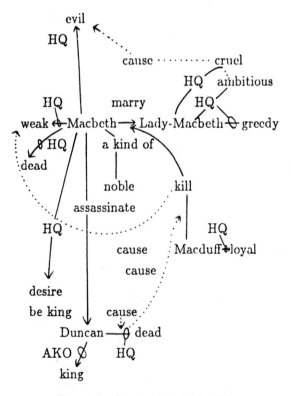

Figure 3.1. Causal networks describe stories

Now suppose that a number of other stories have been previously analyzed and stored in causal network form (e.g., Macbeth, Hamlet, Julius Caesar, and the Taming of the Shrew, as discussed in Winston, 1980), and that none of these previous plot summaries used the word *assassinate*. (Alternatively, the *Macbeth* story could be considered unknown, as long as other examples of murders, say, in *Hamlet*, were already analyzed.)

A causal network representation can be built for each of these stories. For the old Macbeth and Hamlet stories, this network will be nearly identical to the network built previously, but with some key differences that flow from the lack of understanding of *assassinate*. Still, as we see, syntactic constraints permit the entire network to be built, because the connections between objects and actions are actually syntactic.

The learning procedure then takes the causal network descriptions of each of the candidate stories and runs an analogy matching program, pairing objects and relations in the new story against objects and relations in each of the candidates until the best match is obtained. Note that the system can use either similar stories for an attempted match or exactly the same story (but with unknown words).

This is a graph matching problem. It tries all possible combinations of nodes (objects) and links (labeled with verbs, prepositions, or CAUSE) until it finds one that lines up best with the old story. This best match will pair up corresponding objects and links in the network representation of the new Macbeth story and the network of one of the other stories. In this case, the best match weds *murder* and *assassinate*, because these have the most causal links in common. This is the first step in forging a representation of the meaning of the new verb *assassinate*.

This is what we want our system to do; the rest of the chapter says just how it is done. In the first Section, following much recent work on concept acquisition, I discuss why dictionary definitions are inappropriate for this task. The next section follows with an outline of a causal description language that does seem more suited for representing verb meanings and a definition of semantic similarity. The third section outlines the syntactic constraints used by the acquisition program and their connection to semantic representations. A detailed discussion of the program implementation and some examples of the system in action is given in the fourth section. It also compares the current system to an earlier attack on this problem, by Granger (1977). The final section is a discussion of current limitations and some proposed extensions for the learning of Nouns.

THE INADEQUACY OF DEFINITIONS

If the key to any learning program is a good representation of what is learned, then we must have a good representation of word meanings before we can learn them. In fact, this has been the biggest stumbling block for word learning. What is the meaning of a word?

One common analysis has been *decompositional*. Words are viewed as chemical compounds, built out of constituent primitives. So for example, *dog* might be labeled Animate, Four-legged, Mammal. . . . This "word chemistry" is a classical technique that aims to account for our apparent "generative" ability with words—our ability to represent the meaning of a potentially unlimited number of words with finite means. Researchers as diverse as Schank and (much earlier) Katz and Fodor have embraced this method. For instance, as should be familiar, Schank takes the "meaning" of verbs as representable by a graphic language consisting of primitives like PTRANS (physical movement) assembled into a picture of the relationship between objects in an event representation of a sentence.

The difficulties with a "pure" compositional account of word meanings are by now well known. There is a familiar skeptical tradition in 20th century philosophy of language, stemming in part from the later work of Wittgenstein, arguing that it is impossible to give definitions—necessary and sufficient conditions—for words. In a classical passage, Wittgenstein observed, for example, that there can be no definition of a *game*, because there is nothing held in common between board games, sports games, and the like. The most that can be said is that there is a kind of "family resemblance" between the members of the group of games. More recently, psychological arguments have been advanced that mitigate against definitional accounts of meaning. Fodor, Garrett, Walker, and Parkes (1980) pointed out that it is impossible to find "if-and-only-if" conditions for words, aside from examples of such words as jargon or kinship terms. (Note that AI programs for word acquisition have often focused on just these sorts of items, such as *bachelor*.) They also provide psycholinguistic evidence—based on reaction time tests—that feature decomposition into primitive elements is not carried out in on-line processing.

. Whatever the status of these experiments and others like them (see, for example, Hayes-Roth and Hayes-Roth, 1977, who present similar evidence against decompositional theories), it is plain that "if-and-only-if" conditions for word definitions must be rejected. Definitions should admit exceptions and graded categorization judgments, as well as networks of family resemblances. What is the alternative? One approach that has been emerging out of work in AI and psychological analysis is that of *prototype* theory. Prototype theory holds that the criterial features of a word—say, *apple*—are described via some paradigm or core example. We picture an apple by conjuring up a familiar red object in our mind's eye. Even so, this prototypical apple admits exceptions and gradations in each of its characteristic qualities: the skin may be green, if the shape is right; the apple may be mis-shapen, if it is otherwise applelike; a huge apple is still an apple, and so on. In the traditional AI parlance, we may connect these various sorts of apples by means of *difference pointers* (Winston, 1975) indicating how and by how much the various members of the apple family deviate from core apple-ness.

Difference-pointer families avoid the pitfalls of necessary sufficient conditions because there are no necessary and sufficient conditions for any definitions. Indeed, there are no definitions at all, in the "if and only if" sense. Viewed this way, what we learn when we learn a new word is not some set of conditions, but a connection of some network of already-known words. This viewpoint is not novel, of course, being part of most network-based theories of semantic representation. What is new is a demonstration of just how this approach can be used for word learning.

At the same time, it is worth pointing out that these claims about word decomposition are controversial. An opposing, long-standing approach attempts to chop up word meanings, particularly those for verbs, into primitives. So for example, *kill* might be written as CAUSE *to die*. This is a tack favored by Gruber (1965), Schank (1973), and Jackendoff (1972), among others. In this chapter we straddle both sides of this difficult fence. Rejecting if-and-only-if conditions, we adopt a family resemblance model for meaning. At the same time, we decompose verbs into causal network diagrams.

THE ACQUISITION PROCEDURE

The Causal Description Language

Having adopted a "family resemblance" model for meaning, we have still to say just what our network descriptors should be. As is well known, the choice of a semantic network vocabulary is a hazardous game. Ideally, one should follow empirical constraints on descriptors, but little is known about what these should be. Is color a basic element of our semantic descriptions? If so, what colors? What about geometric shapes? Such conditions can be multiplied endlessly. It would be useful to have criteria analogous to those for grammatical categories and features that would let us know that *red* is just as much a part of semantic descriptions as *Noun* is for syntactic

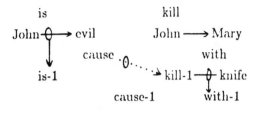

Figure 3.2. A causal network fragment

descriptions. The last section of this chapter explores one way of attacking these problems, based on work by Jackendoff (1977), but we defer the question for now.

Given that we do not know just what the right primitive elements should be, or even that there are primitive elements at all, in this work we have simply adopted the position that *all* elements are allowable as potential descriptors on our semantic network. The actual representation for the simple English stories in our database is called an *extensible-relation* representation. It was developed by Winston (1980).

This semantic net is object oriented, with agents, objects, and qualities serving as nodes and verbs tying them together. If more than one object is involved in an act, additional descriptions can be associated with the act-specifying relation. These additional descriptions are nodes that are related to other nodes. For example, the sentence *John killed Mary with a knife because John is evil* is depicted in Figure 3.2.

Note that in this scheme all individual words such as *knife* or *kill* are considered unanalyzable wholes. Nevertheless, it is still possible to relate one word to another word, by comparing the networks in which each is embedded.

Causality

There is one more ingredient to add to our representational language that is a primitive, however. One of the key elements in describing a situation seems to be *causality*. To know what an event is about it is important to know what causes what and what is caused by what. Evidence for this view comes from a variety of sources. Developmental psychologists have discovered that even very young children are disposed to analyze complex mechanical scenes in causal terms, and they can do so correctly (Gelman & Gallistel, 1979). For example, a long row of standing dominoes can be successfully analyzed as capable of knocking open a jack-in-the-box, if the leftmost domino is rapped with a rigid swinging stick long enough to reach it. Evidently quite young children know enough about causality to reason about even these complex situations.

Then too, the ability to explain what happened depends on a causal description. It is no surprise that many AI programs that reason about physical processes rely on causal descriptions. Causality plays a prominent role in other representational languages for predicates, particularly in the work of Schank and Wilks. Finally, causality adds an implicational structure to an otherwise static description network. Without before-and-after links of some kind, it is impossible to describe a chain of events. Otherwise, words are just linked to each other without any directionality.

Given the central role of causality in the description of events, special *cause* links are included in the network description language. Because causes are so important, there is an extra mechanism, demons, associated with them. The following conventions for CAUSE demons are obeyed:

- If A causes B, then B is caused by A, where A can be people, relations, or objects and B can be other relations or acts. The caused-by links are automatically generated when causal relations are inserted in the database. In our previous example, there should be a caused-by link from kill-1 to is-1.

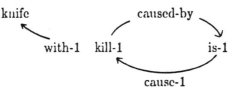

- If A persuades B to do C, then clearly, A causes C and C is caused by A. The appropriate links are added to the database. For example, *Mary persuaded John to eat a cookie* is pictured as:

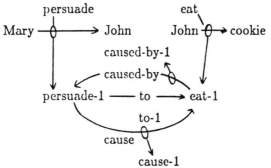

Demons are also used to make certain simple deductions as relations are added to the database. For instance, if we add *Macbeth kills Duncan* to our database, a demon adds *Duncan is dead*. From a theoretical standpoint, these demons are simply meaning postulates, in Carnap's (1952) sense. But why does one add some set of meaning postulates rather than another? Why, for instance, add just "Romeo has-quality dead" rather than a whole list of additional deductions likely to be true if Romeo kills himself? The idea here is that the added deductions are the "simplest" meaning postulates associated with predicates, where "simplest" is a one-step deduction according to a common-sense language of description. In other words, folk psychological terms are used rather than a sophisticated language of scientific descriptions for depicting events: We say that Macbeth killed Duncan because Macbeth is evil, not because of some account averting to biochemical imbalances. To be sure, this way of limiting deduction is not perfect, but it at least aims to stay close to the deductions people make.

Although the AKO and causal-based representation has been a useful testbed, it is not without problems. We use a preexisting set of AKO descriptors, such as *king* or *knife*. Ideally, these too should be learned. Also, it is not clear that *cause* suffices to describe all verbal relationships. Stative verbs like *be* that describe changes in properties or motion verbs like *run* are not so easily cast in terms of causal interactions with objects. A cause-based matcher will have nothing to work with here, and so will fail. In the fourth section of this chapter we propose modifications to handle some of these difficulties.

Thematic Role Structure and Meaning

In addition to the causal network description, there is one other component of word meaning used by the learning program. This is the linguistic notion of *thematic roles,* also called *case frames.* Thematic-role descriptions have been discussed in detail by Fillmore (1968) and Gruber (1965), but in fact are part of almost every linguistic theory. Intuitively, we think of a verb as requiring several thematic arguments that flesh out a picture of the event the verb describes. For example, *eat* takes at least three arguments: the eater, the thing eaten (sometimes tacit); and optionally the manner, instrument, or place of eating. For our purposes here, what is important is that particular thematic roles are ordinarily linked to specific grammatical positions in a particular language. In English, the subject position is canonically the "doer" of the action or the agent. Importantly, the notion of subject is syntactic in English, because it is the first noun phrase under the sentence in a parse tree. Likewise, the object position canonically plays the *affected object* or *patient* role. This correspondence between form and meaning implies that thematic structure can be recovered from syntactic form, at least in clear cases.

Interestingly enough, possible form-meaning assignments vary parametrically within narrow limits. That is, although other languages (unlike English) do not link the subject syntactic position with the thematic role of agent,the allowed variations are quite limited. Linguistic analysis suggests a twofold division of the world's languages, into either the *accusative languages*, with a subject-agent and object-patient connection; or the *ergative languages*, with the reverse object-agent and subject-patient links. Once this pattern is fixed for a given language, it need not be relearned for individual verbs, although there may be exceptions to, for example, the generally accusative character of a language. In English, for instance,there is a systematic class of verbs whose subjects are affected objects rather than agents; this data and the table here are from Levin (1983).

- The glass broke.
- The puddle disappeared.
- The book fell off the shelf.

This analysis carves up English verbs into a few classes according to their argument structure. Basically, there are two argument verbs with the accusative pattern; one argument verbs with a subject-agent link; and the ergative one argument verbs like those just mentioned:

2 arg. verbs	1 arg. verbs (Agent only)	1 arg. verbs (Patient only)
hit	talk	come
kick	cough	break[1]
push	wave	appear
give	sing	fall
take	sniff	go

The learning program exploits these regularities by using the form-meaning correspondence to guide network matching. No matter what the meaning of a novel verb, and unless there are specific syntactic clues that indicate otherwise, one can assume that the subject will be the agent and the object will be the patient. But this means that the subject-verb-object links so crucial for the meaning representation can be partially built even for an unknown verb. Syntactic constraints are enough in most cases. Then, the network matching program can use this information to attempt to pair up only agents with other agents, patients with patients, and so forth. This filtering saves a good deal of effort. For example, if we have that "X kills Y," then naturally X and Y will wind up playing different causal roles later in the story. Given "W assassinates Z" it would thus be a waste of time to try to pair the person killed in one story with the assassinator in the other. Thematic filtering prevents this. Granger (1977) used a similar method within a very different semantic representation. He too found that thematic roles were a crucial factor in looking for a representation for a novel word. Granger did not use thematic roles directly, but instead looked at prepositional types and their noun phrase objects. In English, this amounts to the same thing as a thematic role. For example, *by* plus an animate noun phrase often corresponds to an agent thematic role. This would not work in a language where thematic roles are unmarked by prepositions. It also fails in cases where thematic role varies from its canonical prepositional assignment; for example, in *the vase broke, vase* is not the agent. This is one reason why it is better to work through a mediating syntactic theory that directly defines thematic roles, and then use these for filtering candidate matches.

With the basics of the syntax-semantics connection described, some details are in order. The techniques described in Berwick (1985), based on the Marcus (1980) parser, are used to syntactically analyze the input. Consider a sentence such as *Macbeth assassinates Duncan*. How can we assign the correct thematic roles in this case if *assassinate* is an unknown word?

First of all, we may assume that all normal English sentences are known to be in the form noun phrase—verb phrase. Unless there is evidence to the contrary, the parser will predict that a noun phrase (*Macbeth*) begins this sentence as well. With the NP disposed of, the parser now predicts that an a verb phrase (VP) should be found. Given that English verb phrases must be headed by verbs, *assassinate* is forced to be a verb. In this way, syntax actually constrains the lexical category of the unknown word. (There are, of course, other possibilities. Suppose that an adverb intervened between NP and verb, as in, *Macbeth quickly dispatched Duncan*. In this case, given that *quickly* is known as an adverb, again a VP is predicted, and *assassinate* must be its head. Note that *Duncan* is assumed known as a noun, hence cannot be the verb heading the verb phrase.)

Finally, *Duncan* is parsed as an NP and noted as an object of the unknown verb, as it is by definition. Given the canonical relationship between thematic arguments and syntactic positions, we also know that the object is the patient and that *Macbeth* is the agent. So we already know quite a bit about *assassinate* without really understanding its meaning.

Semantic Similarity and Matching

We are now ready to describe the matching criteria used for judging when two verbs are "close" in meaning. Two verbs are judged semantically identical if:

1. Their thematic role structures and selectional restrictions are the same;
2. The same objects are present in the causal representations of both verbs; and
3. Their causal links overlap exactly.

Selectional restrictions amount to simply the type checking of arguments. For example, *admire* demands an animate subject (*John admires sincerity* but not *Sincerity admires John*). (The final section discusses in more detail how selectional restrictions may be learned.)

These three conditions are identical to what Salveter (1982) used in the MORAN system for learning Schank-type representations of words. Plainly, however, these exact-match conditions are too strong. Similar verbs can violate any or all of conditions (1)–(3). Verbs may differ in argument structure and yet be alike in meaning: *Eat* takes an object argument and *dine* does not (*John ate an apple* vs. *John dined an apple*). Similar verbs may have different selectional restrictions: *Assassinate* differs from *murder* in that it requires the thing killed to be a person and a political figure. The requirement of object identity is also too strong. It is clear that two verbs may be nearly synonymous, and yet one verb might appear in a story mentioning only Hamlet, whereas the other verb occurs with Macbeth. Finally, similar verbs may have causal structures that do not exactly overlap (e.g., *steal* usually leads to a pattern of causes and effects that is distinct from *take*, yet the two verbs are alike in some ways).

All of these considerations suggest that one give up the tight constraint of exact matches for a graded system of inexact matching. Computationally, the problem is one of (directed) graph isomorphism. We want to find the best possible correspondence between graphs G_1 and G_2 labeled with *cause*, verb, and preposition links.

Aside from this labeled correspondence, then, the matching process is completely syntactic; only the pattern of the graphs matters in matching. In addition, two nodes are not considered for matching unless they play the same thematic roles (agent, patient, and so forth) in the graph representations (in particular, two objects may be matched if they denote different instances of the "same" object, e.g., KNIFE-1 and KNIFE-3). (It might also be reasonable to use a weakened condition here that permits two objects to be matched even if they do not fill the same thematic roles, if they are the same object or nearly the same kind of object, but this change has not been investigated.)

The matching process is in general computationally intractable. There are *n* factorial possible 1-1 mappings of *n* nodes to *n* other nodes; there are more possible matches if a 1-1 correspondence is not required. Worse yet, the program must search as many graphs as there are possible stories with candidate verbs. We conclude that some potential matches must be filtered out in advance and the size of matches should be restricted if at all possible. Two heuristics have been adopted to implement this strategy.

The first heuristic limits the number of stories considered by the matcher. It is currently under development. The key idea is to look only at a few stories that are broadly similar to the story with the unknown verb. Similarity of stories is judged in terms of plot units, in the sense of Lehnert (1981). Roughly, plot-unit theory assumes that the causal relationships in a story can be summarized by extracting out the "molecular structure" of the causal network. This is done by imposing a theory of plot "molecular structure" onto the more basic causal network. Given a network description we can form a corresponding description in terms of basic plot units like *loss, gain,* or *intentional problem resolution.* The advantage of this approach is that it boils down entire stories to supergraphs of just a few nodes and links each. For instance, Lehnert showed how a complex story like *The Gift of the Magi* can be reduced to just 10 linked nodes. Applied to our current problem, the idea is to index all stories by their plot summaries and to retrieve only those that happen to closely match the current story under analysis. Of course, this extra indexing and retrieval matching itself takes time, but typically far fewer nodes are involved for matching. One difficulty is that Lehnert's plot summaries are based on a vocabulary of affective reactions, which may not be suitable for indexing causal regularities. What is needed is an approach like Lehnert's but with a different summarization vocabulary. This has not yet been done. Because it is not yet completely implemented, this heuristic currently replaced by an oracle—a programmer who decides what stories to match against the network with the unknown verb.

The second heuristic reduces the number of nodes matched by considering only the local graph structure around the unknown verb. Specifically, we force the matching algorithm to consider only nodes directly linked to the unknown verb plus any nodes linked to these directly connected nodes, but no others. Intuitively, this makes sense: This means that distantly related events and relations are not brought in for matching at all. This is a brute force approach that directly reduces the number of matched nodes. In practice, although a full story could have a 100 or so nodes, this constraint reduces the nodes for matching down to 10 or so—an order of magnitude savings, with a corresponding savings in computation time. Finally, as mentioned, we do not consider match candidates that do not meet the tests of thematic role identity.

Difference Pointers

Having found a match, the last job of the acquisition procedure is to calculate just how the new word differs from the old. This is at least as important as finding the best match, for only by finding differences do we learn anything new. The calculation is straightforward. We take the graphical representation of the local network around the old verb and add an annotated link indicating how the new verb differs from old. Alternatively, one could add pointers to the network representation of the new network, indicating differences. In this way, the system actually builds up a set of family resemblances. Words that are more distant from the "core" member of a family will have more difference pointers than words that are "closer" to the core. Note that this way of storing information already admits a prototype with allowable exceptions. A wormy or overly large apple can still be an apple because it will not violate enough of the prototypical apple qualities to be ruled out.

Constructing the appropriate difference pointers is often difficult. *Assassinate* differs from *murder* in that a political figure is involved, but how is the program to know (or learn) this? Currently, the difference pointer constructed in this example reveals two different AKO structures: for *assassinate* the murdered figure is AKO *king*, whereas for *murder* it is just AKO *person*. Eventually, we would like the system to connect a group of similar *assassinates* by lumping *king*, *president*, and so forth into a more general AKO *political* class.

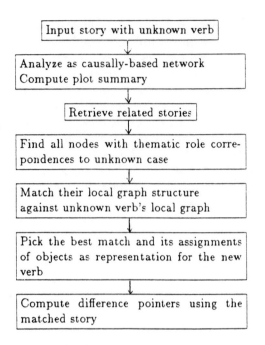

Figure 3.3. Flowchart for word learning

In general, human abilities at forming such natural classes are not well understood; some ways of handling this are discussed in the section on Learning AKO Hierarchies.

Flowchart

We can now give a complete flow diagram of the learning procedure (see Figure 3.3).

IMPLEMENTATION AND EXAMPLES

With the entire acquisition procedure described, this section presents some examples of the system in action. In order to fix the meaning of an unknown verb, stories are first translated into their respective extensible-relation representation. Then it provides our matcher with the unknown verb, the name of the story in which it appears, and the name of the stories to be used as precedents. The pieces of the network local to the known verb (the extent of the pieces is controlled by the user) are superimposed, one at a time, to the piece of the network local to the unknown verb. The verb that is probably the closest in meaning to the unknown verb will have the greatest number of matching links.

The examples use three Shakespearean plots, Hamlet (HA), Macbeth (MA), and Julius Caesar (JU):

HA is a story about a ghost Hamlet Gertrude Claudius and Laertes.

Hamlet is a prince. The ghost is a dead king. Claudius is an evil king. Gertrude is a queen. Gertrude is a naive woman. Laertes is a man. The ghost was married to Gertrude.

Claudius, who is married to Gertrude, murdered the ghost because Claudius wanted to be king and because Claudius was evil. The ghost persuades Hamlet to kill Claudius because Claudius murdered the ghost. The ghost can persuade Hamlet to kill Claudius because Hamlet loves the ghost. Hamlet is unhappy because the ghost is dead. Claudius wants to kill Hamlet because Claudius is afraid of Hamlet. Claudius kills Gertrude. Hamlet kills Claudius because Claudius murdered the ghost and because Hamlet is loyal to the Ghost. Hamlet kills Claudius with a sword. Claudius persuades Laertes to kill Hamlet. Laertes kills Hamlet with a sword. Hamlet kills Laertes.

Remember HA.

MA is a story about Macbeth Lady-macbeth Duncan and Macduff.

Macbeth is an evil noble. Lady-macbeth is a greedy ambitious woman. Duncan is a king. Macduff is a noble.

Lady-macbeth persuades Macbeth to want to be king because she wants him to be king. She wants him to be king because she is greedy. She can convince him because Macbeth loves her and also because Macbeth is wimpy.

Macbeth assassinates Duncan with a knife. Macbeth assassinates Duncan because Macbeth wants to be king. Lady-macbeth becomes insane. She kills herself because she is insane.

Macduff becomes angry because the king was assassinated. Macduff kills Macbeth because Macbeth assassinated Duncan and because Macduff is loyal to Duncan.

Remember MA.

JU is a story about Caesar Brutus Anthony and Cassius.

Caesar is a general. He is an ambitious and foolish emperor. He is a man. Brutus who is an honest and unhappy man loves Rome. Antony is a man. Cassius is a thin man.

Cassius convinces Brutus to murder Caesar because Cassius hates Caesar and also because Brutus is weak. Brutus murders Caesar with a knife. Brutus murders Caesar because Cassius told Brutus that Caesar was evil. Brutus is unhappy because Brutus murdered Caesar and because Brutus loved Caesar. Antony who loved Caesar persuades some people to attack Brutus because Brutus murdered Caesar. Brutus attacks the people because the people attacked him. Cassius also attacks the people. Brutus kills himself. He kills himself because he is unhappy. Cassius kills himself also.

Remember JU.

To begin matching, we need to obtain the relations that are linked to the verbs. An auxiliary function, GET-RELATIONS, returns the root of each different relation linked to each verb. Invoking this function on MURDER-1 returns the list (CAUSE CAUSED-BY). Note that MURDER-1 can be thought of as premeditated, first degree murder.

In this implementation, two nodes or links in a network are possible matches if:

- they are the same object or
- they fill the same thematic roles or
- they are connected by AKO links (i.e., Macbeth and Gertrude are both a-kind-of persons) or

Macaisa (1984) is chiefly responsible for the matcher's implementation, and we follow her description of its next steps:

> Because verbs frequently have multiple instances of the same relations, we risk not finding the best match were we to pair up the instances randomly. How do we decide whether CAUSE-15 or CAUSE-21 matches better with, say, CAUSE-2000? We make this decision by matching the objects of each relation to the objects of the relations of the candidate verbs. In practice, most conflicts are settled at this level. However, if there is still uncertainty, we choose the first match. The consequences of this choice will be examined later.
>
> The routine that performs the steps indicated above is called DO-MATCH, and it returns the matching relations and matching objects. Returning the objects is necessary because we allow the user to control the extent of the local network which is to be matched. The variable controlling the locality of the match is *MATCH-LEVEL, and if its value is greater than 1, DO-MATCH is called on each pair of matching objects. The matching relations are collected into a list by the procedure calling DO-MATCH. This procedure checks membership before adding a new pair of matching relations since our extensible-relation representation allows cycles. When there are no more new matches, or when we have reached the specified *MATCH-LEVEL, the scoring function is applied to the list of matching relations. We use a simple scoring function, one which merely counts the number of pairs of relations. (p. 5)

Let us run through an example. Let us assume that *Hamlet* is retrieved as the story closest to *Macbeth* in terms of plot summaries or causal similarity. We then try to find a verb closest to *murder*, where the *score* is defined as described previously, by the number of matching pairs of relations.

```
(setq *match-level 1)
1.
(define-verb 'murder-1 'ha 'ma)
Matching MURDER-1 with KILL-1 scores 1.
Matching MURDER-1 with ASSASSINATE-1 scores 2.
(setq *match-level 2)
2.
Matching MURDER-1 with ASSASSINATE-1 scores 3.
```

Two verbs score well: KILL-1 and ASSASSINATE-1. If we increase the local distance of matching, then ASSASSINATE-1 does better still. Most relations are eliminated by the case filter: 41 out of 66 in this example.

If we carry out the symmetric match we get this:

```
(setq *match-level 1)
1.
(define-verb 'assassinate-1 'ma 'ha)
Matching ASSASSINATE-1 with KILL-7 scores 1.
Matching ASSASSINATE-1 with MURDER-1 scores 2.
Matching ASSASSINATE-1 with KILL-4 scores 1.
```

Next, the program adds difference pointers connecting *murder* and *assassinate*. In this case, there really is no difference at all. All figures in both plots play political roles; indeed, both persons killed/assassinated (as matched) are rulers. A more interesting example is the matching of *assassinate* to *murder* in, for example, Romeo and Juliet. Here also, the match scores 2, but this time the players are not political. A difference pointer is constructed to indicate this subtlety (see Figure 3.4).

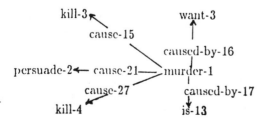

Figure 3.4. Two networks with difference pointers

Further stories should prompt the relevant generalization of the A K O RULER difference to a political classification. Note how this method builds up prototypes automatically. A causal network that reappears in many different plots will be richly connected to other networks of verbs, whereas a rarely occurring verb will be woven only weakly to other stories. Thus, what a "typical" verb is falls out automatically as a consequence of the matching procedure: it is simply a densely connected verb. (It will therefore be easily accessible, under whatever measure of access one uses, again as suggested by psycholinguistic work.)[1]

Macaisa (1984) carried out some other interesting experiments with the matcher. *Love* and *hate* were similar, as were *persuade* and *convince*. Macaisa's summary table runs as follows. The *score* is defined as previously stated, as the number of matching relations. The column labeled *filter* shows the number of relations in the two stories before and after a subcategorization filter is applied that removes relations that do not have the same case frame structure. Some of these results deserve further comment. Note that *attack* and *kill* are considered to match each other in *Julius Caesar* and *Hamlet*. Careful examination of the relevant subnetworks reveals that this conclusion is correct. *Attack* plays a big role in *Julius Caesar*. Here is the relevant excerpt:

> Antony who loved Caesar persuades some people to attack Brutus because Brutus murdered Caesar. Brutus attacks the people because the people attacked him.

This is similar to *kill* in *Hamlet* because of a similar causal role. Both verbs are the result of a persuasion prompted by a death and love of another entity:

> The ghost persuades Hamlet to kill Claudius because Claudius murdered the ghost. The ghost can persuade Hamlet to kill Claudius because Hamlet loves the ghost.

Initial tests of this method proved successful enough to encourage a full-scale test with a large verb computer database currently being

---

[1]Jackendoff (1983) correctly observed that because brains are finite we cannot store an infinite number of such prototypes. However, it is still possible to store rules to generate an arbitrary number of prototypes. It remains to investigate a "grammar" of this kind.

Verb	Story and Precedent	No. of Rels Before and After Filter	Matching Verbs	Score
murder-1	HA, MA	66, 25	kill-1	1
			assassinate-1	2
murder-1	HA, JU	70, 25	kill-10	1
			murder-2	2
assassinate-1	MA, HA	83, 31	kill-7	1
			murder-1	2
			kill-4	1
attack-1	JU, HA	83, 30	kill-7	1
			kill-4	1
love-1	MA, JU	70, 25	hate-3	1
hate-1	JU, MA	66, 24	love-1	1
persuade-4	JU, HA	83, 21	persuade-2	2
			persuade-3	1

developed by the MIT Linguistics Department. This database includes languages other than English. Among these are some ergative-
type languages whose different syntactic-thematic linkages should
provide a good test of the flexibility of the approach.

LEARNING NOUNS AND CLASS HIERARCHIES

Having seen the learning procedure in action, it is time to step back
and assess its competence. One complaint might be that people certainly do not learn the meaning of verbs in the manner suggested.
For example, one could just use a dictionary. But this comment
misses several points. Miller (1984) noted first of all that many verbs
are learned before mastery of reading. Even so, examination of dic-
tionary-reading behavior reveals that children will substitute known
words rather than say an unknown word that is being defined by the
very entry they are reading. This is only suggestive, but it hints that
context-learning plays a dominant role even given learning from
dictionary definitions. It certainly fulfills Wittgenstein's admonition
"don't tell me the meaning, tell me the use" of a word.

More pointedly, there are many other aspects of the procedure
subject to question. In this section, we review two parts of the learning systems behavior that are most open for revision. The first weak
point is our choice of representational language, and the second our
predefined set of AKO relationships. Two corresponding remedies
are suggested: a modified representational language with some primitives, and a systematic method of generating class hierarchies.

Beyond Causal Verbs

The system as designed so far performs adequately on verbs that have a rich causal structure, primarily verbs such as *love, murder,* or *persuade.* This is to be expected. The matcher uses causal relations, and so is sensitive to them. Verbs without rich causal relationships cannot be distinguished, because there is nothing to match. It is not clear, then, a simple causal structure is the right way to describe stative verbs like *be* or *become,* or motion verbs like *run.*

One alternative here is a description language outlined by Jackendoff (1983), originally proposed by Gruber (1965) and extended by Schank (1972) and Jackendoff (1972). It decomposes verbs of state or motion into primitives along a few principle axes or semantic "fields" such as temporal, possessional, or identificational, combined with three primitive verb types: STAY, GO and BE. BE denotes a state, STAY lack of motion, and GO, motion (over the semantic field). Jackendoff observed that a wide variety of verbs are modeled on the same scaffolding as these three verbs, but with modifications depending on the semantic field involved. For example, consider the temporal field. We find the following sorts of verbs:

is: BE *The book is on the table*
move: GO *John moved the book to the table*
kept: STAY *The book was kept on the table*

The same three primitives work for possessional verbs:

give: GO *John gave a book to Mary*
sell: GO object to recipient; "money" from recipient to agent
keep: STAY *John kept the book*

Finally, we have identificational examples:

is: BE *John is a teacher*
become: GO *John became a teacher*
remain: STAY *John remained a teacher.*

How can we graft this modified vocabulary onto our previous word-learning algorithm? All that really must be done is to expand our formerly atomic verb names such as *become* or *give* into their parts. This alters just the arc labels on the network descriptions. Matching will be modified to take note of GO, STAY, and BE labels, as well as semantic subfields. Consider the following example. *Macbeth got a*

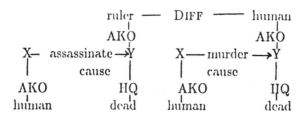

Figure 3.5. Old and new representations for *got*

knife has the two representations depicted in Figure 3.5. Now consider a verb like *obtain*. Not only does it participate in the same causal network as *get*, but it decomposes in the same way. The question is: How is this learned? Once again, we can simply use the network matching algorithm to tell us that *obtain* and go POSSESS are paired up.

What are the advantages to this modification? Evidently, to fix a verb decomposition we must fix (at least) two parameters: first, one of the proto-verbs GO, BE, or STAY; second, one of the semantic fields. One positive example fixes one possible variant of the verb's meaning, but it is easy to get others simply by choosing another parameter. For instance, if we set the semantic field to IDENTIFICATIONAL, then we get the verb *get* used in the sense, *Macbeth got religion*. Thus, given this decomposition, we can delineate a space of parametric variation outlining the space of possible verbs of this kind.[2]

It is interesting to compare this approach with another model for word acquisition, that of Granger (1977). Granger also determined the meaning of an unknown word via a matching procedure that extracted similar network representations across stories. Granger's work is founded on the same nondefinitional, context-based theory of meaning as ours, but differs in significant ways. Unlike our causally based representation, Granger's model used a conceptual dependency representation of a story. As mentioned earlier, Granger filtered story matches by (indirectly) computing the thematic roles for nouns, and retaining only those candidate matches whose thematic roles align with those of the unknown input. This representation language takes a stronger stand on decomposition than the one we adopted earlier, but is otherwise is would be quite close to the modified decomposition model as just suggested. Granger's system had more trouble with verbs than nouns because its matching procedure

---

[2]Miller and Johnson-Laird (1976) probed further into a decompositional approach of this kind.

was grounded on a conceptual dependency representation that in turn required one to know what verb one was analyzing. With an unknown verb, much information is absent, and so it is difficult to start matching. In addition, the system explicitly does not build a syntactic representation of a sentence; this makes it all the more difficult to bootstrap a match. In contrast, the system described in this chapter makes explicit use of syntactic constraints to drive matching. It also directly uses thematic role constraints. Finally, the causally based description says that what causes what is more important to a word's meaning than any primitive decomposition into a series of "physical transfers."

Both models benefit from a parameter-setting approach. First, the essentially combinatoric character of parameter setting immediately accounts for the productivity of word meanings. If recursive devices are some kind are allowed, then an indefinite number of word meanings can be accommodated. Second, a theory of parameter setting translates directly into a learning theory. "All" that must be learned is the settings of the various parameters. Berwick (1985) presented one model of parameter setting under the restriction that only positive examples are given. The key idea is that if positive-only examples are used, then at no time should the learner make a general guess that leaves open the possibility that the correct answer is a *subset* of the guess just made. The reason for this constraint should be apparent. If a subset of the hypothesis *can* be the correct "target," then there is now no way for the learner to find this out. Why? If the correct target is indeed a subset of the hypothesis, then any *positive* example will be compatible with the now overly general hypothesis. In fact, the constraint that one cannot interpolate a subset between one guess and the next turns out to be necessary and sufficient for learning using positive examples.

Learning AKO Hierarchies

The second weak point of the learning model is that it depends on a preexisting set of AKO descriptors. It would be better if these could themselves be learned. Why, for instance, should be class RULER or HUMAN be given rather than POLITICAL? Yet the choice of these descriptors figures crucially in what the matcher does and what difference pointers are created.

In the remainder of this section we outline one possible method of inducing the AKO categories themselves. The central idea rests on

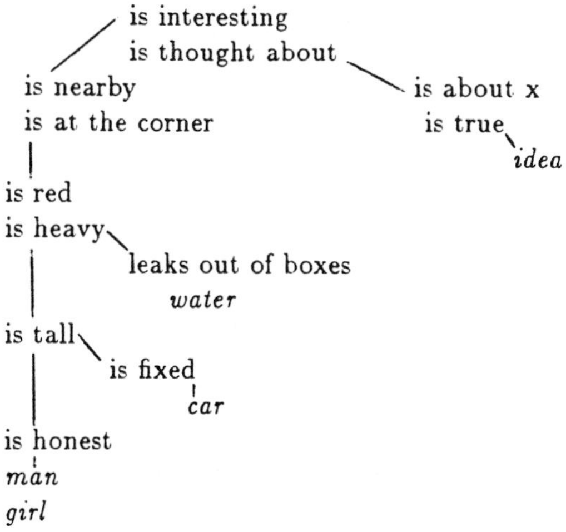

```
        /  is interesting
       /      is thought about
   is nearby                    ↘ is about x
   is at the corner               is true
   |                                    ↘
   is red                                idea
   is heavy↘
   |        leaks out of boxes
   |            water
   is tall↘
   |        is fixed
   |            |
   |           car
   is honest
   |
   man
   girl
```

Figure 3.6.   The M constraint

an observation of Sommers (1971) about semantic networks, explored in detail by Keil (1979).

Briefly, Sommers has suggested that if one arranges terms such as *dog, cat, love,* and so on into a graph structure whose terminal leaves are terms and where each node is an item that can sensibly be predicated of all terms below it in the graph, then one never, or rarely, finds human intuitions of sensibility resulting in M shaped graphs—the so-called "M" constraint. Rather, the graph structures take the form of hierarchical trees. For instance, the tree in Figure 3.6 (reproduced from Keil 1979, p. 15, Figure 1) is typical of one that comports with human intuitions; an idea can be predicated as being true, hence lies under a node labeled true in a predication tree, but cannot be at the corner, or red, hence does not lie under nodes labelled with these predicates. In contrast, a car can be nearby, at the corner, red, tall, and fixed, but not true. The resulting tree of predicates is called a *predicability* tree.

The "M" constraint relates to acquisition in the following way. Keil found through empirical studies of children that the hierarchical tree structures demanded by the "M" constraint developed the foliation of the trees—that is, children formed new categories by splitting old ones, rather than creating entirely different tree structures. For instance, at the earliest ages studied (5–6 years), some children's predicability trees looked like that in Figure 3.7.

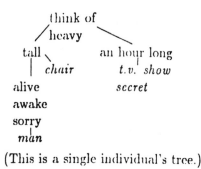

(This is a single individual's tree.)

Figure 3.7. Tree at early age

When second graders were tested, their trees were foliated versions of initial trees of this kind. Figure 3.8 shows the result.

We can use the foliation constraint to learn new AKO categories as follows. Assume at step n that the system has built some predicability tree. For concreteness, we shall use the tree given in Figure 3.9.

The root node corresponds to a universal predicate P_0 that applies to all things. Several layers below it is a chain of predicates that apply Duncan, Macbeth, Romeo, and Juliet. That is, these predicates apply to all these items as a class; we could call this the class HUMAN. Call the last predicate node dominating all of these P_i.[3]

Now suppose that the system acquires a network representation of *assassinate*. The network indicates explicitly that *Duncan* can be assassinated, and the difference pointer notes this as distinct from *Romeo's* murder. To abide by the "M" constraint, the predicability tree should be bifurcated at P_i, carving *Duncan* away from its old class. Now we have the situation as depicted in Figure 3.10.

We could name the new category "political entity," but actually there is no need to name it explicitly. The class is *defined* by the predicates that can apply to it. A "ruler," for example, is simply something to which one can apply the predicates ALIVE, CAN REIGN, CAN BE ASSASSINATED, and so forth. Class formation follows the general principle of acquisition from positive evidence cited earlier. Suppose we define a predicability tree as a set of direct domination relations among predicates P_i: We say that $dom\ (P_i, P_j)$ if and only if

---

[3]One remark in passing: this way of defining a noun in terms of the predicates that can apply to it is quite close to Montague's (1973) analysis.

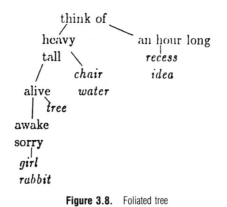

Figure 3.8. Foliated tree

P_i directly dominates P_j. Then according to the class refinement scheme defined earlier, any new predicate is not permitted to destroy existing *dom* relations; it can only add new *dom* relations (between it and old P's).

The justification for this monotonic refinement follows from the general principle of acquisition from positive-only evidence cited earlier.[4] Recall that if a learner is not to overgeneralize, then a new hypothesis should not allow the possibility of a correct target that is a proper subset of the new hypothesis. But this precisely the situation previously described: If a correct target predicability tree could include interpolated P_i's then such trees would be subsets of the hypothesized trees (see Figure 3.11). The criterion of learning from positive-only examples would be violated.

To a certain extent, then, the empirical fact that the evolution of children's predicability trees does *not* allow for interpolated new predicates constitutes evidence that the constraint of acquisition from positive evidence has played a role. To make predicability trees learnable, they are constrained to obey the "M" principle. By following this constraint, the learning procedure too can make use of positive-only example, without relying on explicit negative correction. This is just a particular illustration of the general point that if negative examples are not allowed, then additional constraints are required.

---

[4]For examples of monotonic refinement in other domains of learning, see Berwick (1985).

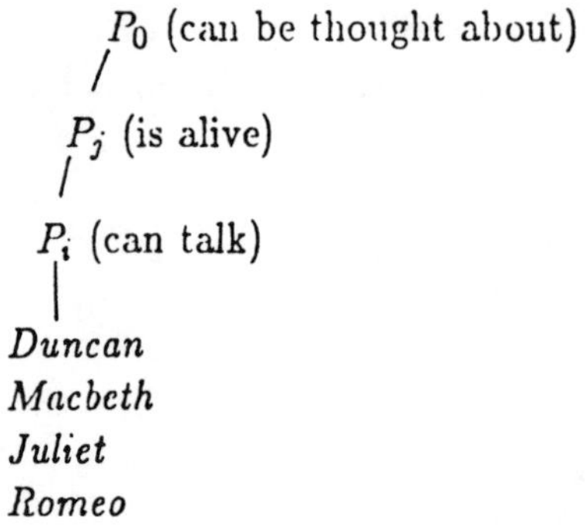

P_0 (can be thought about)

P_j (is alive)

P_i (can talk)

Duncan
Macbeth
Juliet
Romeo

Figure 3.9. A predicability tree fragment for the Shakespeare world

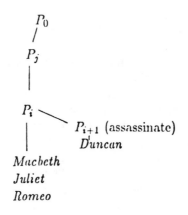

P_0

P_j

P_i — P_{i+1} (assassinate)
  Duncan

Macbeth
Juliet
Romeo

Figure 3.10. New predicability tree

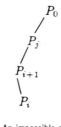

P_0

P_j

P_{i+1}

P_i

Figure 3.11. An impossible predicability tree

CONCLUSIONS

To sum up, the acquisition theory for words described here seems to meet Wittgenstein's challenge for a theory of word meaning that does not depend on dictionary definitions, but instead on a "family resemblance" model of word relationships. It successfully acquires causally based network models of verbs by the analogical analysis of story contexts containing them. Some extensions of the method for noncausally based verb descriptions were also presented. A method for learning AKO hierarchies (class descriptions) using positive-only evidence was presented. All of these learning procedures work because they are tightly constrained. The verb-learning model uses only causal links and syntactic filtering to guide it. The extension to other verbs depends on a limited set of descriptors closely linked to a spatial vocabulary. Finally, AKO learning depends on monotonic tree refinement obeying the "M" constraint. Future success of natural-language learning hinges on the discovery of constraints like these that make learning possible.

REFERENCES

Berwick, R. (1979). Learning structural descriptions of grammar rules from examples. *Proceedings of the 5th International Joint Conference on Artificial Intelligence* (pp. 56–58). Tokyo, Japan.

Berwick, R. (1980). Computational analogs of constraints on grammars. *Proceedings of the 18th Annual Meeting of the Association for Computational Linguistics* (pp. 49–53).

Berwick, R. (1982). Locality principles and the acquisition of syntactic knowledge. Unpublished doctoral dissertation, Department of Electrical Engineering and Computer Science, MIT. Cambridge, Massachusetts.

Berwick, R. (1985). *The acquisition of syntactic knowledge.* Cambridge, MA: MIT Press.

Carnap, R. (1952). Meaning postulates. *Philosophical Studies, 3,* 65–73.

Fillmore, C. (1968). The case for case. In E. Bach & R. Harms (Eds.), *Universals in linguistic theory* (pp. 1–88). New York: Holt, Rinehart, and Winston.

Fodor, J., Garret, M., Walker, E., & Parkes, C. (1980). Against definitions. *Cognition, 8,* 263–367.

Gellman, R., & Gallistel, C. (1979). *The young child's understanding of numbers.* Cambridge, MA: Harvard University Press.

Granger, R. (1977). Foul-up: A program that figures out meanings of words from context. *Proceedings of the 5th International Joint Conference on Artificial Intelligence* (pp. 172–178). Tokyo, Japan.

Gruber, J. (1965). Studies in lexical relations. Unpublished doctoral dissertation, Department of Linguistics, MIT. Cambridge, MA.

Hayes-Roth, B., & Hayes-Roth, F. (1977). The prominence of lexical information in memory representations of meaning. *Journal of Verbal Learning and Verbal Behavior, 16*, 119–136.

Jackendoff, R. (1972). *Semantic interpretation in generative grammar.* Cambridge, MA: MIT Press.

Jackendoff, R. (1977). *X̄ syntax: A study of phrase structure.* Cambridge, MA: MIT Press.

Jackendoff, R. (1983). *Semantics and cognition.* Cambridge, MA: MIT Press.

Katz, B., & Winston, P. (1982). Parsing and generating English text using commutative transformations. MIT A.I. Lab Memo 677.

Keil, F. (1979). *Semantic and conceptual development.* Cambridge, MA: Harvard University Press.

Landau, B., & Gleitman, L. (1985). *Language and experience: Evidence from the blind child.* Cambridge, MA: Harvard University Press.

Lehnert, W. (1981). Plot units and narrative summarization. *Cognitive Science, 4*, 293–331.

Levin, B. (1983). On the nature of ergativity. Unpublished doctoral dissertation, Department of Electrical Engineering and Computer Science, MIT, Cambridge, MA.

Macaisa, M. (1984). Learning word meanings from examples. Unpublished Bachelor's thesis, Department of Electrical Engineering and Computer Science, MIT, Cambridge, MA.

Marcus, M. (1980). *A theory of syntactic recognition for natural language.* Cambridge, MA: MIT Press.

Miller, G. (1984). How to misread a dictionary. Proceedings of the 10th International Conference on Computational Linguistics (p. 462). Stanford, CA.

Miller, G. & Johnson-Laird, P. (1976). *Language and perception.* Cambridge, MA: Harvard University Press.

Montague, R. (1973). The proper treatment of quantification in ordinary English. In R. Thomason (Ed.), *Formal philosophy* (pp. 188–221). New Haven: Yale University Press.

Salveter, S.C. (1982). Inferring building blocks for knowledge representation. In W. Lehnert & M. Ringle (eds.), *Strategies for natural language processing*, (pp. 327–344). Hillsdale, NJ: Lawrence Erlbaum Associates.

Schank, R. (1972). Conceptual dependency: A theory of natural language understanding. *Cognitive Psychology, 3*(4), 552–631.

Schank, R. (1973). Identification of conceptualizations underlying natural language. In R. Schank & K. Colby (Eds.), *Computer models of thought and language.* San Francisco: W. H. Freeman.

Sommers, F. (1971). Structural ontology. *Philosophia, 1*, 21–42.

Winston, P. (1975). Learning structural descriptions from examples. In P. Winston (Ed.), *The psychology of computer vision* (pp. 157–210). New York: McGraw-Hill.

Winston, P. (1980). Learning and reasoning by analogy. *Communications of the Association for Computing Machinery, 23*, 12.

APPENDIX 1: THE STORIES

```
;;This is for the Shakespeare story file - slavish attention to consistent
;;usage was avoided on the ground the programs should be robust enough
;;to deal with some variety and some error -- much of the initial
;;stuff sets up demons and establishes the A-KIND-OF tree

;;initialize


(reset)

;;do not insert PART relation automatically

(setfv *insert-part* nil)

;;read new-style demons

(fread "<analog>demons.lsp")

;;read demons for Macbeth-WW analogy

;;(fread "<analog>xcross.lsp")

;;create some demons

(make-if-affirmed murder
    (affirm reference 'cause (affirm subject 'kill object))
    (affirm subject 'hate object))

(make-if-affirmed kill
    (affirm reference 'cause (affirm object 'is 'dead)))

(make-if-affirmed cruel (when (eq relation 'is) (affirm subject 'is
'evil)))

(make-if-affirmed loyal (when (eq relation 'is) (affirm subject 'is
'good)))

(make-if-affirmed honest (when (eq relation 'is) (affirm subject 'is
'good)))

(make-if-affirmed married
(cond ((eq (relation reference) 'is)
      (let ((partner (get-one-object reference 'to)))
 (cond ((and partner (true? (consider reference 'to partner)))
```

```
(affirm (affirm partner 'is 'married)
'to
(subject reference))))))))
```

```
;;build ako tree
```

Person is an instance of a people.
Man woman and masochist are instances of a person.
Father son boy gentleman and bastard are instances of a man.
Mother daughter girl lady hag and witch are instances of a woman.
Shrew is an instance of a bitch.
General and colonel are instances of a soldier.
Emperor Empress King and Queen are instances of a ruler.
Prince Noble Ruler Emperor and King are instances of a man.
Prince is an instance of a noble.
Empress Queen and Princess are instances of a Woman.
Knife and sword are instances of a weapon.

```
;;insert PART relation automatically
```

```
(setfv *insert-part* t)
```

```
(make-if-affirmed ako
  (loop for class in (get-classes subject)
```

do (affirm subject 'ako class)))

APPENDIX 2: THE MATCHING FUNCTION

The following code is from Macaisa (1984).

```
(p '|Matching | verb '| with | rel '| scores | score))
    (setq *given-matches current-matches)
    ))
  ()
  ))
```

```
;; Is the given verb in story1 "close in meaning" to any verb in story2?
```

```
(defun word-match (word1 word2)
  ;; MATCHES contains all the matching objects; NEXT-MATCHES contains
  ;; the matching objects at each level, including ones which are
  ;; already in MATCHES; NEW-MATCHES contains all the matching objects,
  ;; not already in MATCHES, at each level.
  (declare (special *nesting-level))
```

```
    (if (not (or (matching? word1 word2) (subj-obj-match? word1 word2)))
()
      (add-to-matches word1 word2) ;;  Assume the two words match.
      (let ((matches (list (list word1 word2)))
    (new-matches (list (list word1 word2)))
    (new-match? nil))
(loop for i from 1 to *nesting-level
      with relations and next-matches
      do (let ((rels-and-objs (get-next-matches new-matches)))
    (add-matches (car rels-and-objs) 'relations)
    (setq next-matches (cadr rels-and-objs))
    (setq new-match? nil) (setq new-matches nil)
    (loop for match in next-matches
 do (if (add-match match 'matches)
(progn
 (setq new-match? T)
 (setq new-matches (cons match new-matches)))))
 ))
      if (and (not new-match?) (> i 1) relations)
      ;;do (p '|***No matches past level| i) and return relations
      return nil
      finally (return relations)
))
  ))


(defun get-next-matches (old-matches)
;;  (print old-matches)
  (loop for match in old-matches
with relations and next-matches
do (let ((rels-and-objs (do-match (car match) (cadr match))))
;;       (p '|Rels:| (car rels-and-objs) '|Objs:| (cadr rels-and-objs))
    (setq relations (append relations (car rels-and-objs)))
    (setq next-matches (append next-matches (cadr rels-and-objs))))
finally (return (list relations next-matches))
))


(defun do-match (word1 word2)
  ;; Works with all relations one link away from word1 and word2;
  ;; Adds the matching relations to *matching-relations;
  ;; Adds the matching  objects to *matching-objects;
  ;; Returns an alist of the matching objects at this level.
  (declare (special *uninteresting-relations *uninteresting-objects))
  (let ((rels1 (get-relations word1))
(rels2 (get-relations word2))
(matching-rels1) (matching-rels)
(matching-objs1) (matching-objs))
    (setq matching-rels (lists-match
```

```
(list-difference rels1 *uninteresting-relations)
(list-difference rels2 *uninteresting-relations)))
   (loop for rels in matching-rels
with objs1 and objs2
do (let ((objs1 (get-objects word1 (car rels)))
  (objs2 (get-objects word2 (cadr rels))))
     (setq matching-objs
   (lists-match
    (list-difference objs1 *uninteresting-objects)
    (list-difference objs2 *uninteresting-objects)))
      ;; MATCHING-RELS1 will contain the actual instanstiations
      ;; of the matching relations.  MATCHING-OBJS1 will contain
      ;; a list of objects matched at this level.
      (loop for objs in matching-objs
    do (let ((rel1 (consider word1 (car rels) (car objs)))
      (rel2 (consider word2 (cadr rels) (cadr objs))))
(if (not (subj-obj-match? rel1 rel2)) ()
    (add-match (list rel1 rel2) 'matching-rels1)
    (add-match objs 'matching-objs1))
))
      ))
   (list matching-rels1 matching-objs1)))


(defun add-match (item list-name)
  (let ((fcn-value t)
(list (eval list-name)))
    (loop for item1 in list
  if (or (equal (car item) (car item1))
 (equal (cadr item) (cadr item1)))
  do (setq fcn-value nil) and return fcn-value
  finally (set list-name (cons item list)))
    fcn-value))

(defun add-matches (list1 list-name)
  (loop for item in list1
do (add-match item list-name)
))

(defun add-to-matches (word1 word2)
  (declare (special *given-matches*))
  (add-match (list word1 word2) '*given-matches*)
  (let ((root1 (get word1 'root))
(root2 (get word2 'root)))
    (if (and root1 root2)
(add-match (list root1 root2) '*given-matches*))
    ))
```

```
(defun apply-filters (verb relations)
  (let ((root (get verb 'root))
(properties (list 'transitive))
(pattern) (rels))
    (loop for prop in properties
  do (setq pattern (cons (get root prop) pattern)))
    (setq rels (&sort-relations relations properties pattern))
    (car rels)
    ))

(defun lists-match (list1 list2)
  (let ((match-list))
    (loop for element1 in list1
  do (loop for element2 in list2
   when (matching? element1 element2)
   do (setq list2 (delq element2 list2)) and
   return (setq match-list
(cons (list element1 element2) match-list))
  ))

    match-list))

(defun subj-obj-match? (node1 node2)
  (let* ((subj1 (get node1 'subject)) (obj1 (get node1 'object))
 (subj2 (get node2 'subject)) (obj2 (get node2 'object)))
    (and (matching? subj1 subj2) (matching? obj1 obj2))
    ))

(defun matching? (object1 object2)
  (let ((answer (matching1? object1 object2)))
    (if answer ()
(setq answer (matching1? (get object1 'root) (get object2 'root))))
    answer))

(defun matching1? (object1 object2)
  (declare (special *given-matches*))
  (cond ((or (null object1) (null object2)) nil)
((eq object1 object2) T)
((or (member (list object1 object2) *given-matches*)
     (member (list object2 object1) *given-matches*)) T)
((a-kind-of-join object1 object2) T)
(t nil)))

(defun sublist? (list1 list2)
  (let ((b1 (sublist1? list1 list2))
(b2 (sublist1? list2 list1)))
    (if (and b1 b2)
```

```
nil ;; return nil if the two sets are "equal"
b1) ;; otherwise, return the value of the first boolean
    ))

(defun sublist1? (list1 list2)
  (cond ((null list1) t)
((member (car list1) list2) (sublist? (cdr list1) list2))
(t nil)
))

(defun scoring-fcn (matching-rels)
  (let ((true-matches (eliminate-inverses matching-rels)))
    (length true-matches)))


(defun eliminate-inverses (matching-rels)
  (let* ((sorted-rels (sort-rels matching-rels))
 (cause-rels (car sorted-rels))
 (caused-by-rels (cadr sorted-rels))
 (other-rels (caddr sorted-rels)))
    (loop for cb-rels in caused-by-rels
  do (let ((cb-rel (car cb-rels)))
       (loop for c-rels in cause-rels
     do (let ((c-rel (car c-rels)))
  (if (inverse? c-rel cb-rel) (del c-rels 'cause-rels))
  ))
       ))
    (append cause-rels (append caused-by-rels other-rels))
    ))

(defun sort-rels (matching-rels)
  (loop for rels in matching-rels
with cause-rels and caused-by-rels and other-rels
do (let* ((rel (car rels))
  (root (get rel 'root)))
     (cond ((eq root 'cause) (add rels 'cause-rels))
    ((eq root 'caused-by) (add rels 'caused-by-rels))
    (t (add rels 'other-rels))
    ))
finally (return (list cause-rels caused-by-rels other-rels))
))

(defun inverse? (rel1 rel2)
   (and (eq (get c-rel 'subject)
    (get cb-rel 'object))
 (eq (get c-rel 'object)
    (get cb-rel 'subject))
))
```

CHAPTER 4

An Introduction
to Plot Units

WENDY G. LEHNERT
CYNTHIA L. LOISELLE
Department of Computer and Information Science
University of Massachusetts

UNDERSTANDING AND REPRESENTATION

Representational Systems for Text Understanding

If a computer is to be said to understand a story, we must demand of it the same demonstrations of understanding that we require of people. When a person reads a story, an internal representation for that story is constructed in memory. For a computer to read and understand a story, it too must represent the story's content in memory. We can test both human and computer understanding by using various natural-language tasks such as answering questions or summarization. Each task will help us examine a different piece of the understanding process and the underlying representation. Question answering provides us with a method for examining the contents of the memory representation, but tells us very little about how it is structured. We can only guess at how the various pieces fit together. Summarization, on the other hand, requires concentration on the central elements of a story while ignoring peripheral information. As such it provides an excellent tool for investigating the global structure of a memory representation.

A variety of techniques for representing the information (both explicit and implicit) in narratives have already been proposed including predicate calculus formalisms (Kintsch, 1974; Woods, 1970), case grammars (Fillmore, 1968; Graesser, 1981; Rumelhart & Norman, 1975; Winograd, 1972) and systems of decomposition into primitives (Lehnert, 1979; Schank, 1975; Wilks, 1978). None of these systems alone can adequately represent the many facets of a large memory structure. Because we often find it necessary to deal with such large representations, there is clearly a need for a new approach. To handle these problems we must turn to multilayered representations, where the various levels specialize in describing aspects of the text ranging from physical events to general thematic patterns (Dyer, 1983, and chap. 1 this volume). In this chapter we present a model for narrative summarization. Our model includes a high-level representational system for story content that is particularly well suited for summarizing stories. This system of *plot units* will allow us to see not only how such a memory representation might be structured, but also how it can be used in a process model for generating summaries.

Understanding and Inference

What does it mean to understand something we have read? Does it mean the same thing to say a computer "understands" a text? A narrative is more than the sum of its individual sentences; readers supply their own inferences (Reiger, 1975; Schank & Abelson, 1977; Wilensky, 1980), idiosyncratic interpretations and personal belief systems (Carbonell, 1978) during the understanding process. A tremendous amount of knowledge is needed to understand even a simple sentence. For example, to fully understand the sentence "Tod hit Bill" we have to know more than the definitions of the words used. We expect that Bill felt pain and that Tod was probably angry at him. We also know that Tod probably did not punch Bill in the knee—the upper body is a much more likely target. These *default assumptions* come about as a result of our combined lexical, linguistic, and general world knowledge, and may be further refined by idosyncratic experiences and situation-specific information. If we had just read that Tod and Bill were boxers or karate experts, our corresponding assumptions would change dramatically. It has been estimated that the ratio of implicit information derived from a text to explicit information present in the text is something like 8 : 1 (Graesser, 1981). If a text understander (human or otherwise) is not generating these inferences, we cannot say in what sense that the text has been understood.

It is widely conceded that concepts from a text must be stored in memory in some form that differs from the original sentences, although there is no general agreement as to what this form must be. The necessity of including the inferences generated in story understanding as well as the explicitly present information, has forced us to move away from sentence-driven propositions (Kintsch, 1974) to a more integrated representational scheme (Dyer, 1983). In addition to describing the physical events and situations mentioned in the text, we must also be able to handle inferred goals, likely plans to attain those goals, and affective reactions of characters in the narrative. Although sentences will continue to be a necessary starting point, the conceptual information that we must represent will also strongly depend on causal relations and typical character interactions present in the narrative.

Computer Modelling of Human Understanding

It may at first seem strange to study computers in order to learn more about human understanding and memory representation. Why don't we just study people? The answer to this has many parts. First of all, people are "black boxes." We can ask them to perform some task and observe what they do, but we cannot get inside their heads to see what is actually going on. By constructing computer models of what we believe is happening in a person's mind, we cannot only check the model's behavior against the human subject's, but we can also examine its inner workings. Computer models are easy to manipulate. By changing a few parameters we can experiment with the limits of our model and our theory. And we often find that we learn a great deal simply through the process of implementing our model. To program a computer to behave according to our model we must specify each segment of our theory, each rule and each step with great precision. This mandatory level of detail forces us to be very exact about what our model involves.

The cycle of theory formation, implementation, and refinement is never ending. After we have implemented our model in a computer and tested our prototypes, we must return again to human subjects for verification. From our observations of human experiments we can then refine our theory and adjust our model. In this way, each process helps the other. The knowledge we gain from psychological experiments on human information processing helps us to build better and more capable computer models, and our experiences with these programs give us more understanding of human information processing. In our examination of the plot-unit representation and the summarization process reported in this chapter we hope to gain more insight into the phenomena of human and computer understanding.

THE PLOT UNIT REPRESENTATIONAL SYSTEM

Affect States

Plot units are constructed from smaller entities called *affect states*. We use affect states to represent a character's mental plans, goals, and reactions to external events. Affect states do not attempt to describe subtle or complex emotions; they merely mark gross distinctions between "positive" events (represented by a +), "negative" events (−), and "mental" events of neutral affect (M). At first glance it may seem that such a simplified representation of affect cannot be of much use in narrative processing tasks. This is probably true for tasks such as generating inferences or question answering that require in-depth understanding to be successful. But constructing a summary necessitates a loss of detail. Although we do not contend that this system is adequate to fully represent the vast range of human emotion, it is nevertheless instructive to see how far this very simple scheme can take us in our search for summarization algorithms.

As we process a story we construct an *affect state map*—a sequence of chronologically ordered affect states for the characters in the story. Each affect state occurs with respect to a single character, so events involving more than one character require multiple affect states. Thus, if Jason is in an accident and breaks his arm, we can assume that this event is negative for him, whereas Linda (who despises Jason) may experience his accident as a positive event.

Causal Links

The second component of plot units and affect state maps are *causal links*. Causal links always connect two affect states and indicate the different relationships that exist between various affect state pairs. For example, a link running from a negative event to a mental state describes motivation (in this case, intention to correct the negative event), whereas a link running from a mental state to a positive event describes actualizing a goal.

link used to indicate
motivation

link used to indicate
actualisation

To make such distinctions explicit we employ four separate link types: motivation (m), actualization (a), termination (t) and equivalence (e). M-links describe causality behind mental states and a-links indicate intentionalities behind events. T-links indicate a change over time. We use t-links with positive and negative states when the affective impact of an earlier event is displaced by a reaction to a later event. The use of a termination link does not necessarily indicate that the initial event itself has been terminated. It is important to remember that t-links refer to affective reactions and not directly to events. Thus, Brenda's marriage to Tom may be a very joyous event for her, but when she discovers Tom is having an affair, her anger may "terminate" her prior happiness, but not the marriage itself. T-links connecting mental states indicate that a prior goal has been displaced, signifying a change of mind. E-links describe multiple reactions to or perspectives on a single event when used with positive and negative states, but represent the reinstantiation of a previous goal when used with mental states.

We impose some syntactic restrictions on the use of causal links to constrain them to our intended meanings. Because we intend m-links to represent the motivation underlying mental goals and plans, they must point to a mental state. Similarly, because a-links indicate intentionalities behind events, they must point from a mental state to a positive or negative event. These two restrictions are the same as those placed by Schank (1975) in his representation of action-state causal chains. In this segment of Conceptual Dependency theory, Schank noted two constraints on how mental states and actions may be linked: (a) states or acts can initiate mental states (equivalent to restrictions on m-links; anything can motivate a mental state) and (b) mental states can be reasons for actions (equivalent to restrictions on a-links; actualizing a goal produces action). T-links and e-links must point from an event to an event, or from a mental state to a mental state as they indicate relationships between like kinds of affect states. These constraints reduce the set of legal pairwise configurations of our three affect states and four link types from 36 possible arrangements to 15 legal arrangements.

$$\text{M} \atop \text{M}\Big\rangle_m \qquad\qquad \text{M} {\atop -}\Big\rangle_a$$

m-link indicates	*a-link indicates*
motivation for a goal	*intentionality*
(must point to an M-state)	*(must point from an*
	M-state to a + or −)

Causal links have been given a temporal orientation for intuitive convenience. M-links and a-links point forward in time (down the affect state map) from an antecedent to its consequence. With t-links and e-links the pointer goes back in time since each is in essence a reference to a previous affect state.

$$+ \atop -\Big\rangle_t \qquad\qquad + \atop -\Big\rangle_e$$

t-link indicates	*e-link indicates*
change over time	*different reactions*
	to a single event
(must connect	*(must connect*
like states)	*like states)*

Cross-Character Links

In addition to the four links used to connect affect states for a single character, we also use a cross-character link (c-link) to connect affect states experienced by two different characters. Although c-links preserve the temporal order of an affect state map, they have no inherent orientation. Cross-character links can connect any combination of states and events across two characters, and like e-links, their interpretation depends on the specific affect states involved.

Events resulting in positive or negative reactions for the second character give us one kind of c-link interpretation. Here we are able to work with only two general templates: positive-reaction and negative-reaction. (C-links are not labeled because they are the only type of link involving two characters.)

| *positive-reaction* | *negative-reaction* |

In labeling such events we do not distinguish among the many different affect states that could occur in the initial position, causing the specified reaction. Different events in the text will yield different configurations, however, each having a slightly different interpretation. A mental state leading to a negative state represents a threat, whereas a mental state leading to a positive state represents a promise. When the connected states are combinations of positive and negative states we simply have reactions on the part of two characters in response to a single underlying event. Thus, the example of Linda's glee over Jason's broken arm might be represented as:

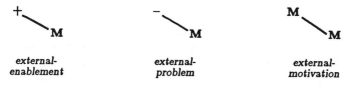

Often a character will initiate a goal state as a direct response to another character's situation. Configurations of this type make up the second group of cross-character interactions.

| *external-enablement* | *external-problem* | *external-motivation* |

In the case of external-motivation, the resulting mental state usually occurs in response to a request. The responding character may agree to the wishes of the instigator, or may oppose them. This configuration does not commit us to any assumptions about the contents of the two mental states or how they are related. In the cases of external-enablement and external-problem, we have mental states brought on by vicarious events. For example, a desire to celebrate is normally enabled by a positive event, whereas a desire to help out is typically motivated by a negative event.

In the same manner that we represent shared reactions or goals for two characters, we can also indicate how three or more characters respond to a given event. In all such cases we consider these states to occur in response to a single event. So if three characters share a goal state, we use three M-states c-linked together. If two characters have a positive reaction to some event and a third experiences a negative reaction to the same event, the affect state map would include two positive states and one negative state c-linked across. When such a configuration arises, we treat the c-links as if they were "transitive," enabling us to represent the interactions between all pairs of characters using a minimum number of links. So in the following example, this configuration represents not only external motivation between Ken and Sue and between Sue and Debra, but also between Ken and Debra.

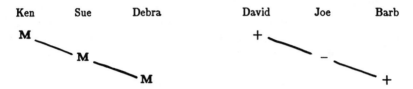

This interpretation becomes important when intervening affects states would otherwise prevent us from realizing a certain relationship was present. Thus, in the example just given, if David's success angers Joe but thrills Barb, we can recognize Barb's positive reaction to David's triumph only if we permit the transitive interpretation of c-links.

Primitive Plot Units

The 15 legal configurations of two affect states connected by a single link plus the five two-character pairs just listed form the set of primitive plot units. Each unit's name is meant to be suggestive of its interpretation, although they should not be taken too literally.

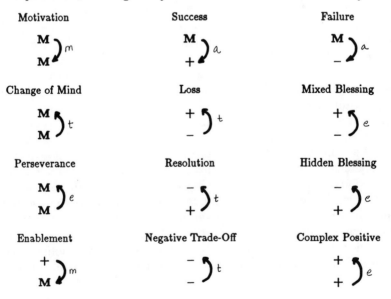

Problem	Positive Trade-Off	Complex Negative

External Motivation	External Problem	External Enablement

M
 ↘
    M

 −
  ↘
    M

 +
  ↘
    M

Postive Reaction	Negative Reaction

?
 ↘
   +

?
 ↘
   −

Some Examples

Enablement: A positive event motivates a goal
You inherit some money and decide to buy a house

Motivation: A goal motivates a subgoal
You want to buy a house so you decide to save money

Success: A goal is successfully actualized
You want to save money and then you do

Failure: A goal is unsuccessfully actualized
You want to save money but end up spending it

Problem: A negative event motivates a goal
You get fired and need a job

Resolution: A positive event terminates a prior negative one
You get fired, but then are offered another job

Loss: A negative event terminates a prior positive one
You are offered a job, but then they give it to someone else

Perseverence: Reinstantiation of a goal
You reapply to a college after being rejected

Change of Mind: A new goal terminates a previous goal
You want to go to Yale, but then decide to go to Harvard

Although the set of primitive plot units contains all the possible relations between affect states, they do not, by themselves, give us all the recognition abilities we need. Just as we build the set of primitive plot units from affect states and links, we can now construct more complex plot configurations using the primitive units as building blocks.

Complex Plot Units

Complex plot units are made up of overlapping configurations of primitive plot units. But unlike the set of primitive plot units that consisted of every possible arrangement permitted by the syntax of links and affect states, the complex plot units correspond only to situations commonly found in narratives.

Because many stories are about a protagonist's attempts to solve a problem we need to construct plot units to represent the various possible attempts and outcomes. For example, if a character realizes an initial success, only to have it terminated by a later loss we have the *fleeting success* plot unit. If this loss motivates the character to try for the same goal again we have a case of *starting over*. But if an attempt fails, resulting in a change of plans, we get *giving up*.

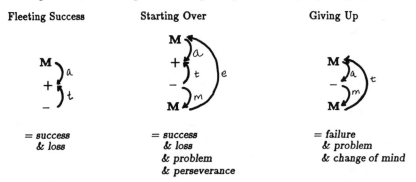

Fleeting Success	Starting Over	Giving Up
= success & loss	= success & loss & problem & perseverance	= failure & problem & change of mind

Other complex plot units dealing with goals and outcomes include *top-level failure* (a subgoal is achieved, but one fails in achieving the top-level goal), both *intentional problem resolution* and *fortuitous problem resolution* (differing only in the intentionality behind the positive outcome) and *half loaf* (a goal is only partially achieved).

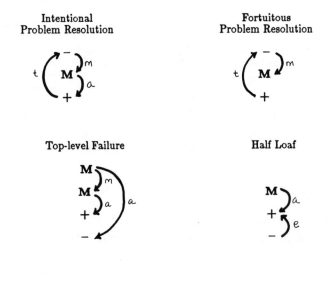

Intentional Problem Resolution	Fortuitous Problem Resolution

Top-level Failure	Half Loaf

Frequently a character will develop rather intricate plans to achieve a goal. This level of detail can be represented by the *nested subgoals* and *sequential subgoals* plot units.

Sequential Subgoals	Nested Subgoals

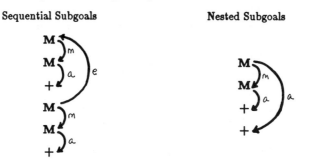

A great many important events occurring in narratives involve multiple characters, so it is not surprising that a large number of complex plot units also involve more than one character. Some of the most common of these are those that involve cooperative agreements and behavior. In the simplest case, a request is made and responded to. The respondent may cooperate (*honored request*), refuse (*denied request*), or fail in an attempt to fulfill the request (*bungled request*).

Honored Request	Denied Request	Bungled Request

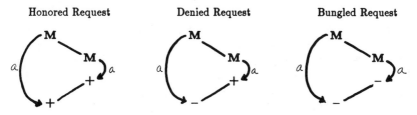

In some cases, the agreement or promise itself is sufficiently interesting to be included in an affect state map. Of course, we also need to be able to represent the eventual outcome of such an agreement—did the respondent fulfill the promise?

Promise	Honored Promise	Reneged Promise

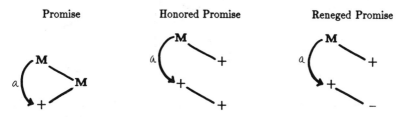

Competition, retaliation, and *reward* serve as the basis for many storylines and therefore also occur commonly as plot units. In the

case of competition, two characters must each be pursuing a unique
goal (obviously, if they both desired the same outcome they would
not be in competition with each other). The critical component of
competition is that one person's success must result in the second
person's failure. Two drivers attempting to win a race is a clear
example of competition. In both, the retaliation and reward plot
units, an unspecified external event either negatively or positively
affects a second character. When this reaction is negative, the responding character instantiates a goal to retaliate. Successfully actualizing this goal produces the desired negative reaction in the first
character. Similarly, when the initial event yields a positive reaction, that character forms the goal of rewarding the instigator. This
time, achieving that goal results in a positive reaction for the starting
character.

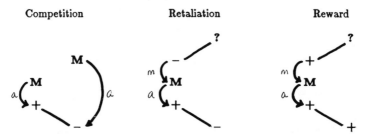

In addition to cooperative and antagonistic reactions, people people often respond in unsolicited ways. The act of setting up and
carrying out a plan to please or hurt another individual yields either
the *kind act* or the *malicious act* plot unit. When the second character acts to alleviate a problem state for the first character, we get
unsolicited help. In all of these cases we assume that no specific
request is made.

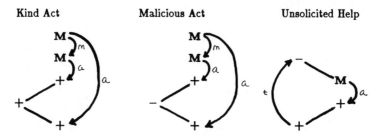

We sometimes come across situations where more than one affect
state configuration seems to capture the desired thematic interaction. If one of the drivers mentioned before wins the race only to be
disqualified when his opponent files a complaint, we maintain a

sense of competition even though the failure component has been replaced by fleeting success. Unsolicited help can also incur a slight modification. If Peter offers to help Bob get his car started because he needs to ride into work with Bob that day, we still have a case of unsolicited help because Bob has not requested any assistance. Here Peter is acting to alleviate both Bob's problem and his own, so we substitute intentional problem resolution for success in our definition of unsolicted help to arrive at the new version of this plot unit. These "flexibly defined" plot units capture the thematic sense of an interaction even when slight variations occur in the action. The substitutions used here—fleeting success for failure and intentional problem resolution for success—are common ones and can be used in many different situations, while still preserving the gist of a particular plot unit.

Competition-2   Unsolicited Help-2

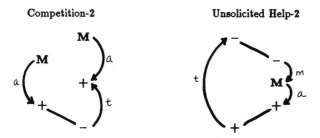

An Example

The best way to see how the different components (affect states, causal links, primitive and complex plot units) are used is to walk through a quick example. By comparing the story, the affect state map and the following explanation, one should be able to get a feel for the system. (For a more detailed treatment of guidelines and heuristics used in constructing affect state maps see Brooks, 1984.)

The History Project

Jennifer and Allison both had a crush on Mark. Because they were all in the same history class, it was natural for Mark to ask Jennifer to help him with his class project. Jennifer was afraid, however, thaf if Mark thought of her only as a study partner, he wouldn't consider her for a date, so she turned him down. Mark didn't know what to do. With only 3 days left before the project was due he was afraid he'd never get it done in time. Allison, overhearing the conversation with Jennifer, volunteered to help Mark with his project. Naturally, Mark was quite relieved. As they worked together on the project, Mark discovered that he really liked Allison's company, so he asked her to go with him to the big rock concert that weekend. When Jennifer found out, she realized how mistaken she'd been.

Affect State Map

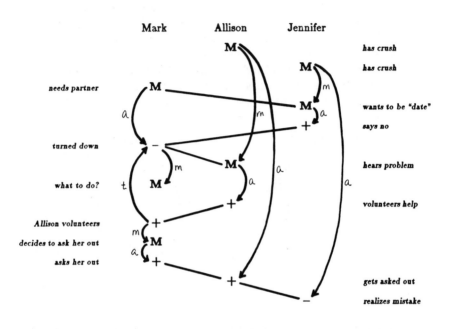

Explanation. The story begins by stating a goal for each of the three characters. Jennifer and Allison want to date Mark, whereas he wants to complete his history project. We represent these goals with mental states. When Jennifer refuses to help Mark we have an example of a denied request, motivated in this case by her previously stated goal. This instantiates a problem for Mark because he now has no one to work with. Allison's crush on Mark motivates her offer of assistance. Because Mark did not plan this as a solution or request her help we represent this with the unsolicited help and fortuitous problem resolution plot units. Mark's gratitude prompts him to reward Allison by asking her out. With this act, Allison's initial goal of dating Mark is achieved, thwarting Jennifer's plans and establishing her as the victor in their competition over Mark. We further note that although each girl realized her subgoal, Allison was successful in achieving her top-level goal (giving us the nested subgoals unit), whereas Jennifer was not (resulting in top-level failure.)

SUMMARIZATION FROM PLOT UNITS

Now that we have some familiarity with the plot-unit representational system, let us examine how such a scheme can be used for narrative summarization. This process involves several steps beyond constructing an affect state map. These are (a) recognizing all the plot units present in the map, (b) sifting out the "top-level" plot units, (c) building a connectivity graph, and (d) using structural features of this graph to identify the components from which we can generate a summary. In this section, we present each of these steps in more detail as well as discuss the various factors that can influence the structure of this graph, and therefore the summary itself.

Identification of Plot Units

The recognition of plot units proceeds from the top to the bottom of the affect state map (Lehnert & Loiselle, 1983). As we encounter each affect state in the map, we form predictions for the states and links we expect to encounter next. These predictions take the form of demons that attempt to recognize plot units by matching the states and links in the map with templates for the anticipated plot units. We form predictions only when we have seen enough structure to justify such expectations. Thus, when we encounter an M-state in the map, we only form predictions for the primitive plot units with an initial M-state. When we recognize a primitive unit such as success, we form predictions for complex plot units that begin with the success configuration. By ordering our predictions hierarchically, we minimize the search time spent considering possible structures. Once we have identified all the plot units in a given affect state map we proceed to construct the *plot-unit graph*.[1]

The Plot-Unit Graph

As we have seen in the "History Project" story in the last section, plot units can overlap with one another at shared affect states. When a plot unit totally envelops a smaller unit we say that the smaller unit is *subsumed* by the larger plot unit. (We have seen this before—complex plot units subsume the primitive units from which they are

---

[1]In actuality, the identification of top-level plot units (discussed in the next subsection) occurs concurrently with the recognition of all the units present in the affect state map.

built.) We use the top-level plot units (those units not subsumed by any other unit) to construct the plot-unit graph.[2] Each top-level plot unit is represented by a node in the graph. Nodes are linked together when two plot units overlap at at least one affect state. We say that two such nodes are *related*. Two plot units or nodes are *connected* if they are related, or if there is some path through any number of related units that joins them. This partial affect state map from the "History Project" story shows how plot units can overlap and subsume one another.

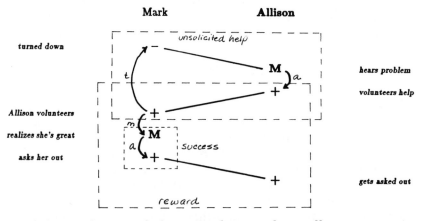

In this map, the reward plot unit subsumes the smaller success unit, whereas unsolicited help and reward overlap, sharing two positive affect states. The plot-unit graph for this partial map contains two nodes linked together, representing the two overlapping units. Success does not appear on the graph because it is subsumed by the reward plot unit.

By using structural features of the resulting graph we are able to identify the critical nodes in the plot-unit graph. It is these nodes that contain the units central to the narrative and from which we can generate a summary. The process of identifying these critical nodes forms a retrieval algorithm for summarizing the given narrative. Different types of stories will produce different plot-unit graph structures. We have identified three core classes, each with corresponding retrieval algorithms (Lehnert, 1983).

---

[2]Primitive plot units may still rise to top level in a given affect state map if they are not subsumed by a larger unit, although by convention, the dyadic (cross-character) primitives are not included in the plot unit graph, even when they appear as top-level units.

Structural Classes of Plot-Unit Graphs

One class of graphs exhibit unique nodes of maximal degree. We label such a graph a *simple cluster*. Although this class seems to be restricted to smaller graphs, we can reliably look to such pivotal nodes for the concepts most central to the story as a whole. Here we use the maximal node to generate a baseline summary, augmented by the concepts contained in the immediate relatives of that node. Let us look at a simple example to see how this might proceed.

The Broken Engagement

Doug was thrilled when Becky accepted his engagement ring. But when he found out about her father's illegal mail-order business, he felt torn between his love for Becky and his responsibility as a policeman. When Doug finally arrested the old man, Becky called off the engagement.

Affect State Map

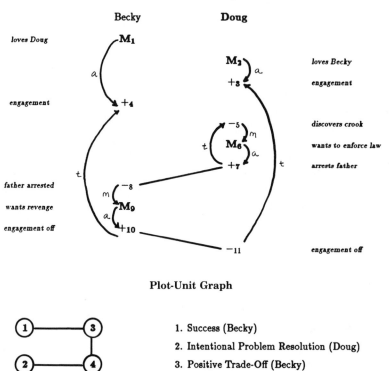

Plot-Unit Graph

1. Success (Becky)
2. Intentional Problem Resolution (Doug)
3. Positive Trade-Off (Becky)
4. Retaliation (Becky against Doug)
5. Fleeting Success (Doug)

Individual Plot Units

1. Success (Becky)

3. Positive Trade-Off (Becky)

**2. Intentional Problem
Resolution (Doug)**

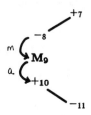

**4. Retaliation
(Becky against Doug)**

$$\mathbf{M_2} \quad a$$
$$+s \quad t$$
$$-11$$

5. Fleeting Success (Doug)

The plot-unit graph for this story is a simple cluster. The node representing the retaliation plot unit has maximal degree and is therefore the central concept for our summary. This seems to match our intuitive sense of the story's main point as well, but a summary containing only that idea would be too weak. We need to augment this unit with its immediate neighbors (positive trade-off, intentional problem resolution, and fleeting success) to produce an acceptable summary. Leaving out any one of these units out will weaken the summary:

Becky got back at Doug for hurting her.
    (retaliation only)

When Doug arrested Becky's father, she interfered with his wedding.
    (no trade-off for Becky)

When Doug arrested an old crook, Becky called off their engagement.
    (no retaliation)

When Becky's father was arrested, she called off their engagement.
    (no fleeting success for Doug)

But a summary that includes all four plot units provides an accurate description of the story:

When Doug arrested Becky's father, she called off their engagement.

(all units present)

As stories get longer and more complex, the top-level plot-unit graphs follow suit. Here we often encounter graphs with multiple pivots (nodes of maximal degree). This class of graphs can be further divided into smaller subsets, each group still having its own summarization algorithm.

In one subset are the graphs where the maximal nodes provide the key concepts for summarization, much like the simple cluster graphs just discussed. This is especially common when the pivotal nodes are adjacent to one another. The "History Project" story falls into this class.

The History Project

Jennifer and Allison both had a crush on Mark. Because they were all in the same history class, it was natural for Mark to ask Jennifer to help him with his class project. Jennifer was afraid, however, that if Mark thought of her only as a study partner, he wouldn't consider her for a date, so she turned him down. Mark didn't know what to do. With only 3 days left before the project was due he was afraid he'd never get it done in time. Allison, overhearing the conversation with Jennifer, volunteered to help Mark with his project. Naturally, Mark was quite relieved. As they worked together on the project, Mark discovered that he really liked Allison's company, so he asked her to go with him to the big rock concert that weekend. When Jennifer found out, she realized how mistaken she'd been.

Using the affect state map in the last section, we can derive the following plot unit graph:

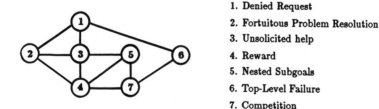

1. **Denied Request**
2. **Fortuitous Problem Resolution**
3. **Unsolicited help**
4. **Reward**
5. **Nested Subgoals**
6. **Top-Level Failure**
7. **Competition**

Nodes 3 and 4 (unsolicited help and reward) both have maximal degree and therefore are the critical nodes for this graph. A simple summary that contained only these units might be:

> Mark asked Allison out (*reward*) after she volunteered to help him with his history project (*unsolicited help*).

This summary feels better than the one generated from the critical node in the "Broken Engagement" story because we are starting with two key nodes this time. If we want to, however, we can fill this out with these nodes' relatives (denied request, fortuitous problem resolution, nested subgoals, and competition). A summary including all these units might be:

> Allison beat out Jennifer (*competiton*) and got her wish (*nested subgoals*) when Mark asked her out (*reward*) after she volunteered to help him with his history project (*unsolicited help*). This got him out of a jam (*fortuitous problem resolution*) caused by Jennifer's earlier refusal to work with him (*denied request*).

This graph is a good example of how we can use connectivity to select the nodes from which we will generate a summary. Including all four relatives of our two critical nodes forces us to include six of our seven top-level units in the summary. We note that although each of these relatives has degree three, only two (fortuitous problem resolution and nested subgoals) are linked to both of our critical nodes. This suggests a third possible variation for this graph using only the two critical nodes and their most tightly connected relatives:

> Allison got her wish (*nested subgoals*) when Mark asked her out (*reward*) after she got him out of a jam (*fortuitous problem resolution*) by volunteering to help him with his history project (*unsolicited help*).

In other cases, we see graphs in which the pivotal plot units partition the graph into two subgraphs. Here we find that the nodes on the boundary between these units are the critical ones. We can use the degree of these boundary nodes as a general guide in selecting the essential units when many such boundary nodes exist.

This unusual structure shows up nicely in O. Henry's *Gift of the Magi*. This is a story about a young couple who want to buy each other Christmas presents. They are both very poor. Della has long, beautiful hair, and Jim has a prized pocket watch. To get money for the presents, Della sells her hair and Jim sells his watch. Then, she buys him a gold chain for his watch, and he buys her an expensive ornament for her hair. When they find out what they have done, they are consoled by the love behind each other's sacrifices.

The story's affect state encoding exhibits an extreme symmetry:

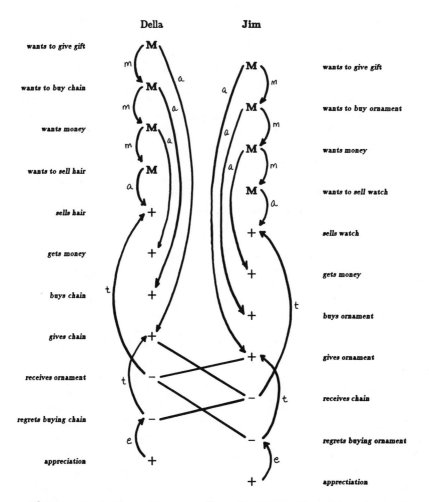

This symmetry is quite naturally reflected in the plot unit graph:

1. Nested Subgoals (Della)
2. Nested Subgoals (Jim)
3. Fleeting Success (Della—receiving gift)
4. Fleeting Success (Jim—receiving gift)
5. Fleeting Success (Della—giving gift)
6. Regrettable Mistake (Della to Jim)
7. Fleeting Success (Jim—giving gift)
8. Regrettable Mistake (Jim to Della)
9. Hidden Blessing (Della)
10. Hidden Blessing (Jim)

Because of this symmetry, we see the same units appearing for both Della and Jim. There are two nodes of maximal degree in the graph (regrettable mistake for both characters). These nodes and their immediate families form two distinct subgraphs with nodes 1, 2, 3, and 4 on the boundary. The two nested subgoals units represent each character's plans to sell a precious possession in order to buy their spouse a gift. The two fleeting success units on the boundary are those for Della and Jim each receiving a gift they know they cannot use. Although these are certainly key events in the story, they are not sufficient for a good summary. Because of the story's complexity in this case, we might want to use all the top-level plot units in a summary. We can use our retrieval algorithm to order their appearance in the summary, placing our critical nodes early in the story:

> A woman sold her long locks of hair so she could buy her husband a watch chain for Christmas (*nested subgoals* (1)). But when she gave him the chain she found out that he had sold his watch (*fleeting success (4 & 5)*) so he could buy her a comb for her hair (*nested subgoals (2), fleeting success (3 & 7)*). Initially they regretted their expensive gifts (*regrettable mistake (6 & 8)*), but then they realized how much love was signified in the sacrifices made (*hidden blessing (9 & 10)*).

Our third class of graphs is made up of very large graphs (more than 50 nodes) composed of subgraphs that can be separated by deleting a single node called an *articulation point*. Any such articulation point whose removal would result in the separation of at least 10% of the graph, becomes a pivotal unit for the story. When multiple articulation points exist, the path connecting all such nodes becomes the basis for a summary. The shortest such path is usually preferred, although the degree of the nodes along the path can also be a factor. (See Lehnert, Alker, & Schneider, 1983, for a detailed discussion of one such graph.)

Influences on Plot-Unit Graph Structure

Several modifications in how an affect state map is constructed can change the plot-unit graph, and possibly the resulting summary as well. Such alternate encodings result from two main variations: (a) level of detail and (b) inferences made by the story understander (Brooks, 1984).

Obviously, if we include more detail in an affect state map we will produce a larger map, and also a larger plot unit graph. Our main concern is whether such a change will affect the critical nodes of the graph, thereby changing the summary. To answer this, we must examine how we can vary the level of detail in an affect state map. We will use the story of the "Czar's Daughters" as our example.

The Czar's Daughters

Once there was a Czar who had three lovely daughters. One day the three daughters went walking in the woods. They were enjoying themselves so much that they forgot the time and stayed too long. A dragon kidnapped the three daughters. As they were being dragged off they cried for help. Three heroes came and fought the dragon and rescued the maidens. Then the heroes returned the daughters to their palace. When the Czar heard of the rescue, he rewarded the heroes.

First we present an affect state encoding corresponding to the level of detail we have been using up to now:

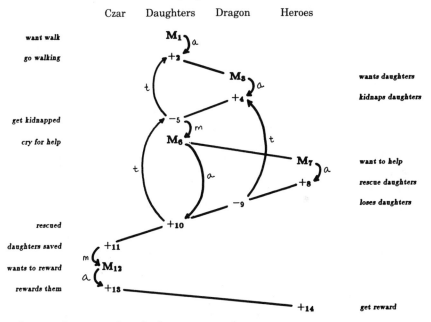

The resulting top level plot-unit graph is:

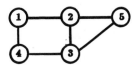

1. Competition-2 (Daughters & Dragon)
2. Competition (Heroes & Dragon)
3. Honored-Request (Daughters & Heroes)
4. Intentional Problem Resolution (Daughters)
5. Reward (Czar & Heroes)

And its individual plot units are:

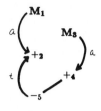

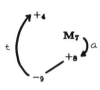

1. Competition-2
(Daughters & Dragon)

2. Competition
(Heroes & Dragon)

5. Honored Request
(Daughters & Heroes)

4. Intentional Problem
Resolution (Daughters)

3. Reward
(Czar & Heroes)

We have two adjacent nodes of maximal degree (competition between the heroes and the dragon and honored request between the daughters and the heroes). Following our summarization algorithm for this case we would select these as our critical nodes on which to base a summary. Our main interest in this section is to see if modifications to the affect state map will change our choice of critical nodes and thus the summary itself.

We have followed our usual convention of representing intentional acts with the success unit. The girls' going for a walk, the dragon's capturing the girls, and the heroes' conquering of the dragon are all represented in this way. Some of these events can easily be broken down into several acts increasing the level of detail included in the map. For example, we know that the daughters went for a walk and then stayed out too late. We can represent this as:

goal:	want to go for a walk	$\mathbf{M}$) a
event:	go walking	$+$ } m
goal:	want to stay longer	$\mathbf{M}$
event:	stay longer	$+$) a

chaining the events together. Similarly, we could expand upon the heroes' battle with the dragon. First they hear the daughters' cry for help. Deciding to help them motivates a goal of defeating the dragon, which they then carry out.

goal:	want to save daughters	
goal:	want to defeat dragon	
event:	defeat dragon	
event:	daughters are saved	

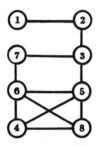

When we make these two changes in the affect state map, we end up with the following plot-unit graph:

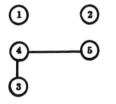

1. Success (Daughters)
2. Enabled Success (Daughters)
3. Competition (Daughters & Dragon)
4. Nested Subgoals (Heroes)
5. Competition (Heroes & Dragon)
6. Honored Request (Daughters & Heroes)
7. Intentional Problem Resolution (Daughters)
8. Reward (Czar & Heroes)

We have added a few new units to the plot-unit graph, but we notice that honored request and competition are still our pivotal units. The resulting summary would probably not differ markedly from one generated from the original plot-unit graph.

The other main factor to consider involves the inferences made by the reader or story understander. The three t-links included in the previous graph reflect one type of inference made by the reader. In this encoding, we infer that being kidnapped terminates the daughters' joy in walking, being defeated terminates the dragon's glee over capturing the daughters, and being rescued terminates the daughters' unhappiness from being kidnapped. These are all reasonable assumptions, yet a story understander may not make them all. When we leave them all out we obtain the following top-level plot unit graph:

1. Success (Daughters)
2. Success (Dragon)
3. Success Born of Adversity (Daughters)
4. Honored Request (Daughters & Heroes)
5. Reward (Czar & Heroes)

In this version we have lost many of the complex plot units (here replaced by the two primitive success units) and much of the connectivity as well, although we still retain the honored request as a pivotal node. Deleting the three t-links provides a good example of how drastically a graph can change in appearance as the result of including or excluding certain inferences. But we also can note here the robustness of this representation. Even with such a major change in the top-level plot unit graph, we still select the same concepts as being crucial to the narrative.

Often inference and level of detail are closely intertwined in an affect state map. One reader may infer unspecified motives behind events whereas another may only include the affective impact of the events alone. The character of the dragon is a good subject to experiment with for this modification. At the two extremes we can infer either no motivation behind the dragon's acts, or conclude that each event was motivated by some mental goal. In the first case we might hypothesize that kidnapping fair maidens is a purely instinctive act for dragons, as is fighting any young heroes who try to rescue them. In the second case we infer that the dragon had instantiated goals both to first capture, and second, retain the daughters.

The affect state representation for the dragon's character would then correspond to one of these maps:

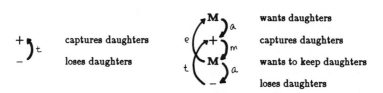

Note that we consider the two inferred goal states to be enough alike to consider one a reinstantiation of the first, thus setting up a perseverance plot unit. To see how these changes might affect our summary, let us examine the corresponding plot unit graphs obtained from each new version:

No Motivation

1. Fleeting Success (Daughters)
2. Loss (Dragon)
3. Honored Request (Daughters & Heroes)
4. Intentional Problem Resolution (Daughters)
5. Reward (Czar & Heroes)

Extended Motivation

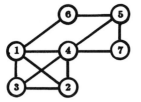

1. Competition (Daughters & Dragon)
2. Perseverance (Dragon)
3. Enablement (Dragon)
4. Competition (Heroes & Dragon)
5. Honored Request (Daughters & Heroes)
6. Intentional Problem Resolution (Daughters)
7. Reward (Czar & Heroes)

With no motivation, we lose both competition units. With both goal states inferred we add several primitive units for the dragon. In the first case, the honored request unit remains a pivotal node, although it now shares that spot with the daughters' intentional problem resolution. In the second case, the competition units return and once again take a central position. Although honored request still has a fairly high degree, it is not as critical to this graph as the two competition units.

Summarization Research

In this section we have shown how to identify the key concepts in a narrative using structural features of the plot-unit graph. The production of natural-language summaries from the information contained in the pivotal units is a very interesting but distinct problem that we discuss in the final section. Identifying appropriate retrieval algorithms and encoding heuristics are some of our major concerns in our current research effort.

To date we have examined approximately 25 stories in detail. For each text we have constructed many different affect state maps, each corresponding to the various inferences or levels of detail that could be used by different readers. The plot-unit graphs generated for these stories show very favorable results. Most of these graphs fit nicely into one of the structural classes just described, with the corresponding retrieval algorithm successfully identifying the key concepts for summarization. Our results also support the robustness of the representation. Despite the wide variety of assumptions used in their encoding, the identification of critical node has remained quite stable within each story.

Future research plans are primarily exploratory, calling for us to expand our library of stories and plot-unit graphs, and to continue our study of how encoding variations may influence summarization. We also plan on refining our classification of plot-unit graph structures. We believe that such a taxonomy can serve as a basis for establishing equivalence classes for narratives based on summarization algorithms (Lehnert, 1983).

EVIDENCE FOR THE PSYCHOLOGICAL VALIDITY OF PLOT UNITS

In addition to the task of summarization, the plot-unit memory representation lends itself to many other narrative-processing tasks. In this section we see how affect analysis in general, and plot units in particular, can be used in computational and cognitive models of comprehension, inferencing, memory retrieval, reminding, and story generation and classification.

Inference Generation

The plot-unit representation system grew out of experience with the BORIS story understanding system (Lehnert, Dyer, Johnson, Yang, & Harley, 1983) and its analysis of affect. After first examining Roseman's (1979) model for representing affective states, it was determined that higher level knowledge structures were needed to handle the necessary inferences (Lehnert, 1981). Initial efforts in this direction led to the development of Thematic Abstraction Units (TAUs, Dyer, 1981), but plot units also contain a great deal of information that can aid inferencing.

Much of what we know about social and goal relationships is thematic in nature, and therefore relatively invariant across different situations. For this reason, such information is quite useful in text understanding. Plot units capture knowledge about social and goal relationships that is not dependent on the particular activity or situation involved. Recognition of a particular plot unit allows us to infer this additional information, aiding the understanding of events already processed as well as creating expectations for future goals, actions, and emotional reactions of the characters. Such inferences will almost always be valid, regardless of the specifics of that interaction.

For example, once we recognize a situation to be a competition, we have a great deal more information available to aid in understanding the text. We can predict that the loser will probably feel angry or disappointed. It is also likely that the two opponents are not friendly toward one another (or if they were, they may not be anymore). Because such inferences are also thematic, they will need to be integrated with situation-specific knowledge. We would expect a retaliatory strike from the loser to take a different form when two men fight over a woman than when two children fight over a candy bar, although such revenge would not come as a surprise in either case. In order to achieve a complete understanding of the story, we need to include inferences from both levels (Dyer, 1983).

Memory Retrieval

Remembering a story that contains more than a few sentences requires condensing information and selectively ignoring details. The plot-unit representation accomplishes both of these tasks. If such a knowledge structure is indeed used in understanding and remembering narratives, we would expect its influences to be felt during retrieval as well. In fact, the connectivity of plot units has been found to be a better predictor of retrievability than position in a structural hierarchy (Lehnert, Black, & Reiser, 1981).

In this experiment, subjects were asked to produce a short written summary for one of three variations of a particular narrative. Each variation was encoded using both the plot unit (causal connectivity) and the story grammar (position in a structural hierarchy) systems. The experimenters identified predictions made by both models regarding the retrievability of the concepts in memory and compared those predictions to the data. Plot units were found to be a better predictor of a concept's inclusion in a summary than were story grammars.

Reminding and Classification

Closely related to retrieval from memory is the process of reminding. What sort of memory structure allows us to be reminded of other experiences? Schank (1979, 1982) has explored how an experience might remind one of another experience, and how a story might remind one of another story, suggesting that the thematic structure of the story or experience could plan an important role. When a thematic pattern is recognized, other stories or experiences processed using that thematic structure may be brought to mind. In text understanding, reminding can aid in making predictions about what is likely to occur. In this respect, reminding is like an inference process. Unlike inferencing, however, we must extrapolate from individual past experiences to the current situation. For example, suppose we had processed several stories involving retaliation after a double-cross. If we are then asked to read another story with a double-cross, we should expect to be reminded of the previous stories, and would probably form a prediction for a retaliation in this case, also.

We can be reminded of previously read stories in many different ways. Two such possible bases for reminding are story content and story structure. This phenomenon allow us to classify stories accordingly. We can group stories according to the kinds of events that occur (content). For example, we can divide stories into those with successful and unsuccessful exertion of a plan. A story's structure may also be used for comparison. Stories with deeply nested goal chains might be distinguished from those with a simple sequence of events. At a higher level, stories with a single critical happening could be separated out from those with multiple key events. Plot units may be useful in classifying narratives on both contentive and structural grounds.

In a clustering experiment, Reiser, Lehnert, and Black (1981) asked subjects to sort 36 stories into groups with the "same kind of plot." Many dimensions could concievably influence the subjects' judgment in grouping the stories (type of plan generated by the protagonist, contextual settings, desirability of the story situation, etc.), yet the six clusters of stories found in the data corresponded very well with the six groups of stories predicted by the plot-unit representations. Further, some of the subjects' labels accurately reflected the gist of a plot unit (e.g., "broken promise" and "revenge" for the plot units reneged-promise and retaliation, respectively) at the same level of abstraction. Higher level clusters corresponded to thematic judgments of a more abstract nature than that represented by plot units. At this level subjects made discriminations based on factors such as the nature of the outcome and the "fairness" of the protagonist.

In another series of experiments, Gee and Grosjean (1984) used spontaneous pausing during the telling of a story to determine if such empirical data could reflect narrative structure. Specifically, they tested to see whether the duration of pauses between sentences in a story could be used as an indication of narrative complexity. Using the theory of plot units as a model of narrative complexity, Gee and Grosjean hypothesized that there should be shorter pauses between sentences that describe the same plot unit, than between sentences that cross plot-unit boundaries. In fact, pausing during sentence breaks was found to be highly correlated with the importance of these breaks as predicted by a plot-unit analysis of the story. Gee and Grosjean cautioned us that any model we now have of narrative structure can be only a rough approximation, but hope that pausing data may help refine these theories. We believe that by exploring the different strategies used to summarize various stories, we can develop a taxonomy of narrative complexity where stories that can be summarized by the same retrieval algorithm would form an equivalence class.

Higher level structures such as TAUs (Dyer, 1981) and MOPs (Schank, 1979) may also serve as a basis for forgetting. These structures involve more complex thematic patterns than those represented by plot units and may be more useful for encoding the major theme of a story. Dyer pointed out that these structures often are nicely captured in adages. A common thematic pattern involving a planning failure is "executing a plan when it is too late to do any good." The adage for this would be "closing the barn door after the horse has fled." Because adages often are used to summarize stories, it appears that TAUs could provide a basis for qualitatively different types of summaries than plot units are prepared to provide.

Story Generation

Plot units may also serve as guides for writing stories. The use of high-level thematic structures such as plot units and TAUs as the basis for a story writing system has not yet been explored, although both representations seem to offer reasonable starting points for story generation. Recent theories of writing suggested that the writing process consists of the stages of idea generation, translation, and editing (Bruce, Collins, Rubin, & Gentner, 1980; Hayes & Flower, 1980). Hayes and Flower (1980) found that the idea-generation phase consists of the production of conceptually related chunks of ideas. Plot units may provide the right kind of "chunks" for such idea generation. For example, if one decides to write a story about a custody fight involving the retaliation of the loser, we would expect to see the various components of the retaliation unit (the triggering incident, the plan, and the act of revenge) present in the story.

In a related experiment, subjects were asked to write stories thematically similar to a set of prototypes (Reiser, Black, & Lehnert, 1983). Although the subjects' stories varied widely in setting and context, when analyzed into their component plot units they were largely composed of the same units as the prototype stories. Subjects often embedded a plot unit from the prototype story into a larger and more complex unit in their versions. For example, the threat plot unit was often incorporated into an ineffective coercion unit. When the prototype narratives contained a pivotal plot unit, that particular unit appeared very frequently in the subjects' versions. Subjects also tended to focus more on the protagonist's plans than on the motivating situation, so the plot units corresponding to the protagonist's actions appeared more often in the subjects' stories, than those relating to the establishment of the problem situation itself.

Conclusion

Plot units seem to well represent the memory structures used in understanding, remembering, summarizing, composing, and relating narratives. Plot-unit representations appear to capture the salient aspects of whatever internal representation humans use when asked to perform some task requiring a thematic analysis. People use these kinds of concepts when dealing with narratives, whether writing original stories or remembering previously read texts.

Plot units also provide a useful level of representation for computational models of human memory and natural language processing. Thematic structures such as TAUs, MOPs, and plot units have been used in a wide variety of computer models ranging from a program that models long-term reconstructive memory (Kolodner, 1983) to one that handles the in-depth understanding of stories in a "soap opera" domain (Lehnert et al., 1983). Plot units in particular were developed with the goal of achieving a process model of narrative summarization and have been implemented in such a program (Lehnert & Loiselle, 1983).

It should be pointed out that plot units were designed to describe the structure of the thematic interactions in a story, only. Higher levels of abstraction such as a narrator's purpose in telling a story or a character's perspective on the events in a narrative are not covered by this representation. Because affect states are based on information about plans, goals, and themes, affect analysis will not be appropriate for expository text or passages. Using this approach we will not be able to handle descriptions of sunsets or comparisons of different forms of government. In fact, it is not clear that people can comfortably summarize such texts, either. The applicability of plot units to a given text might provide us with a means of classifying types of texts, or at least in distinguishing expository text from narratives.

Plot units, MOPs, and TAUs provide fertile ground for future research in modeling human memory and understanding. Thematic structures such as these will certainly continue to play an important role in such computational models. The evidence presented here suggests that such a thematic analysis permeates the processing of narratives, regardless of task.

AN OVERALL VIEW

Where Do Plot Units Fit In?

The plot-unit system resides on one level of a multilayered representational scheme. Because they use a thematic level of description, plot units work well for examining larger, structural aspects of a narrative, but are ill-suited for analyzing the fine details of a story's content. Plot units can, however, play an important role in an integrated representational system. Thorough comprehension of a narrative involves understanding at all levels.

The Plot-Unit Graph Generator

We have implemented the plot-unit model for summarizing stories in a computer program. This program—the Plot-Unit Graph Generator (PUGG, Lehnert & Loiselle, 1983)—handles the conceptual portion of narrative summarization. Its level of representation (affect states and plot units) must be built on top of lower levels of memory representation. Much work has been done developing these lower levels of memory representation, in particular the BORIS system (Lehnert et al., 1983) provides a good picture of what such representations must entail. We do not discuss such systems here except to note that the knowledge structures they employ (see, for example, Schank & Abelson, 1977) provide us with enough information for constructing affect state maps. PUGG accepts input in the form of an affect state map, as opposed to English prose. (Affect state maps are currently hand-generated by trained encoders; for more information on this process see Brooks, 1984.)

Let us look at an example to see how PUGG processes a story. Recall that an affect state map is a chronological ordering of the simple affective reactions for the main characters in a story. By comparing the input to and output from PUGG, we can get a good feel for what it accomplishes. Consider the following story and affect state map:

> John wanted to make a lot of money so he decided to go to college and become a doctor. While in college he decided that he liked working with computers better than he liked working with people so he

changed his mind and decided to become a computer professional. When he graduated he looked for a position with a high-ranking computer firm and landed a good job at IBM. John ended up making a doctor's salary anyway.

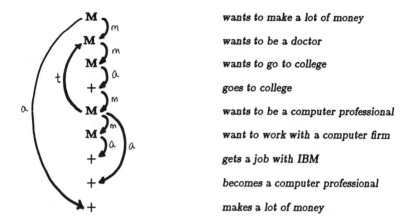

M	*wants to make a lot of money*
M	*wants to be a doctor*
M	*wants to go to college*
+	*goes to college*
M	*wants to be a computer professional*
M	*want to work with a computer firm*
+	*gets a job with IBM*
+	*becomes a computer professional*
+	*makes a lot of money*

This affect state map is fed into PUGG. We can see that we start out with a simple list of events, goals and reactions. As this stage, each node and arc are of equal importance. The result from PUGG is the following plot unit graph:

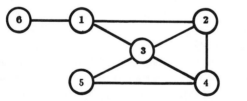

1. Motivation
2. Motivated Success
3. Change of Mind
4. Enabled Success
5. Nested Subgoals

Here we have a hierarchy of concepts (represented by nodes in the graph.) The most important node can be determined purely from the structure of the graph. Because this is a simple cluster we can use the summarization algorithm presented in the section on Structural Classes of Plot-Unit Graphs. The most important node for our summary is therefore change of mind. PUGG has taken an unranked, chronological list of states and events as input and produced a ranked set of plot units as output for our summary generation.

But how do we actually get that summary from this stage? Again, because PUGG deals only with the conceptual stage of this process, we will have to hook up another processor to the output to handle the details of generating the English summary.

Generation of English Language Summaries

To this end we are developing an interface between PUGG and MUMBLE, a natural language generation program (McDonald, 1983). Because MUMBLE can produce the English sentences but cannot determine how they should be ordered or what concepts from PUGG's output should be included, we are creating a text planner named PRECIS to stand between these two facilities (Cook, Lehnert, & McDonald, 1984).

In its role of text planner, PRECIS decides what should be mentioned and what should be left for the reader to infer. Thus, PRECIS interfaces between the purely conceptual and the purely linguistic and must have knowledge both of plot units and linguistic considerations. PRECIS associates different planning rules with different plot units or plot-unit combinations. One such rule for the competition plot unit might be: mention both characters, the goal, and the winner. We know that by naming the winner the reader will also make the natural inference that the other player necessarily lost. Let us consider a typical example. Suppose Betty beats out Nick for a higher ranking job that they both wanted:

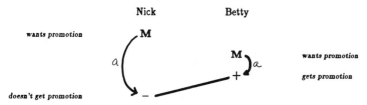

We could express this by stating "Nick wanted to get the promotion and Betty wanted to get the promotion, but Betty got it and Nick didn't." This sounds awkward and contains much more information than a reader needs. The sentence "Both Nick and Betty wanted the promotion, but Betty got it" is much more natural and is actually easier to understand. The reader is able to infer that because Betty got the promotion, Nick must not have, so we need not explicitly mention it. MUMBLE can handle such issues as pronominalization and the use of "both," but PRECIS must decide whether to explicitly include the loser.

PRECIS has been under development for only a short time and its stock of such rules is still small. We are currently developing more tactical rules and experimenting with the existing set to test the limits of their applicability. Eventually we will almost certainly need "metarules" to tell us which rule to choose when more than one might apply in a given situation.

Comparisons to Other Models

Several other systems for representing narrative structure or summarizing stories have been developed. Each takes a slightly different approach from the one we have taken here. A quick look at some of these models will help to point out their strengths and weaknesses, as well as some of the good and bad points of the plot-unit representational system.

The only other extensive attempt to implement a computer model of text summarization was within the FRUMP system (DeJong, 1979). FRUMP analyzed UPI stories in about 50 domains, and provided summaries based on a top-down extraction of relevant information in those domains. The summaries were all based on an a priori set of expectations about the domain and did not exhibit much variation. For example, an earthquake story was summarized in terms of (a) where it occurred, (b) what the Richter scale registered, and (c) how many people were hurt. All earthquake summaries described these three components when available. This style of summarization was completely top-down and driven by specific expectations. FRUMP could not deal with unexpected information, and its summaries reflected total ignorance of anything unexpected, regardless of that information's importance.

With the plot-unit approach, we do not form expectations until we have enough information to warrant their anticipation. In this way, unexpected information can be easily incorporated. FRUMP was specifically designed to handle news stories where, given a particular domain, the content is often quite predictable, and thus can work quite efficiently in such situations. Plot units are better suited to a less constrained input.

Another popular approach to the summary problem involves the notion of a story grammar (Rumelhart, 1977; Simmons & Correira, 1979; Thorndyke, 1977). Although many different story grammars have been proposed, the general idea is that stories are a linguistic form in much the same sense as sentences, and like sentences, can be described in terms of their constituent structure. In other words, just as we use a sentence grammar to identify the various parts of a sentence, we can use a story grammar to "parse" a story. Rummelhart pointed out that a number of short stories fall into what he called the "EPISODE" schema. The EPISODE schema about protagonist **P** consists of:

1. Event **E** causes **P** to desire goal **G**
2. **P** tries to get **G** until outcome **O** occurs.

Each of the relational terms in this schema (cause, desire, and try) refer in turn to other schema that will likewise be instantiated by particular variables within a given story. Using these schema we can construct a hierarchical tree (with the EPISODE schema at its root) to represent the story.

Story grammar approaches to summarization try to anticipate these structural components, using them as a basis for forming a summary. Both story grammars and plot units can be used to predict human summarization behavior in terms of internal memory representations. Lehnert et al. (1981) conducted a series of experiments comparing predictions of human summaries made by both the plot unit and story grammar approaches. The experimenters concluded that plot units predicted structural influences in the internal representation more effectively than story grammars. Story grammars have been criticized on many levels (Black & Wilensky, 1979) but the most basic limitation as a summarization model derives from being a purely top-down processor. As with FRUMP, story grammars are totally unable to handle input that does not conform to their expectations.

One theory of stories that seems to have much in common with the plot-unit system is the theory of story points (Wilensky, 1982, 1983). Story points purport to capture the "storiness" of a narrative by representing those events in a story with high intrinsic interest. Such events are often "human dramatic situations" involving a problem for a character in the text. Although he does not propose the theory of story points as a model of summarization, Wilensky claimed that a summary should consist of the point-related events of a narrative.

Unfortunately, Wilensky failed to provide us with a substantive strategy for text analysis with regard to story points. We are given no general method for determining what is interesting in a text. Wilensky characterized the story point approach as being primarily concerned with the affective reactions of the reader, whereas the plot-unit approach deals with the emotional reactions of the story's characters, without considering the strong relationship between the two. It is reasonable to expect that a reader's response will be largely determined by the affective reactions (inferred or otherwise) of the characters in the story.

Both systems provide a high-level memory representation for narratives. However, because the plot-unit approach is motivated by the task of narrative summarization, it explicitly addresses the question of effective memory organization for efficient retrieval. This aspect of the problem has no counterpart in the points approach; Wilensky has nothing to say about the problem of many points in competition for primary salience. His model must go one step further in this regard before it will be comparable to plot units.

Thematic Abstraction Units (Dyer, 1983) are a closely related scheme for representing abstract information about a story. First developed in the context of BORIS (Lehnert et al., 1983), TAUs contain knowledge about planning and expectation failures often found in narratives. These kinds of errors in planning are often effectively expressed in adages, such as "closing the barn door after the horse has fled."

TAUs contain an abstract planning structure consisting of (a) the plan used in a situation, (b) the intended effect of the plan, (c) why the plan failed, and (d) how to avoid similar planning failures in the future. The TAU "Unsupported-Plan" provides a good example of this structure:

X has a goal G1

X formulates plan P1 to achieve G1

X believes that P1 will succeed so X initiates plan P2 for achieving G2 based on the belief that G1 has been (or will be) achieved

G1 fails; and since P2 depended on G1, P2 fails and therefore G2 also fails

In TAU-UNSUPPORTED-PLAN, a character executes a plan based on some future result. When this result does not turn out as expected, the secondary goal is also defeated.

Although both plot units and TAUs represent abstract information about a narrative, TAUs tend to characterize a whole story or large segments of a story. Plot units usually represent smaller components of narratives. Additionally, TAUs are concerned mostly with plans and outcomes; plot units also involve states and reactions. Plot units and TAUs should be viewed as complementary representations, however. Both schemes are useful for summarizing stories, although each places its own perspective on the task. Summaries based on TAUs emphasize planning failures, whereas those based on plot units emphasize the structure of the story. And because expectation failures often produce strong affective reactions, plot units would seem to be useful in recognizing TAUs in narratives.

Summary

We started by saying we wanted our research to teach us more about understanding, both in machines and in people. Have we been successful? We have seen that understanding requires analysis of both the explicit and implicit content of a text. This analysis must occur at many levels ranging from descriptions of simple physical acts or events to the consideration of overall thematic patterns. These various levels seem to require different representational systems. Examining these representational schemes permits us to explore some of the possible inner workings of the understanding process.

Plot units provide one such system of representation at a fairly high level, because they are concerned with thematic patterns occurring in a text. We build these patterns up from smaller affective reactions and goal states. Plot units work well both as a computer program and as a cognitive model: PUGG is able to identify the key concepts in a story and its output agrees well with summaries produced by human subjects.

We recall that the only real way we can evaluate understanding is to test for it through tasks like question answering or summarization. Applying the test of summarization to stories represented by the plot unit system gives us results very similar to human generated summaries. In this sense, then, we seem to have discovered one useful mechanism for both machine and human understanding. Although we cannot say that people use plot units exactly as described here in their internal processing of a text, the evidence clearly indicates that people do employ some level of thematic processing in understanding narratives. Our simulations with PUGG seem to be a step in the right direction toward computational models of complex text-processing phenomena.

REFERENCES

Black, J. B., & Wilensky, R. (1979). An evaluation of story grammars. *Cognitive Science, 3*(3), 213–230.

Brooks, J. M. (1984). Generation of affect state maps. *Proceedings of the First Annual Workshop on Theoretical Issues in Conceptual Information Processing* (pp. 107–116). Atlanta, GA: Georgia Institute of Technology.

Bruce, B., Collins, A., Rubin, A. D., & Gentner, D. (1980). A cognitive science approach to writing. In C. H. Frederiksen, M. F. Whiteman, & J. D. Dominic (Eds.), *Writing: The nature, development, and teaching of written communication* Hillsdale, NJ: Lawrence Erlbaum Associates.

Carbonell, J. G., Jr. (1978). POLITICS: Automated ideological reasoning. *Cognitive Science, 2*(1), 27–51.

Cook, M., Lehnert, W. G., & McDonald, D. D. (1984, July). *Conveying implicit content in narrative summaries.* Paper presented at COLING-84, Palo Alto, CA.

DeJong, G. F. (1979). Skimming stories in real time: An experiment in integrated understanding (Research Rep. No. 158). New Haven, CT: Yale University, Department of Computer Science.

Dyer, M. G. (1981). The role of TAU's in narratives. *Proceedings of the Third Annual Conference of the Cognitive Science Society.*

Dyer, M. G. (1983). *In-depth understanding: A computer model of integrated processing for narrative comprehension.* Cambridge, MA: MIT Press.

Fillmore, C. (1968). *The case for case.* In E. Bach & R. Harms (Eds.), *Universals in linguistic theory* New York: Holt, Rhinehart & Winston.

Gee, J. P., & Grosjean, F. (1984). Empirical evidence for narrative structure. *Cognitive Science, 8*(1), 59–85.

Graesser, A. C. (1981). *Prose comprehension beyond the word.* New York: Springer-Verlag.

Hayes, J. R., & Flower, R. S. (1980). Identifying the organization of writing processes. In L. Gregg, & E. R. Sternberg (Eds.), *Cognitive processes in writing,* Hillsdale, NJ: Lawrence Erlbaum Associates.

Kintsch, W. (1974). *The representation of meaning in memory,* Hillsdale, NJ: Lawrence Erlbaum Associates.

Kolodner, J. L. (1983). Reconstructive memory: A computer model. *Cognitive Science, 7*(4), 281–328.

Lehnert, W. G. (1979). Representing physical objects in memory. In M. Ringle (Ed.), *Philosophical perspectives in A. I.* Atlantic Highlands, NJ: Humanities Press.

Lehnert, W. G. (1981). Affect and memory representation. *Proceedings of the Third Annual Conference of the Cognitive Science Society,* Berkeley, Ca.

Lehnert, W. G. (1983). Narrative complexity based on summarization algorithms. In *Proceedings of the Eighth International Joint Conference on Artificial Intelligence,* Karlsruhe, West Germany.

Lehnert, W. G., Alker, H., & Schneider, D. (1983). Affective plot structure of Toynbee's *Christus Patiens.* In *Proceedings of the Sixth International Conference on Computers and the Humanities.* Washington, D.C.

Lehnert, W. G., Black, J., & Reiser, B. (1981). Summarizing narratives. *Proceedings of the Seventh International Joint Conference on Artificial Intelligence,* Vancouver, British Columbia.

Lehnert, W. G., Dyer, M. G., Johnson, P. N., Yang, C. J., & Harley, S. (1983). BORIS—An experiment in in-depth understanding of narratives." *Artificial Intelligence, 20,* 15–62.

Lehnert, W. G., & Loiselle, C. L. (1983). Plot unit recognition for narratives. (Tech. Rep. No. 83-39) Amherst, MA: University of Massachusetts, Department of Computer and Information Science.

McDonald, D. D. (1983). Natural language generation as a computational problem—An introduction. In M. Brady, & R. Berwick (Eds.), *Computational models of discourse* (pp. 209–265). Cambridge, MA: MIT Press.

Reiser, B. J., Black, J. B., & Lehnert, W. G. (1983). Thematic knowledge structures in the understanding and generation of narratives. *Discourse Processes, 8,* (3), pp. 357–359.

Reiser, B. J., Lehnert, W. G., & Black, J. B. (1981). Recognizing thematic units in narratives. *Proceedings of the Third Annual Conference of the Cognitive Science Society,* Berkeley, Ca.

Rieger, C. (1975). *Conceptual memory and inference.* In R. Schank (Ed.), *Conceptual information processing* (pp. 157–288). Amsterdam: North-Holland.

Roseman, I. (1979). *Cognitive aspects of emotion and emotional behavior.* Paper presented at the meeting of the American Psychological Association, New York.

Rumelhart, D. E. (1977). Understanding and summarizing brief stories. In D. Laberge & S. Samuels (Eds.), *Basic processing in reading, perception, and comprehension.* Hillsdale, NJ: Lawrence Erlbaum Associates.

Rumelhart, D., & Norman, D. (Eds.). (1975). *Explorations in cognition.* San Francisco, CA: Freeman.

Schank, R. C. (1975). *Conceptual information processing.* Amsterdam: North-Holland.

Schank, R. C. (1979). Reminding and memory organization: An introduction to MOPs (Research Dept. of Computer Science. Rep. No. 170). New Haven, CT: Yale University.

Schank, R. C. (1982). *Dynamic memory: A theory of reminding and learning in computers and people.* New York: Cambridge University Press.

Schank, R. C., & Abelson, R. P. (1977). *Scripts, plans, goals, and understanding.* Hillsdale, NJ, Lawrence Erlbaum Associates.

Simmons, R. F., & Correira, A. (1979). Rule forms for verse, sentences and story trees. In N. Findler (Ed.), *Associative networks—Representation and use of knowledge by computers.* New York: Academic Press.

Thorndyke, P. W. (1977). Cognitive structures in comprehension and memory of narrative discourse. *Cognitive Psychology, 9,* 77–110.

Wilensky, R. (1980). *Understanding goal-based stories.* New York: Garland.

Wilensky, R. (1982). Points: A theory of the structure of stories in memory. In W. Lehnert & M. H. Ringle (Eds.), *Strategies for natural language processing* (pp. 345–374). Hillsdale, NJ: Lawrence Erlbaum Associates.

Wilensky, R. (1983). Story grammars versus story points. *The Behavioral and Brain Sciences, 6*(4), 519–623.

Wilks, Y. (1978). Good and bad arguments for semantic primitives. *Communication and Cognition, 10,* 181–221.

Winograd, T. (1972). *Understanding natural language.* New York: Academic Press.

Woods, W. (1970). Transition network grammars for natural language analysis. *Communications of the ACM, 13*(10).

CHAPTER 5

Natural Language Description of Time-Varying Scenes

BERND NEUMANN
Fachbereich Informatik,
Universität Hamburg

OVERVIEW

This work explores the border area between vision and natural language with respect to a particular task: obtaining verbal descriptions of scenes with motion. The task involves image understanding as we assume that the time-varying scene to be described is represented by an image sequence. Hence, part of the problem is image-sequence analysis. We focus on high-level aspects: recognizing interesting occurrences that extend over time. Very little is said about lower level processes that constitute the scope of vision in a narrow sense. The concepts and representations proposed in this work can be viewed as extending the scope of a vision system beyond the level of object recognition. In this respect, our work is a contribution to the question raised by Waltz (1979): What should the output of a (complete) vision system be?

Another aspect of this work concerns the connection of vision and natural language. Both disciplines have been studied rather independently from each other. Hence, little is known about how the semantics of a verbal scene description relate to a description derived from visual input. This work shows that visual motion analysis can lead to representations that easily map into deep case frames of natural-language utterances. Apart from the technical aspects, this is interesting because semantic categories developed in natural-language research turn out to have clear physical (and visual) connotations, computable from an image sequence.

The problem of generating a natural-language utterance from an appropriate deep structure is not our concern. Our work does however, touch upon the problem of composing a coherent description (i.e., selecting and ordering possible utterances). The general idea of our approach is to use the anticipated visualization of the hearer for speech planning.

These are, in brief, three major problem areas addressed by this contribution. We now give an overview of the system NAOS that implements our ideas.

The acronym stands for "NAtural language description of Object movements in a Street scene". This indicates our domain of interest: traffic scenes. In particular, we are concerned with the following scenario. Person A (looking out of a window) observes a street scene over a certain time span. Then A turns to some person B (who knows the street but cannot see it) and describes what he has seen. NAOS attempts to generate natural-language scene descriptions according to this scenario.

The raw input data are black-and-white TV images taken from a fixed viewpoint. Figure 5.1 shows 4 images out of a sequence of 64, covering a time span of approximately 13 seconds. The events of interest are pedestrians standing, walking, and crossing the street, cars starting and stopping, turning right, and so on.

Scenes like this have been used for many years as experimental data for image-understanding research at the Universität Hamburg, primarily for low-level motion analysis, object tracking, and motion stereo. In project NAOS we are interested in high-level interpretations. For this purpose, all low-level processing up to a complete recovery of the scene geometry (including classified objects) is simulated by human interaction. The output of this first stage of processing is called *geometrical scene description* (GSD). A precise definition of this intermediate-level scene representation is given in the next section.

The core of NAOS is a program that recognizes *events* in a GSD. An event is a subset of the scene that can be described by a certain verb of locomotion (e.g., "overtake"). A priori knowledge about event types is provided by *event models*. They consist of propositions about the scene that must be satisfied if an event can be said to have occurred. Event recognition is very much like proving the exis-

Figure 5.1. Images of a traffic scene to be described by NAOS

tence of an event based on facts provided by the GSD and rules provided by the event models. In implementing the proof procedure (using the programming language FUZZY), several techniques have been developed that may have relevance beyond this task. For example, relational matching has been extended to deal with constraints arising from time intervals. Event models are discussed in the third section; event recognition is discussed in the fifth section.

Events are conceptual units that are designed to capture the semantics of verbs of locomotion. The next step toward a natural-language scene description is filling the "case frames" associated with such verbs (Fillmore, 1968). For example, the agent case corresponds to a certain object in the event. Similarly source, path, and goal cases correspond to locations readily available from the event description. For verbalization, these objects that fill case roles have to be referenced according to certain rules of natural language use. For example, locations are referenced using spatial prepositions and nearby objects of reference ("at the traffic lights"). In our view, the construction of such references is the critical step from a visual to a verbal representation.

Although bottom-up scene description is the central goal of NAOS, we also consider question answering involving top-down processing. In this case, an inverse mapping is required: Natural-language input is transformed into a deep-case structure from which a constrained event recognition task can be derived. This process is described in the third section. After event evaluation, a case frame is filled in a manner similar to bottom-up verbalization. Answer generation requires, however, several special processes (e.g., provisions for generating cooperative answers). This distinguishes the task from unconstrained verbalization. All issues concerning the mapping between events and case frames are discussed in the section on verbalization.

The core processes of natural-language understanding and generation were not developed as part of the NAOS-project. We make use of components of the natural language dialogue system HAM-ANS (Hoeppner et al., 1983, Hoeppner et al., 1984), in particular of a generator written by Busemann (1984). These components are not discussed in detail in this contribution. We are concerned, however, with another issue on the natural-language side: composing a coherent, natural description from a set of possible utterances. This is the theme of the fifth section. We assume that the computer is always trying to perform a single kind of "speech act": to inform its user of some situation or event. Many other "speech acts" (Searle, 1969) are possible: requesting, reminding, connecting, ordering, promising, apologizing, or many others. In order to perform appropriately, the system must anticipate the effect of each utterance on the hearer. We present a "standard plan" for scene description that is a first approximation to speech-act planning based on the hearer's anticipated visualization.

The final section of this contribution presents a discussion of related work and points out future directions planned for our research.

REPRESENTING THE SCENE

In this section, we describe the data that are used as input for the NAOS system. Eventually, we would like NAOS to generate verbal descriptions from the output of some existing vision system whose input would be raw images. This would clearly demonstrate the intended scope of our work: to extend vision to higher levels of representation that connect to concepts of natural language. Unfortunately, there do not yet exist vision systems that can analyze real-world image sequences with sufficient reliability and speed to provide the input for NAOS. Our group is indeed working on analyzing image sequences of traffic scenes (Dreschler and Nagel, 1981).

An intermediate level of representation has been defined that bypasses the problems of low-level vision. This level represents the output of a vision system in the narrow sense: it tells "what is where" (Marr, 1981). More specifically, this level provides a representation of the 3D scene geometry, and photometric scene properties, plus a classification of all objects of interest. This seems to be also in agreement with the intended output of a vision system as proposed in Ballard and Brown (1982): an explicit, meaningful description of physical objects. In NAOS, this representation is called the *geometrical scene description* (GSD) to emphasize the prevalence of geometrical information and the absence of high-level concepts.

Clearly, a vision system will hardly ever be able to recover the complete 3D geometry of a scene, as the shape of surfaces may remain guess-work, particularly if they are hidden. But as higher level scene interpretations seem to be based on what one knows about a scene rather than on what one does not know, it is appropriate to choose a canonical representation containing all information which could possibly be available. To really obtain such information requires considerable perceptual inference facilities, including viewpoint and light source geometry.

By similar reasoning, all photometric scene properties are assumed to be known (e.g., light source characteristics and surface reflectivity). Although these data are not essential for NAOS (except, perhaps, of object colors), they guarantee completeness of the GSD in the following sense: The data suffice, in principle, to regenerate the raw images. In other words, the scope of this representation does not presuppose loss of information along the way from raw images to the GSD.

In more detail, a GSD contains

—for each frame of the image sequence:

- instance of time
- visible objects
- viewpoint
- illumination

—for each object:

- 3D shape
- surface characteristics (color)
- class (automobile, person, tree)
- identity (VW1, Person1)
- 3D position and orientation in each frame

By far the most important information for NAOS is the list of positions and orientations attached to each object. Based on these data, high-level motion concepts are recognized (e.g., one car overtaking another). Position refers to some fixed reference point of an object coordinate system (usually the centroid) and is given with respect to a fixed world coordinate system. Similarly, orientation refers to a distinguished direction in the object coordinate system (usually the 'front').

Shape and surface information is provided by models based on polyhedra and cones (Brooks, 1981). The repertoire of possible shapes is in no way adequate for representing highly irregular bodies. Also there are only very crude provisions for encoding photometric surface properties. More sophistication, however, is currently not required in NAOS where shape information will be mainly used for computing qualitative spatial relations.

How is a GSD obtained for a real-world traffic scene? NAOS deals with traffic scenes observable from our laboratory window. The major stationary components of such scenes are known to the system: It has access to a model of the environment as part of its knowledge base.

The first step in processing an image sequence is to determine the viewpoint (camera position, orientation, and focus) with the help of the street model. This is done by finding point correspondences (currently by hand) and then employing a standard calibration technique (Yakimovsky & Cunningham, 1978). Using the viewpoint information one can identify those stationary objects of the street model that are visible in the scene. To obtain the 3D trajectories of moving objects, automatic and human-aided change detection and tracking procedures developed for other motion analysis tasks can be employed (Nagel & Rekers, 1982). Figure 5.2 shows a synthetic view of trajectories obtained manually for a scene involving 3 cars

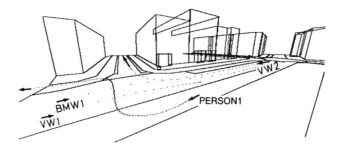

Figure 5.2.   Synthetic view of a scene with 4 moving objects.

and a pedestrian. The intersection shown in Figure 5.1 is visible on the right.

EVENTS

Given an intermediate-level representation of a scene in terms of objects and their positions, it is not all clear where further processing should lead. One might be interested, for example, in finding out whether a certain object configuration is present or not (e.g., a parked red Mercedes). Or else one might want the system to communicate its observations to humans. There are clearly as many tasks as there are uses for visual data, and each task would suggest certain abstractions—high-level "conceptual units"—to be computed from the scene data. If one is finding a path for a robot, for example, it might be useful to compute an explicit representation of free space. As obvious guidelines for structuring high-level vision do not seem to be around the corner, some motivation for the approach taken in NAOS must be given.

We introduce conceptual units that are useful for talking about scenes with motion. Clearly, an intermediate-level representation of motion in terms of objects and their positions—the GSD introduced in the preceding section—would be inappropriate for this purpose. Natural language gives some indication of motion concepts that may be generally interesting, namely concepts for which succinct expressions are available.

In the remainder of this section, we discuss 'events' that are the conceptual units for motion description in NAOS. First, event models are introduced, and then procedures for event recognition are described.

Event Models

Events are interesting subspaces of the four-dimensional space–time continuum (much in accord with Webster's definition). We consider events that describe "changes of the kind people talk about" (Miller & Johnson-Laird, 1976). More specifically, an event is a subspace of a scene that can be described by a verb of change (in our domain: locomotion).

Events are organized into classes according to the verb that is associated with the event. Event classes are defined by event models. An event model is a schema that specifies what we are looking for in a scene. Events are particular instantiations of event models.

Event models consist of a head, which is a predicate about a scene, and a body, which specifies how to verify the predicate. The following is the model for 'overtake' events.

Head: (OVERTAKE OBJ1 OBJ2 T1 T2)
Body: (MOVE OBJ1 T1 T2)
(MOVE OBJ2 T1 T2)
(APPROACH OBJ1 OBJ2 T1 T3)
(BESIDE OBJ1 OBJ2 T3 T4)
(RECEDE OBJ1 OBJ2 T4 T2)

The semantics of OVERTAKE can be paraphrased as follows: "OBJ1 overtakes OBJ2 during the time interval (T1 and T2) if

- both objects are in motion throughout the time interval (T1 T2),
- OBJ1 approaches OBJ2 during the time interval (T1 T3),
- there follows a time interval (T3 T4) where OBJ1 is beside OBJ2,
- and finally OBJ1 recedes from OBJ2 throughout the remaining interval (T4 T2)."

It is not claimed that this definition captures the semantics of all 'overtake' situations that one might think of (for example, an airplane passing overhead another). The point is to demonstrate that the representational formalism is adequate for the street example.

Some comments on the syntax are in order. Predicates are written in a relational notation. The first element is a predicate identifier, the other elements are arguments. Arguments are usually variables which must be instantiated, but may also be constants, for example, numbers. (All arguments in this example are variables.) If there can be any doubt as to whether an identifier denotes a variable or a constant, a '?' will be attached to the variable identifier.

The variables T1 to T4 are time variables denoting interval boundaries. Events are taken to extend over a nonzero time interval in all but degenerate cases in accord with the notion of a 'four-dimensional subspace' of a time-varying scene. Hence, the head of an event model always involves a time interval. A predicate about one time interval does not necessarily imply anything about another time interval, even if the latter is a subinterval of the former. Nevertheless, there are many predicates that do allow the subinterval implication (e.g., MOVE, BEHIND). They are called *durative* corresponding to the linguistic notion. Durative predicates have also been introduced in Allen (1981) by means of the HOLDS predicate. To be precise, a predicate P is durative if

(P . . . T1 T2) => (P . . . T1' T2') for T1 ≤ T1' < T2' ≤ T2.

Similarly, there are *inchoative* and *resultative* predicates. The event model 'stop,' for example, is resultative. It is defined as follows:

> Head: (STOP OBJ T1 T2)
> Body: (MOVE OBJ T1 T2)
> (STAND OBJ T2 T3)

For a resultative predicate P the following implication holds:

(P . . . T1 T2) => (P . . . T1' T2) for T1 ≤ T1' < T2.

Inchoative predicates are discussed in the second part of this section.

The 'overtake' event is hierarchical (i.e., the body is composed of predicates that must be verified if the head predicate is to be true). The predicates of the body may be events (e.g., APPROACH) or other predicates (e.g., BESIDE). Predicates are called 'primitive' if they cannot be decomposed further. The body of each primitive predicate is a procedure to be evaluated with the GSD as data. The event model MOVE, for example, is primitive. So is the predicate BESIDE.

Some motion concepts are like events except that there is no verb available for describing such motion. For example, it proved useful to define the primitive predicate SYM-APPROACH ("symmetrical approach"):

> Head: (SYM-APPROACH OBJ1 OBJ2 T1 T2)
> Body: <test whether the distance between
> OBJ1 and OBJ2 decreases>

Using this predicate, APPROACH may be defined as follows:

> Head: (APPROACH OBJ1 OBJ2 T1 T2)
> Body: (SYM-APPROACH OBJ1 OBJ2 T1 T2)
> (MOVE OBJ1 T1 T2)
> (IN-FRONT-OF OBJ2 OBJ1 T1 T2)

APPROACH is an event model that closely corresponds to the meaning of the natural-language verb 'approach.' Not only must the distance decrease, but OBJ1 is also required to move toward OBJ2. The predicate IN-FRONT-OF tests whether OBJ2 is located within a certain sector relative to the 'front' of OBJ1.

Similarly, RECEDE is defined in terms of SYM-RECEDE (increasing distance) and BEHIND.

Event models have clear logical interpretation. They specify that the head is logically equivalent to the body:

$$\langle\text{head}\rangle <=> \langle\text{body}\rangle$$

All variables are existentially quantified. The body is given by a conjunction of predicates or by a procedure that is equivalent to a single predicate. Event recognition can be viewed as inferring certain predicates about the scene using the GSD for facts and the event models for inference rules. For event recognition the implication

$$\langle\text{body}\rangle => \langle\text{head}\rangle$$

will be extensively exploited.[1]

Event models form an implication hierarchy. As customary, general events are considered "higher" than special events. Hence, the top of the hierarchy corresponds to 'happen' which is implied by all other events. The structure of the hierarchy is determined by the implications that follow from

$$\langle\text{head}\rangle => \langle\text{body}\rangle$$

when decomposing the body into the individual conjuncts. For example, we get

---

[1] The event models presented so far do not use the full power of predicate calculus notation. In particular, there are neither explicit disjunctions nor explicit universal quantifications. As it turns out, none of the other 50 verbs currently considered in NAOS (see Appendix A) requires an extension of the notation in this respect (there will be other extensions). Hence, one may wonder whether this must be so. The first thing to observe is that the body of predicates may be procedural, hence unrestricted. Thus, no limitations are imposed in principle. Second, universal quantifications are in fact part of the formalism as far as time intervals are concerned. Whenever a predicate is marked "durative," it implies a predication of all subintervals of the given interval. Regarding disjunctions, it is quite conceivable to define an event model in terms of alternatives. For example, 'turn off' could be broken down into 'turn off right' or 'turn off left'. As there are other intuitive predicates to express the alternative (e.g., 'change of direction'), there is no need to employ a disjunction. Ambiguity of verb meaning also gives rise to alternatives. These can (and should) be handled, however, outside event models, as these alternatives do not constitute a single conceptual unit. In summary, there are no deep reasons for choosing this representational formalism. It just happens to be adequate.

(OVERTAKE OBJ1 OBJ2 T1 T2) => (MOVE OBJ1 T1 T2)
(OVERTAKE OBJ1 OBJ2 T1 T2) => (APPROACH OBJ1 OBJ2 T1 T2)
(etc.)

As all arguments are existentially quantified, the rules can also be written in the weaker form:

OVERTAKE => MOVE

This means: if there is an overtake event in the scene, there must be also a 'move' event. The hierarchy presented in Appendix A is based on such rules. It is useful for event recognition in the free verbalization task (as opposed to question answering). Events are recognized in their order of decreasing generality (i.e., from the top of the hierarchy to the bottom). If at any point in the hierarchy an event model cannot be instantiated, all descendents can also not be instantiated by virture of the implication chains. For example, if nothing moves, no overtake may take place:

NOT (MOVE) => NOT (OVERTAKE)

VERBALIZATION

We are interested now in clarifying the connection between events and natural language. We first consider bottom-up verbalization (i.e., the task of obtaining a verbal scene description from a GSD). In this section, we restrict our discussion to single utterances.

The main contribution of this section is to describe how case frames can be filled by events and other scene data, and how event recognition is triggered by a filled case frame in the context of question answering. The remaining problem of generating surface strings from deep case frames and vice versa is handled by processes that have been developed for the natural language system HAM-ANS. They are not discussed further here.

Figure 5.3 gives an overview of the major processing steps.

Filling Case Frames

The target structures into which the GSD and the events will be transformed for verbalization, are deep case frames for verbs of locomotion.

Given a GSD and an 'overtake' event recognized in the scene, how

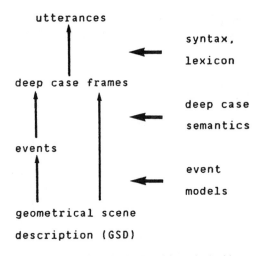

utterances

syntax,
lexicon

deep case frames

deep case
semantics

events

event
models

geometrical scene

description (GSD)

Figure 5.3. Overview of connection between vision and natural language system

can one obtain the deep case structure for a natural-language utterance that describes that event? Consider, for example,

"A yellow VW overtook a truck in front of the FBI."

(FBI is the German abbreviation of the Department of Computer Science.) The sentence is composed of the verb overtake, two noun phrases for the agent and objective cases, and a prepositional phrase for the locative case that also involves a noun phrase. In addition, there is temporal information expressed by the past tense. The referents of the deep cases can be easily expressed in terms of scene data. The verb refers to an 'overtake' event, the agent and objective cases to the two participating objects, the locative case to the locations taken up by the agent during the event, and finally the past tense to the temporal relation of the event interval to a reference time. Thus, filling a case frame for verbalization amounts to constructing references to the constituents of an event so that all constraints are satisfied.

Knowledge that governs this process is called *deep case semantics*. It is represented by case frame models as illustrated here for the example 'overtake.'

The case frame model for 'overtake' is as follows:

```
(VERB "overtake")
(OVERTAKE OBJ1 OBJ2 T1 T2)
(AGENT AGT-EXP)
(REF AGT-EXP OBJ1)
```

```
(OBJECTIVE OBJ-EXP)
(REF OBJ-EXP OBJ2)
(LOCATIVE LOC-EXP)
(LOC-REF LOC-EXP (LOC-PREP OBJ1 LOC-OBJ T1 T2))
(TENSE TNS-EXP)
(TIME-REF TNS-EXP T1 T2)
```

Each case description of the case-frame model consists of two parts: a declaration of an identifier (or constant in case of the verb) for the case expression on the language side, and a predicate (in general a list of predicates) relating the case expression to the scene data. The heart of the deep case semantics are the predicates REF and LOC-REF. They are now described in more detail.

REF relates a natural-language expression (in the format understood by the surface string generator or delivered by the parser) to a symbolic object identifier of the GSD. It works in two ways. Bottom-up, it generates suitable NL expressions for a scene object. This process is called *referencing*. Top-down, an NL expression is given and possible scene objects are generated. This is *dereferencing*. Referencing and dereferencing are well understood in NL research. We have adapted techniques developed in HAM-ANS. For example,

(REF AGT-EXP BUILDING1)

(where BUILDING1 is a certain scene object) will be evaluated as follows. First, the hearer model will be searched; the hearer model records all objects that are known to both speaker and hearer (e.g., by previous mention). If BUILDING1 is found and it has a name, for example "the FBI", its name can be used for reference. If BUILDING1 is found, but it has no name, then the definite article is used and referentiation is accomplished by retrieving class membership and possibly discriminating properties from the GSD. *If* BUILDING1 is not found in the hearer model, it must be newly introduced using the indefinite article, class membership, and discriminating properties similar to the definite case. For example, "a yellow VW" may be returned for a scene object VW1 which is a VW that has not been mentioned before. There are several other issues connected to referencing which are, however, outside the scope of this presentation (e.g., quantization, use of pronouns, and ellipses). The reverse process of dereferencing is discussed in the context of question answering.

LOC-REF is analogous to REF with the difference that an abstract location instead of an object is to be related to an NL expression. The locative case and other spatial deep cases such as source, path, and goal are often misconstrued as referring to names of places or objects. With scene data as a referential data base the spatial deep cases can be defined concisely as follows. The locative case is the union of all positions of the agent during the event (i.e., the volume swept out by the agent's trajectory). To verbalize the locative case means to find a natural language expression referring to that volume. In NAOS we have only considered prepositional phrases so far. Hence, LOC-REF tries to find a reference object in the scene (LOC-OBJ) that is in a prepositional relation to the locative volume. Similarly, source and goal-deep cases are verbalized by relating the source or goal volume to a reference object using a suitable preposition. Note that after finding a reference object in the scene, REF is called to generate a natural language expression for this object.

The semantics of spatial prepositions are not trivial (see, for example, Boggess, 1979, Herskovits, 1985, Waltz & Boggess, 1979). In NAOS, we have currently implemented simplified versions of the most commonly used prepositions. For example, 'in-front-of,' 'behind,' and 'beside' simply test whether the second object is in the appropriate sector of the first object. Sectors originate at the centroid and extend in a fixed direction relative to the 'front' of an object.

We now turn to TIME-REF, which relates time intervals expressed in clock units of scene time to temporal expression in natural language. One effect of TIME-REF is the determination of tense. This is accomplished by comparing the interval boundaries with time marks separating the past from the present. The present time is held fixed and coincides with the end of the scene data. More sophistication will be required when the present time progresses as the description is generated. This is currently outside the scope of NAOS.

In addition to tense, temporal expressions can be used to specify the event interval. The problem of referencing interval boundaries is similar to referencing locations as there are in general no names attached. Hence, an indirect specification has to be generated by referring to a suitable item nearby—in this case in the temporal neighborhood. For example, a 'turn-off' event could be used to mark the beginning of the event in question:

"After the BMW turned off Schlueterstreet, the yellow VW . . ."

If events are described in chronological order, reference to preceding events is particularly easy, as one can use "then" or "after this" or rely on the implicit understanding that the end of one event marks the beginning of the next. This is elaborated further in the next section.

COMPOSING A DESCRIPTION

So far we have described methods for recognizing all events in a
scene that match event models of a given repertoire, and for generating a natural-language utterance for a single event. We now consider
the task of producing a coherent scene description. At several levels
decisions have to be made that determine format and contents of the
description. At the level of events, one has to select from a possibly
large number of instances. For example, any of the events 'move,'
'slow down,' 'leave,' 'turn off,' or others could be selected for a
description of roughly the same subspace of the scene. Furthermore,
one also has to decide the order in which events should be
presented.

At the case-frame level, there are choices concerning optional
deep cases or alternative case fillers. For example, one could say

"A VW turned off"

(which may very well be adequate in certain scenarios) or

"A VW turned off from Schlueterstreet into Bieberstreet after the
BMW had passed the FBI."

One might also consider adverbials or other modifiers, relative
clauses, comparisons, and so on. Finally, decisions have to be made
concerning such matters as voice, use of pronouns, connectives, el-
lipsis, and so on to obtain a pleasant and natural description.

Linguistic theories (see for example, Austin, 1962, or Cohen,
1978) view speech acts as purposeful and planned actions, designed
to achieve certain goals. Planning such actions involves a hearer
model, as the selection of an utterance must be done with regard to
its effect on the hearer.

Speech-act theory is also a useful framework for the description
task in NAOS. Our communication situation is very simple: A speak-
er/viewer 'informs' a hearer about a scene. Informing somebody
means communicating things that are *true* and *new*. These are the
two basic criteria on which speech act planning in NAOS is built.
Other interesting criteria (e.g., focus and level of detail), are considered refinements that play a subordinate role.

What does it mean to convey 'truth'? We follow the semantics of
Barwise and Perry (1983) where *meaning* is defined as a relation
between utterances and situations. The interpretation of an utterance by a hearer is the set of possible situations connected to that

utterance via the meaning relation. Applied to scene description, we define an utterance to be true if its interpretation—the set of possible scenes—includes the actual scene. Thus, utterances leading to a misunderstanding are not true in this sense. Hence, if an utterance is to be true, the speaker must take into account the semantics of the hearer—he must take care that the hearer understands the right thing. In the uncomplicated world of NAOS it is assumed that the hearer always has the same semantics as the speaker, and as no false utterances are intended, the 'truth' criterion is always satisfied.

Considering the interpretations of the hearer is also fundamental for the second requirement, saying something new. As the interpretation of an utterance is defined in terms of possible scenes, a description that is composed of several utterances can be viewed as narrowing down the set of possibilities. This is—conceptually— carried out by set intersection. We define an utterance as new, if the set of possible scenes is strictly reduced by that utterance. One may equivalently speak about a partially specified scene instead of a set of possible scenes. Using this notion, an utterance is new if it conveys additional specifications for a partially specified scene.

In NAOS, a completely specified scene is available to the speaker in terms of the GSD. Thus, the speaker has a representation of what he tries to convey to the hearer. In addition, he needs a representation of what has been achieved at a given time (i.e., what the hearer has learned about the scene from the description received so far). We call this representation a *visualized geometrical scene description* (VGSD), as it can be considered the output of some kind of visualization process.

A comparison of the GSD and the VGSD is the heart of speech-act planning. Informing the hearer means causing his VGSD to approach the GSD. Planning a speech act that informs means anticipating its effect on the hearer's VGSD. This can be done by simulating the hearer's visualization process. We call this method of speech act planning *visualization anticipation*. The general idea is illustrated in Figure 5.4.

The major new component of this scheme is the VGSD. Structure and contents of the VGSD are not at all obvious, as visualized data are in many respects different from the scene data represented by the GSD, but still should be comparable. Internal representations of visualized scene data have been the topic of a long-standing debate among philosophers, psychologists, linguists and, lately, researchers from cognitive science and AI. (See Block, 1981 or Yuille 1983, for recent contributions to this so-called 'imagery debate)').

It would be beyond the scope of this chapter to discuss our ap-

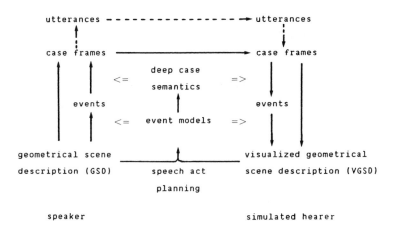

Figure 5.4. Visualization anticipation for speech-act planning

proach relative to the positions taken up in that debate. Our position is pragmatic. The nature of the internal scene representation follows from the tasks which this representation must support. In our case the emphasis is on making two representations comparable, the VGSD that is derived from a NL description, and the GSD that is derived from visual input. Although our task is speech-act planning, we believe that several other tasks such as spatial reasoning or remembering scenes will also require similar representations.

As indicated in Figure 5.4, the VGSD is generated, roughly speaking, by inverting the verbalization path. We assume that case frames can be completely recovered from utterances. Hence, the visualization process begins at the level of case frames. From a case frame, propositions about the scene can be derived using deep-case semantics and event models, following a procedure similar to the top-down event instantiation process described in the previous section. The major difference is, of course, that there is no referential database (the GSD) on which to instantiate the variables of a predicate. Instantiation takes place by creating ("visualizing") scene tokens which satisfy the predicates. Hence, from

"A yellow VW overtook a large truck"

the following primary VGSD propositions are derived:

(CLASS VW1 VW)
(COLOR VW1 YELLOW)
(CLASS TRUCK1 TRUCK)

```
(SIZE TRUCK1 LARGE)
(OVERTAKE VW1 TRUCK1 T1 T2)
        (MOVE VW1 T1 T2)
        (MOVE TRUCK1 T1 T2)
        (APPROACH VW1 TRUCK1 T1 T3)
                (SYM-APPROACH VW1 TRUCK1 T1 T3)
                (MOVE VW1 T1 T3)
                (IN-FRONT-OF TRUCK1 VW1 T1 T3)
        (BESIDE VW1 TRUCK1 T3 T4)
                        *

                        *

                        *
```

Here, VW1 and TRUCK1 are visualized objects. The time variables are constrained according to the past tense of the utterance or whatever temporal information can be extracted from the context of the utterance. The predicates have been expanded down to the level of primitives, and it should be clear that knowledge about the procedural definition of primitives is also available. The primary propositions implicitly define possible scenes compatible with the verbal description.

This is not all there is to a VGSD. We believe that considerable detail must be added by tapping a body of knowledge that has not yet been mentioned in our discussion: knowledge about 'typical events.' A typical event is a scene description composed of an event and of information that is typical for the event but not implied by the event model. We have developed an analogical event representation for this purpose (Mohnhaupt & Neumann, 1988) which is associated with a propositional event model as introduced before and essentially provides typical trajectories in space and time.

There is much to say about typical events, their use in NL understanding and reasoning, their relationship to beliefs, their acquisition by experience, and other interesting issues. This is, however, outside the scope of this chapter. In NAOS, typical event knowledge is used to supply scene data —expectations— beyond the primary propositions implied by the event models. Expectations have a modality different from primary scene data because they need not be true. "Contradictory" primary information overrides (or replaces) expectations. Both primary scene and expectations are part of the VGSD.

We have outlined the process of 'visualization' now. With this process the task of 'informing' is well-defined: describe a scene in such a way that the VGSD approaches the GSD in successive refinements. In the NAOS system we have not yet developed a speech-planning component that actually computes a VGSD. But we have devised a standard plan for the special task of giving a complete, coherent description of all moving objects. The plan is based on the general idea of anticipated visualization, as it monitors to which extent the trajectory of a moving object has been specified so far, and generates further utterances accordingly.

Standard Plan for Scene Description

The first utterance is a standardized summary of all moving objects, using the template:

> "There are $\langle N \rangle$ moving objects in the scene: $\langle N1 \rangle$ $\langle$class-1$\rangle$, $\langle N2 \rangle$ $\langle$class-2$\rangle$, . . . , and $\langle NM \rangle$ $\langle$class-M$\rangle$."

Then a chronological description of each individual moving object is given. The following example is a translation of a German language text generated automatically for the scene in Fig. 5.2 (Neumann & Novak 86).

> The scene contains four moving objects: three cars and one pedestrian.
>
> A VW drives from the old post office to the FBI. It stops.
>
> Another VW drives toward Dammtor station. It turns off Schlueter-street. It drives on Bieberstreet toward Grindelhof.
>
> A BMW drives toward Hallerplatz. Thereby it overtakes the VW which has stopped at Bierberstreet. The BMW stops at the traffic lights.
>
> The pedestrian goes toward Dammtor station. He crosses Schlueter-street in front of the FBI.

The description of an object is generated according to the following rules:

1. The trajectory of the object is described completely except where not visible.
2. The trajectory is described in terms of the "most special events" according to the event hierarchy. This is done by choosing the most special event covering a time interval from the beginning of the scene to some time point, and then proceeding from this time point in the same manner until the trajectory is completely covered.

3. The spatio-temporal location of an event in four-dimensional space-time is specified as follows:
   (a) Spatial deep cases are used except where the location has already been specified by the preceding event or the verb does not allow it. If necessary, additional—less special—events are verbalized to provide spatial information.
   (b) Time specifications are only exceptional. As a rule the temporal distribution of events is given as follows:

- The first event begins at the beginning of the scene if not specified otherwise.
- Events described thereafter immediately succeed the preceding event (chronological coverage).
- The duration of an event follows from location specifications and a typical velocity in case of durative events (e.g., 'walk'). For nondurative events a typical duration is assumed. Exceptional cases arise if no locomotion takes place ('stand') or standard values deviate too much from the actual ones. For the latter case one can use linguistic means to modify standard values, for example adverbials ('quickly'). If it is necessary to explicitly specify a time point, this is done by referring to time points that have already been specified. All start and end times of events that have been previously mentioned according to the standard plan, are considered specified.

Note that temporal specifications rely heavily on typical event data. Thus, knowledge of typical events—common to speaker and hearer—is shown to play a significant part in scene description. Further details about text generation in NAOS are given in Novak (1986).

Question Answering

The possibility of putting questions to a vision system and obtaining answers is certainly an interesting perspective, as questions may radically reduce the required processing compared to general-purpose scene analysis. In NAOS, top-down processing can only be demonstrated down to the level of the GSD. But other systems show the effectiveness of top-down constraints below this level (Brooks, 1983).

Consider the decision question:

"Did a yellow VW overtake a truck in front of the FBI?"

To answer this question, the following steps are executed. First, all noun phrases are dereferenced. That is, REF is called with a noun phrase as input and generates scene objects that fit the description. For example, a set of yellow VWs: VW1, VW3, . . . may be determined as the range of OBJ1. If no such objects exist, an answer such as

"There is no yellow VW in the scene"

will be generated. In general, the second step is a quantization test on referents. Consider the question:

"Did the BMW overtake two trucks?"

If a BMW has not been previously mentioned, the definite article implies that there is exactly one BMW in the scene. Also, there must be at least two trucks. If the quantization test fails, an appropriate answer will be generated.

Although dereferentiation of objects is performed *before* event recognition, all other constraints of a question are evaluated in connection with the event model. LOC-REF takes a locative expression (e.g., "in front of the FBI") and generates the appropriate scene constraint, for example, (IN-FRONT-OF OBJ1 LOC-OBJ T1 T2) with BUILDING1 (which is the FBI) bound to LOC-OBJ. Spatial deep case expressions supplied by the parser are transformed into constraints in a similar way. TIME-REF generates constraints for the interval boundaries. For example, from the past tense of the question one gets

$$\text{T-PAST-BEG} \leq \text{T}1 < \text{T}2 \leq \text{T-PAST-END}$$

where the boundary values are fixed time marks as mentioned earlier. Hence, from the first of the two questions one gets the predicates:

(OVERTAKE OBJ1 OBJ2 T1 T2)
(IN-FRONT-OF OBJ1 OBJ3 T1 T2)

with the following ranges attached to the variables:

OBJ1 = {VW1, VW3, . . .}
OBJ2 = {TRUCK1, TRUCK 2, . . .}
OBJ3 = {BUILDING1}
T1 = (T-PAST-BEG T-PAST-END−1)
T2 = (T-PAST-BEG+1 T-PAST-END)

These constitute a set of constraints on events that can satisfy the question.

Event recognition now takes place as described in the next section. A trace of this process is presented in Appendix B.

Event Recognition

We now turn to the process of event recognition, which is the search of the GSD for events that could match the constraints previously generated. For bottom-up scene description the search is unconstrained.

The GSD and all facts computed about the scene are kept in an associative database. The availability of an associative net was one of the reasons for selecting the programming language FUZZY for our implementation. The basic techniques for event recognition are hierarchical matching (Barrow, Ambler, & Burstall, 1972) and backtracking search. The scheme used in NAOS is particular in several ways as becomes apparent here. The following shows the search strategy of EVENTEVAL. This is the component of NAOS that tries to instantiate a list of predicates with range restrictions with the goal of making all predicates conjunctively true.

EVENTEVAL list of predicates:

- SELECT predicate from list.
- GENERATE all instances.
- Select instance and TEST for compatability.
- Backtrack if not compatible, else
- EVENTEVAL remaining predicates.

Before commenting on this procedure, it is necessary to consider the GENERATE component in more detail. The following steps are carried out:

GENERATE all instances of a predicate:

- Generate all instances of non-instantiated arguments except time variables. Each combination of such instances defines a predicate 'pattern.'
- Skip predicate pattern if generated before,
- EVENTUAL body if predicate is composite, else EVAL body.

GENERATE cycles through all patterns of a predicate by substituting possible instances for noninstantiated variables except for those denoting time intervals. The variable range restrictions are used to generate potential instances. There are provisions for avoiding duplicate computations by keeping a history of all patterns which have been tried before. Evaluation is either carried out by a recursive call of EVENTEVAL or by EVAL that deals with primitive predicates. Each evaluation of a pattern generates all time intervals for which the pattern is true. EVAL can be characterized as follows.

EVAL primitive predicate:

- Compute all maximal time intervals, for which the predicate is true.
- Enter instances into database.

The computations of EVAL are carried out using data of the GSD or facts of the knowledge base. In its simplest form the computation of a primitive predicate is a direct retrieval from the GSD (e.g., CLASS or COLOR). But there are also primitives which require more processing (e.g., SYM-APPROACH, BESIDE).

From the structure of EVENTEVAL and GENERATE one can see that event recognition proceeds in a doubly recursive manner: by recursively instantiating a list of predicates and by recursively decomposing predicates. This should be kept in mind when studying the trace of the 'overtake' example in Appendix B.

So far, very little has been said about instantiating time intervals. Time intervals are different from other data in that they are represented by constraints rather than fixed instances. Consider the proposition

$$(\text{MOVE CAR1 10 30})$$

As MOVE is durative, the interval boundaries 10 and 30 have to be interpreted as constraints marking the range of possible subintervals. Hence if a predicate

$$(\text{MOVE OBJ1 T1 T2})$$

is matched against the MOVE data, OBJ1 is instantiated to CAR1, whereas T1 and T2 are only constrained:

$$10 \leq \text{T1} < \text{T2} \leq 30.$$

As more predicates involving the same time variables are instantiated, more constraints accumulate.

For the following example we assume that all 'move' events have been computed in an initialization step and entered into the database. (This is the usual procedure in NAOS.) Consider the data

```
(MOVE CAR1 1 30)
(MOVE CAR2 7 13)
(MOVE CAR2 20 35)
(IN-FRONT-OF CAR2 CAR1 15 27)
```

and the list of predicates (taken from the event model 'overtake')

```
(MOVE OBJ1 T1 T2)
(MOVE OBJ2 T1 T2)
(IN-FRONT-OF OBJ2 OBJ1 T1 T3)
```

One possible instantiation would give rise to the inequalities:

$1 \leq \text{T1} < \text{T2} \leq 30$
$20 \leq \text{T1} < \text{T2} \leq 35$
$15 \leq \text{T1} < \text{T3} \leq 27.$

Assuming for the sake of simplicity that the three propositions amount to a complete 'overtake' event, what are the temporal constraints of this event? We can solve the inequalities by inspection and get

$20 \leq \text{T1} \leq 26$
$21 \leq \text{T2} \leq 30.$

The resulting 'overtake' event is recorded using the notation:

```
(OVERTAKE CAR1 CAR2 (20 26) (21 30))
```

Hence, the general form for writing a constrained time interval with beginning T-BEG and end T-END is

```
(T-BEG-MIN T-BEG-MAX)  (T-END-MIN T-END-MAX)
```

For durative predicates, the minimal and maximal values coincide except of the fact that zero intervals are not allowed. Thus, the notation introduced earlier

```
( . . . T1 T2)
```

is equivalent to

(. . . (T1 T2-1) (T1+1 T2)).

Inchoative predicates are written

(. . . T1 (T1+1 T2))

which is equivalent to

(. . . (T1 T1) (T1+1 T2)).

Similarly, for resultative predicates

(. . . (T1 T2-1) T2)

is equivalent to

(. . . (T1 T2-1) (T2 T2)).

Note that another instantiation for the example data would result in an inconsistent set of inequalities. Checking the current time constraints for consistency is the task of the TEST component of EVENTEVAL. If the test fails, backtracking ensues and other instantiations are selected.

The fact that recognition of temporal events involves feasibility test and solution of a set of linear inequalities has also been observed in Malik and Binford (1982). They suggest linear programming, in particular the SIMPLEX method, to obtain the desired results. In NAOS, a much simpler procedure is employed. It is based on an inequality net that is maintained for all time variables. Each variable has a current minimum and maximum value and is linked to other variables according to the inequalities. This is shown in Fig. 5.5 for the example used earlier.

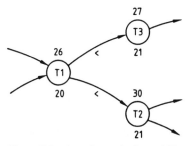

Figure 5.5.   Inequality net for time variables

If a new inequality is encountered, new links are added, and the new constraints are propagated along the links, lower bounds upward and upper bounds downward. Whenever a minimum surpasses a maximum, the inequalities are inconsistent. Otherwise, minimum and maximum are valid bounds and provide the desired solution. Note that all entries are subject to backtracking.

We believe that this incremental constraint propagation method is a key element for dealing with temporal concepts in scenes. It reflects the fact that the basic building blocks of interesting concepts are scene properties extending over some time interval (i.e., durative properties). Taken together, they give rise to systems of inequalities as shown above, and to concepts which need not be durative (e.g., 'overtake' or 'stop').

In conclusion of the discussion of event recognition we describe the SELECT component of EVENTEVAL, as this is another unusual feature of NAOS. SELECT determines the order in which a list of predicates is instantiated. It should be intuitively clear that the size of the search tree and hence the computing costs depend on this order. For example, consider finding all 'stop' events. As 'stop' is composed of 'move' and 'stand,' the question is which to evaluate first. Assuming that no a priori knowledge about motility is available and that there are many more stationary objects than moving ones, it would be advisable to first find moving objects and then the standing ones that were moving earlier.

In NAOS the optimal order for evaluating predicates is determined based on the intrinsic branching factor associated with each predicate (this is a priori knowledge about the likelihood of its occurrence), the actual number of patterns of each predicate (given the variable ranges), and the cost for evaluating a predicate. From this a score is computed which favors predicates with the least chance of success and the smallest cost. After each predicate evaluation the score is recomputed for the remaining predicates (see Neumann, 1984 for details).

DISCUSSION

In this section we compare our work on natural-language motion description with related approaches. We also indicate in which direction current work in NAOS is proceeding.

Our work can be considered as a contribution to high-level interpretation of image sequences. Image sequences with motion have not yet been studied for a long time—the 1979 Workshop on Computer Analysis of Time-Varying Imagery in Philadelphia marked the beginning of general interest in this area. One of the early contributions is the pioneering work of Badler (1975). He investigated the recognition of motion concepts in computer-generated line drawings. His conceptual units are oriented toward natural-language verbs ('swing,' 'bounce') and directional adverbials ('forward,' 'upward'). The focus of Badler's work, however, is not on generating a natural language output but on segmenting trajectories into motion primitives which can be combined into complex motion patterns.

The work of Tsotsos (Tsotsos, 1980; Tsotsos, Mylopoulos, Covvey, & Zucker, 1980) builds on some of the motion concepts developed by Badler, but also improves on Badler's framework in several respects. Most importantly, a hierarchy of domain-independent motion concepts is defined (e.g., 'area-expand,' 'rotate') from which domain-specific motion concepts (e.g., 'posterior-rapid fill,' which is a special left ventricular motion in Tsotsos' domain) can be constructed. Tsotsos also presented a data-driven recognition strategy where hypotheses are generated according to conceptual proximity. Proximity is based on ISA, PART-OF, SIMILARITY, and TEMPORAL-NEXT links in the conceptual database. The implication hierarchy in NAOS plays a similar role: Implication links are used to prevent useless instantiation attempts.

It is interesting to note that Tsotsos, who did not attempt to provide natural language output, based his motion concepts on categories developed by Miller (1972) for motion verbs of the English language. Tsotsos realized that some of Miller's categories cannot be easily incorporated in a vision system (e.g., 'causative' or 'permissive' motion), whereas others have natural visual correlates (e.g., 'inchoative' motion). This was also observed by Marburger, Neumann, & Novak (1981), which is the first report on the NAOS project.

A different set of motion concepts underlies the system SUPP (Okada, 1980), which produces sentences from a short sequence of line drawings showing, for example a bird landing on a tree, a man entering a car, and so on. Okada used 20 semantic features (e.g., 'displacement,' 'deformation,' 'change in quality,' 'start and stop') to decide which of a set of about 1,200 primitive verb concepts applies to a given scene. Usually, many concepts qualify and give rise to as many simple sentences describing the same event. Okada's work seems to be influenced by the feature space paradigm of pattern recognition. It suffers from the lack of structure of feature vector semantics.

There is one issue common to all this work and also to NAOS that is worth emphasizing: the question of what motion concepts should be considered a conceptual unit. Tsotsos stressed the role of taxonomical hierarchies (ISA, PART-OF), hence motion concepts are decompositions of a conceptual space. In NAOS, the conceptual units—events—are subspaces of scenes. They are considered units by virtue of corresponding natural language concepts. Taxonomical units are useful building blocks if parsimonious representations are desired. Events are useful for pragmatical reasons. A combination of both may be advantageous as exemplified by certain event models in NAOS.

The choice of verb-oriented event models has several consequences which are discussed in Neumann and Novak (1983). For example, one is led to deal with concepts that express more than actually can be observed in the subspace of a scene associated with the verb. A striking example is "continue walking," which is the translation of one of the meanings of the German verb "weitergehen." It denotes an uninterrupted walk where stopping has been expected (e.g., "He continued walking in spite of the approaching car"). To recognize such an event, one obviously has to generate expectations about the development of the scene. There are many other verbs of this kind and also other ways of expressing expectations in natural language, for example by negative statements ("The car did not stop"). A framework for generating expectations in NAOS has been devised (Retz-Schmidt 1985). The main idea is to employ script-like conceptual units that represent knowledge about typical sequences of events, for example about typical behavior at traffic lights. Scripts constitute a level of representation "above" events, much in accord with structures proposed in Waltz (1981). Partially instantiated scripts give rise to expectations. Event models may consist of expectations as well as other predicates about the scene.

On the natural-language side our work is influenced by the early NL dialogue system HAM-RPM (von Hahn, Hoeppner, Jameson, & Wahlster, 1980) and its successor HAM-ANS (Hoeppner, Morik, & Marburger, 1984). One of the domains of HAM-ANS is a street scene (in fact: the same street as in NAOS) which has been used to study various NL issues arising from a dialogue about a scene (e.g. focus of attention and referencing). Working close to the HAM-ANS research group was an interesting experience, as they approached NL scene description from the language side, whereas our work is vision oriented. On several occasions we found our ideas and concepts competing with existing linguistic notions, for example when defining deep cases. In the authors's opinion, vision—or for that matter: the physical nature of a scene—is the easier side from which to investigate NL scene description.

ACKNOWLEDGMENTS

The author wishes to acknowledge the valuable work of Hans-Joachim Novak who was the main collaborator in this part of project NAOS. The project has been partially supported by the German Science Foundation (DFG).

REFERENCES

Allen, J. F. (1981). *A general model of action and time.* Technical Report 97, University of Rochester, Rochester, NJ.

Austin, J. L. (1962). *How to do things with words.* New York: Oxford University Press.

Badler, N. I. (1975). *Temporal scene analysis: Conceptual descriptions of object movements.* Report TR 80, Department of Computer Science, University of Toronto, Toronto/Canada.

Ballard, D. H., & Brown, C. M. (1983). *Computer vision.* Englewood Cliff, NY: Prentice Hall.

Barrow, H. G., Ambler, A. P., & Burstall, R. M. (1972). Some techniques for recognizing structures in pictures. In J. K. Aggarwal, R. O. Duda, & A. Rosenfeld (Eds.), *Computer methods in image analysis,* (pp. 397–425). IEEE Press.

Barwise, J., & Perry, J. (1983). *Situations and attitudes.* Cambridge, MA: The MIT Press.

Block, N. (Ed.) (1981). *Imagery.* Cambridge, MA: The MIT Press.

Boggess, L. C. (1979). *Computational interpretation of English spatial prepositions.* University of Illinois-Urbana, Illinois.

Brooks, R. A. (1981). Symbolic Reasoning Among 3-D Models and 2-D Images. In J. M. Brady (Ed.), *Computer vision* (pp. 285–348). Amsterdam: North-Holland.

Brooks, R. A. (1983). *Model-based three-dimensional interpretations of two-dimensional images.* IEEE Trans. PAMI 5 (pp. 140-150).

Busemann, S. (1984). Surface transformations during the generation of written German sentences. In Bolc. L. (Ed.), *Natural language generation systems.* Heidelberg: Springer.

Cohen, P. R. (1978). *On knowing what to say: Planning speech acts.* Ph.D. Thesis, Dept. of Computer Science, University of Toronto.

Dreschler, L., & Nagel, H.-H. (1981). *Volumetric model and 3D-trajectory of a moving car derived from monocular TV-frame sequences of a street scene.* Proceedings of the IJCAI-81 (pp. 692–697). Vancouver, B.C., Canada: University of British Columbia.

Fillmore, C. J. (1968). The case for case. In Bach, E., & Harms, R. T. (Eds.) *Universals in linguistic theory* (pp. 1–88). New York: Holt, Rinehart, and Winston.

Herskovits, A. (1980). *On the spatial uses of prepositions.* Proceedings 18th Annual Meeting ACL, 1-5, Philadelphia, PA.

Herskovits, A. (1985). Semantics and pragmatics of locative expressions. *Cognitive Science, 9,* (pp. 314–378).

Hoeppner, W., Christaller, T., Marburger, H., Morik, K., Nebel, B., O'Leary, M., & Wahlster, W. (1983). *Beyond domain independence: Experience with the development of a German language access system to highly diverse background systems.* Proceedings of the IJCAI-83 (pp. 588–594). Los Altos, CA.: M. Kaufmann.

Hoeppner, W., Morik, K., & Marburger, H. (1984). *Talking it over: The natural language dialog system HAM-ANS.* (Report ANS-26) Hamburg: Research Unit for Information Science and Artificial Intelligence, Hamburg.

Malik, J., & Binford, T. O. (1982). *Representation of time and sequences of events.* Proceedings of a Workshop on Image Understanding (pp. 15-16). Palo Alto, CA.

Marburger, H., Neumann, B., & Novak, H.-J. (1981). *Natural language dialogue about moving objects in an automatically analyzed traffic scene.* Proceedings of the IJCAI-81 (pp. 49-51). Vancouver, B.C., Canada: University of British Columbia.

Marr, D. (1981). *Vision.* San Francisco, CA.: Freeman.

Miller, G. A. (1972). English verbs of motion: A case study in semantics and lexical memory. A. W. Melton & E. Martin (Eds.), *Coding Processes in Human Memory* (pp. 335–372). Washington D.C.: V. H. Winston and Sons.

Miller, G. A., & Johnson-Laird, P. N. (1976). *Language and perception.* Cambridge, MA.: Cambridge University Press.

Mohnhaupt, M., & Neumann, B. (1988). *Some aspects of learning and reorganization in an analogical representation.* Proceedings International Workshop on Knowledge Representation and Knowledge (Re)organisation in Machine Learning, K. Morik (Ed.). Heidelberg: Springer.

Nagel, H. H., & Rekers, G. (1982). *Moving object masks based on an improved likelihood test.* Proceedings of the ICPR-82 (1140-1142). Silver Spring, MD.: IEEE Computer Society Press.

Neumann, B., & Novak, H.-J. (1983). *Natural language oriented event models for image sequence interpretation: The issues.* (CSRG Technical Note 34) Toronto, Canada: Department of Computer Science, University of Toronto.

Neumann, B., & Novak, H.-J. (1986). NAOS: *Ein System zur natuerlichsprachlichen Beschreibung zeitveraenderlicher Szenen.* Informatik Forschung und Entwicklung, *1,* 83–92. Heidelberg: Springer.

Neumann, B. (1984). *Natural language description of time-varying scenes.* (Report FBI-HH-B-105/84). Hamburg: Fachbereich Informatik, Universitaet Hamburg.

Novak, H.-J. (1986). *Generating a coherent text describing a traffic scene.* Proc. COLING (pp. 570-575).

Okada, N. (1980). *Conceptual taxonomy of Japanese verbs for understanding natural language and picture patterns.* Proceedings COLING-80 (pp. 127-135).

Retz-Schmidt, G. (1985). *Script-based generation and evaluation of expectations in traffic scenes.* (Report FBI-HH-M-136/85) Hamburg: Fachbereich Informatik, Universitaet Hamburg.

Searle, J. (1969). *Speech acts: An essay in the philosophy of language.* Cambridge, MA: Cambridge University Press.

Tsotsos, J. K. (1980). *A framework for visual motion understanding.* (TR CSRG-114) Department of Computer Science, University of Toronto, Toronto, Canada.

Tsotsos, J. K., Mylopoulos, J., Covvey, H. D., & Zucker, S. W. (1980). *A framework for visual motion understanding.* Proceedings IEEE Trans. Pattern Analysis and Machine Intelligence PAMI-2 (pp. 563-573).

von Hahn, W., Hoeppner, W., Jameson, A., & Wahlster, W. (1980). The anatomy of the natural language dialogue system HAM-RPM. In L. Bolc (Ed.) *Natural language based computer systems,* (pp. 119–253). Muenchen: Hanser/McMillan.

Waltz, D. L. (1979). *Relating images, concepts, and words.* Philadelphia, PA.: Proc. NSF Workshop on the Representation of Three-Dimensional Objects, R. Bajcsy (Ed.). Philadelphia, PA.

Waltz, D. L. (1981). *Toward a detailed model of processing for language describing the physical world.* Proceedings of the IJCAI-81 (pp. 1-6). Los Altos, CA.: M. Kaufman.

Waltz, D. L., & Boggess, L. C. (1979). *Visual analog representation for natural language understanding.* Proceedings of the IJCAI-79. Los Altos, CA.: M. Kaufman.

Yakimovsky, Y., & Cunningham, R. (1978). *A system for extracting three-dimensional measurements from a stereo pair of TV cameras.* Computer Graphics and Image Processing, *7, 195–210.*

Yuille, J. C. (Ed.) (1983). *Imagery, memory, and cognition.* Hillsdale, NJ: Lawrence Erlbaum Associates.

APPENDIX A

Event Hierarchy in NAOS

P = parents (or predecessors)
S = sons (or successors)

abbiegen (turn off)
    P: drehen (turn)
    S: —

abfahren (depart)
    P: beschleunigen (accelerate), halten (halt)
    S: —

anfahren (start driving)
    P: beschleunigen (accelerate), halten (halt)
    S: —

anhalten (stop)
    P: bremsen (slow down), halten (halt), stehenbleiben-1 (stop)
    S: einparken (park)

ankommen (arrive)
  P: herankommen (come near)
  S: —

ausweichen (yield, avoid)
  P: bewegen (move)
  S: —

begegnen (meet)
  P: naehern-r (approach)
  S: treffen-r (meet)

beschleunigen (accelerate)
  P: fahren (drive)
  S: abfahren (depart), anfahren (start driving), losfahren (start driving)

betreten (tread on)
  P: gehen (walk)
  S: —

bewegen (move)
  P: existieren (exist)
  S: ausweichen (yield, avoid), drehen (turn), entfernen-r (recede), fahren
      (drive), folgen (follow), gehen (walk), kommen (come), laufen
      (run), naehern-r (approach), rasen (speed), stehenbleiben-1 (stop),
      ueberqueren (cross)

bremsen (slow down)
  P: fahren (drive)
  S: anhalten (stop), stoppen (stop)

drehen (turn)
  P: bewegen (move)
  S: abbiegen (turn off), einbiegen (turn into), umdrehen (turn round)

einbiegen (turn into)
  P: drehen (turn)
  S: —

einholen (catch up with)
  P: naehern-r (approach)
  S: —

einparken (park)
  P: anhalten (stop), parken (park), stoppen (stop)
  S: —

entfernen-r (recede)
  P: bewegen (move)
  S: passieren (pass), verlassen (leave), vorbeifahren (drive past), vor-
      beigehen (go past), vorueberfahren (drive past), voruebergehen (go
      past), wegfahren (drive off)

erreichen (reach)
  P: naehern-r (approach)
  S: ueberqueren (cross)

existieren (exist)
    P: —
    S: bewegen (move), stehen (stand)

fahren (drive)
    P: bewegen (move)
    S: beschleunigen (accelerate), bremsen (slow down), hinterherfahren
        (drive behind, follow), rasen (speed), vorbeifahren (drive past),
        vorueberfahren (drive past), wegfahren (drive off), weiterfahren-2
        (continue driving)

folgen (follow)
    P: bewegen (move)
    S: hinterherfahren (drive behind, follow)

gehen (walk)
    P: bewegen (move)
    S: betreten (tread on), losgehen (start walking), vorbeigehen (go past),
        voruebergehen (go past), weggehen (go off), weitergehen-2 (con-
        tinue walking)

halten (halt)
    P: stehen (stand)
    S: abfahren (depart), anfahren (start driving), anhalten (stop), losfahren
        (start driving), parken (park), stoppen (stop), wegfahren (drive off)

herankommen (come near)
    P: kommen (come)
    S: ankommen (arrive)

hinterherfahren (drive behind, follow)
    P: fahren (drive), folgen (follow)
    S: —

kommen (come)
    P: bewegen (move)
    S: herankommen (come near)

laufen (run)
    P: bewegen (move)
    S: rennen (run fast)

losfahren (start driving)
    P: beschleunigen (accelerate), halten (halt)
    S: weiterfahren-1 (resume driving)

losgehen (start walking)
    P: gehen (walk), stehen (stand)
    S: weitergehen-1 (resume walking)

naehern-r (approach)
    P: bewegen (move)
    S: begegnen (meet), einholen (catch up with), erreichen (reach), pas-
        sieren (pass), vorbeifahren (drive past), vorbeigehen (go past),
        vorueberfahren (drive past), voruebergehen (go past)

parken (park)
  P: halten (halt)
  S: einparken (park)

passieren (pass)
  P: naehern-r (approach), entfernen-r (recede)
  S: vorbeifahren (drive past), vorbeigehen (go past), vorueberfahren
      (drive past), voruebergehen (go past)

rasen (speed)
  P: bewegen (move), fahren (drive)
  S: —

rennen (run fast)
  P: laufen (run)
  S: —

stehen (stand)
  P: existieren (exist)
  S: halten (halt), losgehen (start walking), stehenbleiben-1 (stop),
      stehenbleiben-2 (remain standing), warten (wait), weggehen (go
      off), weitergehen-1 (resume walking)

stehenbleiben-1 (stop)
  P: bewegen (move), stehen (stand)
  S: anhalten (stop), stoppen (stop)

stehenbleiben-2 (remain standing)
  P: stehen (stand)
  S: —

stoppen (stop)
  P: bremsen (slow down), halten (halt), stehenbleiben-1 (stop)
  S: einparken (park)

treffen-r (meet)
  P: begegnen (meet)
  S: —

ueberholen (overtake)
  P: vorbeifahren (drive past), vorueberfahren (drive past)
  S: —

ueberqueren (cross)
  P: bewegen (move), erreichen (reach), verlassen (leave)
  S: —

umdrehen (turn round)
  P: drehen (turn)
  S: umkehren (return), wenden (turn, make a u-turn)

umfahren (drive round)
  P: vorbeifahren (drive past), vorueberfahren (drive past)
  S: —

umgehen (walk round)
    P: vorbeigehen (go past), voruebergehen (go past)
    S: —

umkehren (return)
    P: umdrehen (turn round)
    S: —

verlassen (leave)
    P: entfernen-r (recede)
    S: ueberqueren (cross)

vorbeifahren (drive past)
    P: entfernen-r (recede), fahren (drive), naehern-r (approach), passieren
        (pass)
    S: umfahren (drive round), ueberholen (overtake)

vorbeigehen (go past)
    P: entfernen-r (recede), gehen (walk), naehern-r (approach), passieren
        (pass)
    S: umgehen (walk round)

vorueberfahren (drive past)
    P: entfernen-r (recede), fahren (drive), naehern-r (approach), passieren
        (pass)
    S: umfahren (drive round), ueberholen (overtake)

voruebergehen (go past)
    P: entfernen-r (recede), gehen (walk), naehern-r (approach), passieren
        (pass)
    S: umgehen (walk round)

warten (wait)
    P: stehen (stand)
    S: —

wegfahren (drive off)
    P: entfernen-r (recede), fahren (drive), halten (halt)
    S: —

weggehen (go off)
    P: gehen (walk), stehen (stand)
    S: —

weiterfahren-1 (resume driving)
    P: losfahren (start driving)
    S: —

weiterfahren-2 (continue driving)
    P: fahren (drive)
    S: —

weitergehen-1 (resume walking)
    P: losgehen (start walking), stehen (stand)
    S: —

weitergehen-2 (continue walking)
    P: gehen (walk)
    S: —

wenden (turn, make a u-turn)
    P: umdrehen (turn round)
    S: —

APPENDIX B

Overtake Example

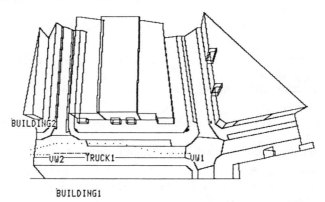

Figure 5.6. Synthetic view of 'overtake' example

Geometrical scene description (GSD) for 'overtake' example:

```
((CLASS BUILDING1 BUILDING) . 1)
((CLASS BUILDING2 BUILDING) . 1)
((CLASS TRUCK1 TRUCK) . 1)
((CLASS VW1 VW) . 1)
((CLASS VW2 VW) . 1)
((NAME BUILDING1 FBI) . 1)
((NAME BUILDING2 (OLD POST)) . 1)
((SIZE TRUCK1 LARGE) . 1)
((COLOR VW1 YELLOW) . 1)
((COLOR VW2 BLACK) . 1)
((LOCATION BUILDING1 (100 -60 70) (0 1 0) 1 40) . 1)
((LOCATION BUILDING2 (-200 350 80) (0 -1 0) 1 40) . 1)
((LOCATION TRUCK1 (50 50 15) (1 0 0) 1 2) . 1)
((LOCATION TRUCK1 (60 50 15) (1 0 0) 2 3) . 1)
((LOCATION TRUCK1 (70 50 15) (1 0 0) 3 4) . 1)
((LOCATION TRUCK1 (80 50 15) (1 0 0) 4 5) . 1)
((LOCATION TRUCK1 (90 50 15) (1 0 0) 5 6) . 1)
```

((LOCATION TRUCK1 (100 50 15) (1 0 0) 6 7) . 1)
((LOCATION TRUCK1 (110 50 15) (1 0 0) 7 8) . 1)
((LOCATION TRUCK1 (120 50 15) (1 0 0) 8 9) . 1)
((LOCATION TRUCK1 (130 50 15) (1 0 0) 9 10) . 1)
((LOCATION TRUCK1 (140 50 15) (1 0 0) 10 11) . 1)
((LOCATION TRUCK1 (150 50 15) (1 0 0) 11 12) . 1)
((LOCATION TRUCK1 (160 50 15) (1 0 0) 12 13) . 1)
((LOCATION TRUCK1 (170 50 15) (1 0 0) 13 14) . 1)
((LOCATION TRUCK1 (180 50 15) (1 0 0) 14 15) . 1)
((LOCATION TRUCK1 (190 50 15) (1 0 0) 15 16) . 1)
((LOCATION TRUCK1 (200 50 15) (1 0 0) 16 17) . 1)
((LOCATION TRUCK1 (210 50 15) (1 0 0) 17 18) . 1)
((LOCATION TRUCK1 (220 50 15) (1 0 0) 18 19) . 1)
((LOCATION TRUCK1 (230 50 15) (1 0 0) 19 20) . 1)
((LOCATION TRUCK1 (240 50 15) (1 0 0) 20 21) . 1)
((LOCATION TRUCK1 (250 50 15) (1 0 0) 21 22) . 1)
((LOCATION TRUCK1 (255 50 15) (1 0 0) 22 23) . 1)
((LOCATION TRUCK1 (260 50 15) (1 0 0) 23 30) . 1)
((LOCATION TRUCK1 (255 50 15) (1 0 0) 30 31) . 1)
((LOCATION TRUCK1 (250 50 15) (1 0 0) 31 32) . 1)
((LOCATION TRUCK1 (245 50 15) (1 0 0) 32 33) . 1)
((LOCATION TRUCK1 (240 50 15) (1 0 0) 33 34) . 1)
((LOCATION TRUCK1 (238 50 15) (1 0 0) 34 40) . 1)
((LOCATION VW1 (-100 70 8) (4 1 0) 1 2) . 1)
((LOCATION VW1 (-80 75 8) (4 1 0) 2 3) . 1)
((LOCATION VW1 (-60 80 8) (4 1 0) 3 4) . 1)
((LOCATION VW1 (-40 85 8) (4 1 0) 4 5) . 1)
((LOCATION VW1 (-20 90 8) (4 1 0) 5 6) . 1)
((LOCATION VW1 (0 95 8) (4 1 0) 6 7) . 1)
((LOCATION VW1 (20 100 8) (4 1 0) 7 8) . 1)
((LOCATION VW1 (40 105 8) (4 1 0) 8 9) . 1)
((LOCATION VW1 (60 110 8) (1 0 0) 9 10) . 1)
((LOCATION VW1 (90 110 8) (1 0 0) 10 11) . 1)
((LOCATION VW1 (125 110 8) (1 0 0) 11 12) . 1)
((LOCATION VW1 (165 110 8) (1 0 0) 12 13) . 1)
((LOCATION VW1 (210 110 8) (1 0 0) 13 14) . 1)
((LOCATION VW1 (260 110 8) (1 0 0) 14 15) . 1)
((LOCATION VW1 (310 110 8) (1 0 0) 15 16) . 1)
((LOCATION VW1 (360 110 8) (1 0 0) 16 17) . 1)
((LOCATION VW1 (410 110 8) (1 0 0) 17 18) . 1)
((LOCATION VW1 (450 110 8) (4 -1 0) 18 19) . 1)
((LOCATION VW1 (490 100 8) (4 -1 0) 19 20) . 1)
((LOCATION VW1 (540 90 8) (4 -1 0) 20 21) . 1)
((LOCATION VW1 (580 80 8) (4 -1 0) 21 22) . 1)
((LOCATION VW1 (620 70 8) (4 -1 0) 22 23) . 1)
((LOCATION VW1 (660 60 8) (4 -1 0) 23 24) . 1)
((LOCATION VW1 (700 50 8) (1 0 0) 24 25) . 1)
((LOCATION VW1 (740 50 8) (1 0 0) 25 26) . 1)
((LOCATION VW1 (775 50 8) (1 0 0) 26 27) . 1)

```
((LOCATION VW1 (805 50 8) (1 0 0) 27 28) . 1)
((LOCATION VW1 (830 50 8) (1 0 0) 28 29) . 1)
((LOCATION VW1 (850 50 8) (1 0 0) 29 30) . 1)
((LOCATION VW1 (865 50 8) (1 0 0) 30 31) . 1)
((LOCATION VW1 (875 50 8) (1 0 0) 31 32) . 1)
((LOCATION VW1 (880 50 8) (1 0 0) 32 40) . 1)
((LOCATION VW1 (-100 55 7) (1 0 0) 32 33) . 1)
((LOCATION VW1 (-80 55 7) (1 0 0) 33 34) . 1)
((LOCATION VW1 (-60 55 7) (1 0 0) 34 35) . 1)
((LOCATION VW1 (-40 55 7) (1 0 0) 35 36) . 1)
((LOCATION VW1 (-20 55 7) (1 0 0) 36 37) . 1)
((LOCATION VW1 (0 55 7) (1 0 0) 37 38) . 1)
((LOCATION VW1 (10 55 7) (1 0 0) 38 39) . 1)
((LOCATION VW1 (20 55 7) (1 0 0) 39 40) . 1)
```

The initialization phase yields the following additional entries:

(MOVE VW2 32 39)
(MOVE VW1 1 32)
(MOVE TRUCK1 1 23)
(MOVE TRUCK1 29 34)

In the following example all OVERTAKE events are to be instantiated. The range of the variables OBJ1? and OBJ2? is {VW1 VW2 TRUCK1}. The trace markers have the following meanings:

G: = generate all instances
T: = test instance
>> = enter proposition into database

SEARCH:

```
        (OVERTAKE OBJ1? OBJ2? (1 40) (1 40))

    G:  (OVERTAKE OBJ1? OBJ2? (1 40) (1 40))
      G:  (APPROACH OBJ1? OBJ2? 1 40)
        G:  (SYM-APPROACH OBJ1? OBJ2? 1 40)
        >>  (SYM-APPROACH VW2 VW1 32 39)
        >>  (SYM-APPROACH VW2 TRUCK1 32 39)
        >>  (SYM-APPROACH VW1 TRUCK1 1 12)
        T:  (SYM-APPROACH VW2 VW1 32 39)
          G:  (IN-FRONT-OF VW1 VW2 32 39)
          >>  (IN-FRONT-OF VW1 VW2 32 40)
          T:  (IN-FRONT-OF VW1 VW2 32 40)
            G:  (MOVE VW2 32 39)
            T:  (MOVE VW2 32 39)
              >>  (APPROACH VW2 VW1 32 39)
              T:  (SYM-APPROACH VW2 TRUCK1 32 39)
          G:  (IN-FRONT-OF TRUCK1 VW2 32 39)
          >>  (IN-FRONT-OF TRUCK1 VW2 32 40)
```

```
            T:  (IN-FRONT-OF TRUCK1 VW2 32 40)
               G:  (MOVE VW2 32 39)
               T:  (MOVE VW2 32 39)
                  >> (APPROACH VW2 TRUCK1 32 39)
                  T:  (SYM-APPROACH VW1 TRUCK1 1 12)
         G:  (IN-FRONT-OF TRUCK1 VW1 1 12)
         >> (IN-FRONT-OF TRUCK1 VW1 1 11)
         T:  (IN-FRONT-OF TRUCK1 VW1 1 11)
            G:  (MOVE VW1 1 11)
            T:  (MOVE VW1 1 32)
               >> (APPROACH VW1 TRUCK 1 1 11)
               T:  (APPROACH VW2 VW1 32 39)
      G:  (RECEDE VW2 VW1 1 40)
         G:  (SYM-RECEDE VW2 VW1 1 40)
         T:  (APPROACH VW2 TRUCK1 32 39)
      G:  (RECEDE VW2 TRUCK1 1 40)
         G:  (SYM-RECEDE VW2 TRUCK1 1 40)
         T:  (APPROACH VW1 TRUCK1 1 11)
      G:  (RECEDE VW1 TRUCK1 1 40)
         G:  (SYM-RECEDE VW1 TRUCK1 1 40)
         >> (SYM-RECEDE VW1 TRUCK1 12 34)
         T:  (SYM-RECEDE VW1 TRUCK1 12 34)
            G:  (BEHIND TRUCK1 VW1 12 34)
            >> (BEHIND TRUCK1 VW1 14 40)
            T:  (BEHIND TRUCK1 VW1 14 40)
               G:  (MOVE VW1 14 34)
               T:  (MOVE VW1 1 32)
                  >> (RECEDE VW1 TRUCK1 14 32)
                  T:  (RECEDE VW1 TRUCK1 14 32)
         G:  (MOVE VW1 1 32)
         T:  (MOVE VW1 1 32)
            G:  (MOVE TRUCK1 1 32)
            T:  (MOVE TRUCK1 29 34)
            T:  (MOVE TRUCK1 1 32)
               G:  (BESIDE VW1 TRUCK1 2 22)
               >> (BESIDE VW1 TRUCK1 9 14)
               T:  (BESIDE VW1 TRUCK1 9 14)
                  >> (OVERTAKE VW1 TRUCK1 (1 10) (15 23))
                  T:  (OVERTAKE VW1 TRUCK1 (1 10) (15 23))
FOUND:

   (OVERTAKE VW1 TRUCK1 (1 10) (15 23))
```

The next trace is for the example "Did a yellow VW overtake a truck in front fo the FBI?" The variable X1?, X2? and X3? are bound to VW1, TRUCK1 and BUILDING1 respectively. The database has been reinitialized.

SEARCH:

```
        (OVERTAKE X1? X2? (1 40) (1 30)
        (IN-FRONT-OF X1? X3? 1 30)


    G:  (OVERTAKE X1? X2? (1 40)(1 30)
      G:  (APPROACH OBJ1? OBJ2? 1 40)
        G:  (SYM-APPROACH OBJ1? OBJ2? 1 40)
        >> (SYM-APPROACH VW1 TRUCK1 1 12)
        T:  (SYM-APPROACH VW1 TRUCK1 1 12)
           G:  (IN-FRONT-OF TRUCK1 VW1 1 12)
           >> (IN-FRONT-OF TRUCK1 VW1 1 11)
           T:  (IN-FRONT-OF TRUCK1 VW1 1 11)
              G:  (MOVE VW1 1 11)
              T:  (MOVE VW1 1 32)
                 >> (APPROACH VW1 TRUCK1 1 11)
                 T:  (APPROACH VW1 TRUCK1 1 11)
        G:  (RECEDE VW1 TRUCK1 1 40)
          G:  (SYM-RECEDE VW1 TRUCK1 1 40)
          >> (SYM-RECEDE VW1 TRUCK1 12 34)
          T:  (SYM-RECEDE VW1 TRUCK1 12 34)
             G:  (BEHIND TRUCK1 VW1 12 34)
             >> (BEHIND TRUCK1 VW1 14 40)
             T:  (BEHIND TRUCK1 VW1 14 40)
                G:  (MOVE VW1 14 34)
                T:  (MOVE VW1 1 32)
                   >> (RECEDE VW1 TRUCK1 14 32)
                   T:  (RECEDE VW1 TRUCK1 14 32)
          G:  (MOVE VW1 1 32)
          T:  (MOVE VW1 1 32)
             G:  (MOVE TRUCK1 1 32)
             T:  (MOVE TRUCK1 29 34)
             T:  (MOVE TRUCK1 1 23)
                G:  (BESIDE VW1 TRUCK1 2 22)
                >> (BESIDE VW1 TRUCK1 9 14)
                T:  (BESIDE VW1 TRUCK1 9 14)
                   >> (OVERTAKE VW1 TRUCK1 (1 10) (15 23))
                   T:  (OVERTAKE VW1 TRUCK1 (1 10) (15 23))
      G:  (IN-FRONT-OF VW1 X3? 1 23)
      >> (IN-FRONT-OF VW1 BUILDING1 4 15)
      T:  (IN-FRONT-OF VW1 BUILDING1 4 15)
```

FOUND:

```
        (OVERTAKE VW1 TRUCK1 (4 10)
        (IN-FRONT-OF VW1 BUILDING1 4 15)
```

Author Index

Subject Index